Bernard MacLaverty

C O N T E M P O R A R Y   I R I S H   W R I T E R S
a   B u c k n e l l   s e r i e s

Series Editor:
John Rickard

Irish studies is currently undergoing a strong renewal, not only in connection to major figures such as James Joyce and W. B. Yeats, but also within a larger framework, with particular
attention to women's issues, nationalism, Northern Ireland and its writers, the Irish language,
and the fiction, poetry, drama, and film of contemporary Ireland.

These short monographs bring newer, more theoretically informed perspectives to a con-
sideration of the work and lives of single authors, and they provide a general discussion of
interpretive issues and strategies for understanding this work. These books will appeal to a
sophisticated but not solely professorial audience — that is, advanced undergraduates, graduate students, and independent readers and scholars as well as professors of Irish literature
and culture.

Forthcoming Titles in Series

Richard Rankin Russell on Bernard MacLaverty

Jonathan Allison on Seamus Heaney

J. Fitzpatrick Smith on Ciaran Carson

Borbála Faragó on Medbh McGuckian

www.bucknell.edu/universitypress

CONTEMPORARY IRISH WRITERS

Bernard MacLaverty

Richard Rankin Russell

BUCKNELL UNIVERSITY PRESS

Associated University Presses
2010 Eastpark Boulevard
Cranbury, NJ 08512

The paper used in this publication meets the
requirements of the American National Standard for
Permanence of Paper for Printed Library Materials
Z39.48-1984.

Library of Congress Cataloging-in-Publication Data

Russell, Richard Rankin.
    Bernard MacLaverty / Richard Rankin Russell.
      p. cm. — (Contemporary Irish writers)
    Includes bibliographical references and index.
    ISBN 978-0-8387-5703-1 (alk. paper)
    1. MacLaverty, Bernard—Criticism and
interpretation. 2. Northern Ireland—Intellectual life—
20th century. I. Title. II. Series

    PR6063.A2474Z85 2009
    823'.912—dc22
                                2009008929

For Hannah, the love of my life

CONTENTS

ACKNOWLEDGMENTS

I am very grateful to the College of Arts and Sciences at Baylor University, which granted me both a full semester sabbatical in the spring of 2006 and a summer sabbatical later that year, during which this project was written. I am thankful for the friendship and encouragement, scholarly and otherwise, given to me by several colleagues in the Baylor English Department, including James E. Barcus, Joe B. Fulton, Clement T. Goode, and J. R. LeMaster. I also am grateful to my former chair in English, Maurice Hunt, and the former Dean of Arts and Sciences, Wallace Daniel, who both have been very supportive of my scholarship over the years. The reader for Bucknell University Press, the late George Watson, made a series of helpful suggestions that greatly improved the manuscript, especially the introduction. I am especially grateful to my mentor Weldon Thornton, at the University of North Carolina, Chapel Hill, the best close reader and teacher I have ever had. Weldon's scholarship, teaching, and generosity in the field of Irish Studies is exemplary. His personal and professional encouragement of my development as a human being, thinker, and writer remains the great boon of my graduate school years at Chapel Hill. Finally, I give great thanks to God for my wife and best friend, Hannah Gray Russell, to whom this project is dedicated: "her price is far above rubies."

The quotations from Seamus Heaney's poems "The Forge," "Whatever You Say Say Nothing," "Personal Helicon," and "The Toome Road" adhere to the fair-use standard for the academic market, as does the quotation from Michael Longley's poem "Wounds."

Permission has been granted from the BBC Northern Ireland Radio Community Archive for the right to reproduce Bernard MacLaverty's quotation from "Whatever You Say Say Nothing."

Permission has been granted from *Nua: Studies in Contemporary Irish Writing* to reprint a portion of my review of Bernard MacLaverty's *The Anatomy School.* Special thanks are due to Gill Coleridge, Bernard MacLaverty's agent, and to Bernard MacLaverty himself for permission to quote from all of MacLaverty's fiction. Bernard has graciously and patiently answered a series of questions from me and helpfully provided me with a partial bibliography of critical sources on his work. This study shows the great value and affection I have for his fiction.

ABBREVIATIONS

MLD. *Matters of Life and Death and Other Stories*

AS. *The Anatomy School*

GN. *Grace Notes*

WD. *Walking the Dog*

GP. *The Great Profundo and Other Stories*

C. *Cal*

TD. *A Time to Dance and Other Stories*

L. *Lamb*

S. *Secrets and Other Stories*

IRELAND HAS PRODUCED A SERIES OF OUTSTANDING twentieth-century novelists
and short story writers, including George Moore, Seumas O'Kelly, and James Joyce.
A second generation of such writers, led by Liam O'Flaherty, Frank O'Connor,
and Sean O'Faolain, followed Joyce and, beginning in the 1960s, a number of fine
new Irish novelists and short story writers emerged such as William Trevor, John
McGahern, and Edna O'Brien. Ben Forkner argues in his introduction to the major
collection of modern Irish short stories that in the work of these latest writers, "the
special virtues of the Irish story announced by Moore and Joyce—strong characterization and vivid, dramatic dialogue—still predominate."[1] Although the reputations of these writers and others—such as John Banville and, more recently, Patrick
McCabe and Roddy Doyle—have generally flourished, the reputations of other Irish
writers, despite strong reviews, have languished, especially those writers who have
been committed to the short story form.

Beginning in the 1970s and continuing to the present, Bernard MacLaverty
has written an impressive series of five short story collections and four novels.
Despite his perspicuous style, sympathetic, penetrating explorations of the human
condition, and an underappreciated humor, along with the "strong characterization
and vivid, dramatic dialogue" commonly found in the best work of contemporary
Irish short story writers, and despite wide public acclaim and his adaptation of his
first two novels, *Lamb* (1980) and *Cal* (1983), into thoughtful films, MacLaverty
has yet to garner the critical acclaim he deserves. Perhaps his best-known work, his
1997 novel *Grace Notes* won the Saltire Award in Scotland and was short-listed for
the Booker Prize. One welcome exception to his relative critical obscurity is his
inclusion in the *Oxford Book of Irish Short Stories* edited by William Trevor.[2] Some
critical essays on MacLaverty's fiction have been published, but the present study
lays claim to being the first monograph on his work.

Part of this comparative critical neglect of his work may stem from problems of generic and national classification. In addition to his outstanding short stories, MacLaverty has written very fine novels, placing him in such good company as McGahern and Trevor, who have both continued to write excellent short and long fiction. Although McGahern's novels are receiving the critical attention they deserve, especially since his recent death, his short stories are usually slighted. Trevor's short fiction, however, has been recognized with important critical work. The reductive critical tendency to identify the majority of authors with a particular form has created a problem for authors such as MacLaverty who excel in two or more genres: because he cannot be generically pigeonholed, the trend is to focus either on his short fiction or his novels, or not on his work at all.

Furthermore, although literature has begun to move away from association with national identities, that designation still holds considerable sway. Classification of such authors as MacLaverty becomes difficult because he manifests an hybridized identity as an author from Northern Ireland, neither fully British nor Irish, who has lived in Scotland since 1975. Even practicing Catholics who have remained in Northern Ireland—unlike MacLaverty, who has left both the church and the province—throughout the Troubles have conflicting opinions about their identity and their Irishness, as Fionnuala O'Connor's 1993 comprehensive collection of interviews of a wide range of fifty Catholics, *In Search of a State: Catholics in Northern Ireland*, has demonstrated. Despite finding an ongoing perception that Northern Irish Catholics feel more Irish than any other identity, O'Connor shows that, as the Troubles progressed, a series of factors has led a significant minority of Northern Irish Catholics to feel less uncomplicatedly Irish. These developments include a gradual, often grudging acceptance (if only mentally) of the border between Northern Ireland and the Irish Republic, a growing revulsion toward IRA violence and that group's monolithic notions of Irishness, and an increasing detachment toward Northern Irish Catholics on the part of the South.[3]

Bernard MacLaverty was born in Belfast on September 14, 1942, to John MacLaverty, a commercial artist, and Molly (Boyd) MacLaverty. When Bernard was only twelve, his father died from lung cancer, an event that has led him to focus on father-son relationships in some of his work. He married Madeline McGuckin on March 30, 1967, and they raised four children—Ciara, Claire, John, and Judith. While working in the laboratory at Queen's University, Belfast, from 1960 to 1970, MacLaverty was encouraged by anatomy professor Jack Prichard and English professor Philip Hobsbaum to develop his short stories for publication. In 1970, he began working toward a Bachelor of Arts degree in English at Queen's, which he attained with honors in 1974; he earned his teacher's qualification with his Education Diploma in 1975. He and his family moved to Edinburgh, Scotland, in August

1975, and he taught at St. Augustine's High School there until October 1978, when they moved to the village of Bowmore on the Inner Hebridean island of Islay, where he served as Head of English at Islay High School. On April 30, 1981, MacLaverty quit teaching to write full-time. He and his family moved to Glasgow on January 20, 1986, where they still live. He has held teaching positions such as Writer in Residence at the University of Aberdeen, Guest Writer at both Iowa State University and the University of Augsburg, Visiting Writer at John Moores University (Liverpool), and Visiting Professor at the University of Strathclyde (Glasgow). Although he is best known for his novels and short stories, he has also written books for children and numerous radio, television, and screenplays based on his short and long fiction. MacLaverty's contributions to literature have been recognized with his induction into *Aosdána*, Ireland's premier association of writers of distinction.

Although MacLaverty had been publishing some of his short fiction in local journals like *Snakes Alive* and *The Honest Ulsterman* in the 1960s and 1970s, he did not really attract critical attention until he published his first book of short stories, *Secrets and Other Stories*, in 1977 with the fledgling Blackstaff Press in Belfast. Up until that time, the two most celebrated short story writers in Northern Ireland were Brian Friel and John Montague. The prominence of Friel and Montague as the leading short story writers from the province is evidenced by the space devoted to their work in what remains the essential study of fiction from the North of Ireland, John Wilson Foster's *Forces and Themes in Ulster Fiction*. However, Montague is now best known as a poet, having never published another short story collection, and Friel as Ireland's best living dramatist, who has also not published a short fiction collection again. In short, there was no Northern Irish short story writer and novelist who seriously treated the issues resulting from individuals living in a divided province in a series of fictional works until MacLaverty became established as a major writer in the 1970s and 1980s.

During the 1960s when the short and long fiction of these writers and others was being published, a young Bernard MacLaverty was participating in Philip Hobsbaum's creative writing group in Belfast. The Belfast Group's inclusiveness across the religious divide and across a variety of vocations enabled MacLaverty to participate in a venture remarkable for its time. Hobsbaum was probably the first critic to note MacLaverty's early promise, despite Hobsbaum's own preference for poetry.

The leading poets in the Belfast Group published pamphlets for the Belfast Festival of Arts in 1965 and quickly became famous after the publication of their first volumes in the 1960s. MacLaverty, however, did not publish a book until *Secrets* in 1977. The reasons for this relatively late "arrival" in contrast to that of his fellow Belfast Group members are various. First, MacLaverty was working full-time during the 1960s in the laboratory at Queen's and had to devote himself to writing in his spare time. Additionally, although he did publish a number of the short stories that appeared in *Secrets* in journals such as *Snakes Alive* and *The Honest Ulsterman*, he waited until he felt he had stories of sufficient heft to publish. There was an additional inhibiting factor as well given the upsurge of the violence in the province starting in 1969.

While Belfast Group poets such as Michael Longley and Seamus Heaney were able to release their first poetry collections before the outbreak of the Northern Irish "Troubles" and thus escape some of the demand to incorporate the atrocities into their poetry, MacLaverty faced such pressure with publishing a collection in the late 1970s after some of the worst bombings and murders of the conflict. The expectation that art will respond to such horror is understandable, but that expectation is compounded by the very immediacy and impersonality of the violent acts themselves, which seem to demand nearly instantaneous, highly individual artistic responses. As Denis Donoghue has argued in his seminal essay, "The Literature of Trouble," atrocities such as the Provisional IRA bombing at the La Mon Hotel in 1978 not only deny humanity, but also outrage us through their immediacy. "What the act gives, without our asking, is immediacy, a quality which we are ready to accept when it comes as an attribute of chance and misfortune but which leaves us baffled when it comes with human motive."[4] Such bombings instilled in the minds of those living in Northern Ireland a similar feeling to that held by an English public that experienced a series of explosions triggered by Irish nationalists in the 1880s. Alex Houen has noted that the "impersonal randomness" of these early acts of modern terrorism "revealed to people that they were *already living as potential statistics*, already living as anonymous figures in a crowd. Dynamite's explosivity underscored the fact that instead of death and its significance being managed and contained within specific private and public spaces . . . death could break into any space at any time."[5] And indeed it did during the Northern Irish Troubles: victims were murdered in pubs, in the countryside, on city streets, even at funerals. These acts of terrorism created an abiding impression that death could visit anyone, anywhere, at any time.

In some salient ways, the formal properties of short fiction seem especially appropriate for depicting the upheaval that Northern Irish society was going through in the 1960s and beyond. One of the contemporary masters of the genre, the English writer V. S. Pritchett, has argued that it "is the glancing form of fiction that seems to be right for the nervousness and restlessness of contemporary life."[6] The charged atmosphere that often obtained on the streets of the province during times of great crisis in this period would seem to lend itself well to reproduction in this "glancing" form.

Additionally, the form's typical taciturnity seems well suited to conveying the tendency toward silence of inhabitants of Northern Ireland, especially its Catholic population,[7] whose civil rights were suppressed from the time of Partition in 1921 until sometime after the outbreak of the violence at the end of the 1960s. Traditionally, the short story has not been a voluble medium but a silently musing one with a tendency toward privacy and a penchant for capturing intensely personal discrete moments. This characteristic makes the appropriate use of dialogue all the more effective in the hands of a gifted writer like MacLaverty, who knows both the intricate pauses inherent to conversational rhythm and how silences are necessary to the pace of effective short stories.

However, Donoghue's point about the immediacy characteristic of terrorist bombings and sectarian murders that makes reflective art about such acts difficult to achieve highlights a pressing problem for the short story writer working in, or gazing on, the frenetic milieu of Northern Ireland during the Troubles. The singular immediacy of the effective story that seems to unfold before our eyes can be hampered by the repetitious nature of the violence such as that experienced in the province at the height of the Troubles in the 1970s and early 1980s. Certainly to those victims and survivors such experiences were unique, but attempting to portray even striking atrocities in short fiction would be complicated by the cumulative effect of events that has led to the gradual battering of the public psyche, which weariness would tend to blur the crispness necessary for short fiction's own version of immediacy—especially for Northern Irish readers and others closely observing the fighting. In the only two stories of MacLaverty's *Secrets* dealing with the Troubles, the ironically titled "Happy Birthday" and "Between Two Shores," the conflict is relegated to the background and is employed mainly to heighten the aimlessness and despair of the characters. In fact, there is a studied reluctance to write about the Troubles in that volume that bespeaks MacLaverty's unease with doing so.

Another sort of immediacy, the urge to write imaginative literature right after a violent event, has also tempted Northern Irish writers seeking to respond to the conflict. The best writers who have explored aspects of the Troubles, such as Longley, Heaney, and Stewart Parker, have often done so with great caution, fearing that too quick a reaction to atrocities may result in an impoverishment of their artistic vision. In a 1994 BBC Northern Ireland radio program on the twenty-fifth anniversary of the Troubles, MacLaverty reflected about the duty of the Northern Irish artist to respond appropriately to the violence. He recalled, "suddenly, this awful thing comes into your life, this new thing, this people being killed, people being maimed. A climate of fear. And as a writer, you have to respond to that in some way. Now, it took a long time for me to respond to that in any kind of creative way."[8] For a variety of reasons, then, it took MacLaverty longer to become an established writer than some of his more famous contemporaries in the Belfast Group. This relatively slower start has undoubtedly created a high degree of artistic integrity in his work, which enabled him to critique the violence effectively when he finally chose to do so directly in his novel *Cal*, a work that privileges the human need for relationships and intimacy over the contrasting human urge toward violence and brutality.

His study of the discipline of short fiction and commitment to the form probably precluded MacLaverty from attempting to publish a novel first. Another inhibiting factor could have been the novel genre's growing association with gory thrillers about the province's violence. As we will see, it is a measure of the artistic integrity of *Cal*, which superficially resembles such works, that it refuses their breathlessness and voyeurism. Serious novels treating the Troubles have been eclipsed, as Elmer Kennedy-Andrews has noted, by the work of "popular fiction writers [who] cashed in early (and continue to do so), exploiting the Troubles to cater for a mass market which feeds voraciously on thrillers and romances." For this reason, he contends that "for serious literary engagement with the Troubles we tend to think of poetry and even drama rather than fiction."[9]

Short fiction was also slow in responding to such a large-scale event as the Troubles. Michael L. Storey's recent work *Representing the Troubles in Irish Short Fiction*, however, wrongly suggests that "the response of Irish [short fiction] writers" to the upsurge in contemporary violence "was to create stories depicting that nightmare in all of its horror."[10] The refusal of such significant writers as MacLaverty to treat the Troubles directly in his early short stories suggests that, in addition to the problems inherent to this genre detailed above, the tradition of realistic short fiction in Ireland, with few exceptions, was initially not amenable to incorporating such content without becoming overwhelmed by it.[11]

Despite a tremendous outpouring of fiction from Northern Ireland—one count covering the period of 1971 to 2000 gives nearly six hundred novels by at least two hundred writers[12]—critical coverage of this genre has noticeably lagged behind that of poetry and drama. Eve Patten suggests that this relative lack of criticism stems from an emphasis on the part of "an English readership" on "the authentic [, which] was identified closely with the poetic. Poetry was prized as the definitive form for the expression of the province's condition, with the Yeatsian legacy of the well-made lyric poem taking precedence first, over the region's less noted though nonetheless successful output of drama and, secondly, over what was considered an intractable, even feeble tradition of fictional prose."[13] This preference for authenticity that Patten identifies valorizes rural life while neglecting narratives of urban life. With some significant exceptions, Heaney's poems of rural life typify this kind of representation. Although several Northern Irish novels fit into this heuristic, such as Joseph Tomelty's *Red Is the Port Light* (1948), John O'Connor's *Come Day—Go Day* (1948), and Sam Hanna Bell's *December Bride* (1951), they have been termed "qualified successes only[14] and were generally critically neglected in favor of shorter, more easily excerpted poetry, especially that written by the major poets, such as Heaney, who emerged from the much-publicized Belfast Group.

Partly because of the conflict, much contemporary Northern Irish literature has become a literature written by authors who have left the province, such as Heaney (the Irish Republic, America), Stewart Parker (Edinburgh, then London), and MacLaverty himself. MacLaverty's voluntary removal to Scotland, although it has been tempered by many crossings across the Irish Sea to the province and by the very nearness of Northern Ireland to Scotland, has helped him attain a positive condition from which his pluralistic fiction issues. Although Edward Said's sense of exile has been markedly more pronounced than MacLaverty's in both Said's geographic distance from Palestine and the great difficulty he would have in returning to that territory, his remarks on the enabling condition created by exile is apposite to understanding MacLaverty's artistic vision. Said notes, "most people are principally aware of one culture, one setting, one home; exiles are aware of at least two, and this plurality of vision gives rise to an awareness of simultaneous dimensions. . . ."[15] MacLaverty's adult ability to dwell in Scotland and, by extrapolation, in a wider, largely secular British culture, while remaining rooted in the communal cultural and religious Catholicism of the Northern Ireland of his childhood and early adulthood, has led him to an artistic position in which he is aware of "simultaneous dimensions," receptive to varying registers of cultural and political expression.

His geographic removal from Northern Ireland has enabled him to create a body of long fiction that defies classification, particularly given the categories that critics have developed for novels focusing on the Troubles. Gerry Smyth has delineated the four major types of Northern Irish fiction dealing with the Troubles—"realist thriller, national romance, domestic [,] and prodigal fiction."[16] MacLaverty's novels, with the exception of *Cal*, which mimics both the realist thriller and the national romance before finally showing the vacuity of these models, can best be described as "prodigal fiction," in the sense that Smyth articulates. Smyth borrows the term from Eve Patten, who defines this type of writing as questioning traditional terms of representation. "Highly conscious of the charged political context from which they emerge and of the received patterns of writing with which their own texts emerge, each of these writers has subjected the heavy contingency of Northern Ireland literature to a series of rearguard tactics, in order to renegotiate its terms of representation."[17] According to Patten's formulation, "prodigal" writers resent the expectation that they will merely represent the realities of their society in their work and engage in revolts of content, style, and even setting, particularly in their predilection for urban narratives over the rural settings favored by poets such as Heaney. Eamonn Hughes's contention that the most successful Northern Irish novelists have "avoided turning the Troubles into a . . . crushing monolith" and generally "locate the Troubles as one strand in a more complex set of stories" suggests how writers such as MacLaverty may attend to the Troubles but refuse to allow that violence to overwhelm the agency of their characters.[18]

Literary influences on MacLaverty abound but perhaps the most important has been Michael McLaverty, a short story writer and novelist from Northern Ireland. The elder writer spoke to the younger one after a talk on the short story he gave in the 1950s that Bernard MacLaverty attended. As the younger writer has recalled, McLaverty emphasized the importance of local dialect in effectively communicating the particulars of province life, citing Joyce as an example. "He must have known that I was writing because he talked to me briefly afterwards and he was questioning me about the funnel and the tundish [in Joyce's *A Portrait of the Artist as a Young Man*]. He wanted to know if I would use a local word like Stephen did or if I would be afraid of the English not understanding it? . . . That weight of Northern Ireland speech is something I was always interested in."[19] McLaverty's insistence on local dialect confirmed Bernard MacLaverty's decision to write not only about his native milieu, but also to do so by using a local dialect that would realistically reproduce that environment.

He turned naturally to examples of reported speech by his family members. Recently he recalled the origins of his facility with such speech, noting that "Those Northern Ireland rhythms and speech are drawn from my own background. When I was sick as a child I would sleep on the sofa and listen to the old people talking by the fire."[20] In Hobsbaum's recollection about the Belfast Group, he cites the vivacity of colloquial language that is "settled in the text" of a short story entitled "Jim Scroggy," rather than "imposed on it."[21] MacLaverty's ability to reproduce realistic, colloquial language has increased over the years and remains a hallmark of his short fiction and novels, placing him in the great tradition of Irish fiction writers, but with a characteristically humorous, wry Ulster twist.

Another characteristic of MacLaverty's fiction is one shared with other writers who emerged from the Belfast Group: a thoroughgoing respect for and concern with form. His immersion in this coterie forced him to consider the integrity of form and to celebrate its varied uses. Just as former Group members such as Heaney have experimented with a variety of forms, such as the sonnet, MacLaverty has too; for example, he does so in the sketches about "your man" interspersed between the more traditional short stories of *Walking the Dog*.

MacLaverty's interest in the formal properties of literature is inseparably connected to the particular content of his work. The present study takes for granted the importance of the formal properties of literature and sees an appreciation of them as integral for understanding the nuances of his meanings or those of any author. Moreover, appreciating the nature of literary form is crucial for realizing how literature that attends to itself can also speak to the conditions of the outer world. As Glenn C. Arbery argues, "A novel that does not succeed in being literature cannot fruitfully address the actual condition of the world. Why? Because it has not addressed, with sufficient awareness and care, its own actual condition as a made thing."[22] MacLaverty's carefully crafted fictional worlds evince a formal integrity that renders them both complete in themselves and capable of imagining solutions to problems in the "real world."

This study of MacLaverty's short fiction and novels draws on both Mikhail Bakhtin's articulation of the intersection of content and form and Theodor Adorno's aesthetic theories. As Bakhtin writes in "Discourse and the Novel," "The study of verbal art can and must overcome the divorce between an abstract 'formal' approach and an equally abstract 'ideological approach.' Form and content in discourse are one. . . ."[23] He further claims, "More often than not, stylistics defines itself as a stylistics of 'private craftsmanship' and ignores the social life of discourse outside the author's study, discourse in the open spaces of public squares, streets, cities and villages, of social groups, generations, and epochs."[24] Bakhtin's balanced approach to ideology and form enables us to understand MacLaverty's marriage of form and content and how his fiction becomes part of "the social life of discourse outside the author's study," while preserving its imaginative independence.

MacLaverty's authorial integrity is closely linked to art's relative autonomy, by virtue of its form, from the empirical world, despite maintaining the connection between them, as Adorno has shown is typical of art generally. "Art negates the categorical determinations stamped on the empirical world and yet harbors what is empirically existing in its own substance. If art opposes the empirical through the element of form—and the mediation of form and content is not to be grasped without their differentiation—the mediation is to be sought in the recognition of aesthetic form as sedimented content."[25] The "sedimented content" of MacLaverty's work, such as the subtext concerning the 1981 Irish republican hunger strikes in *Cal*, formally enables him to imagine another world in which frankness and open dialogue replace secrecy and silence. In this sense, his fiction's humane honesty accords with Adorno's conviction: "Artworks participate in enlightenment because they do not lie: They do not feign the literalness of what speaks out of them. They are as real as answers to the puzzle externally posed to them."[26]

MacLaverty has always linked his choice of short stories to their content, noting in an interview, "It's something to do with the weight of the idea. When you pick up a thing, you know by the weight of it whether it's going to be a novel or a short story."[27] Generally speaking, he has chosen to write short fiction to capture moments in the lives of his characters through apt images. For example, he told the present writer that when he first began, "I would see that I was trying to emulate what Michael McLaverty was doing because I admired him so much as a writer . . . that kind of slice of an accurate image that he would use every so often. For example, 'In the duck's nest, the egg was as cold as a cave stone.'"[28] The abbreviated form of short fiction seems especially suited to portraying such images. MacLaverty told Rosa Gonzalez in an interview that he sees short stories as having "the concentration of a poem."[29] His short stories are concentrated snapshots of lives, and they demonstrate how the best short fiction suggests "a spectrum of human behaviour and response, and intelligence, and sensitivity."[30]

When taken collectively, MacLaverty's memorable characters do convey this full "spectrum of human behavior," yet his short fiction most often explores the state of deracination. Living in Scotland has enabled him to depict successfully the lives of his many displaced characters, who often illustrate Frank O'Connor's famous dictum in *The Lonely Voice:* "Always in the short story there is this sense of outlawed figures wandering about the fringes of society. . . . As a result there is in the short story at its most characteristic something we do not often find in the novel—an intense awareness of human loneliness."[31] O'Connor further argues that the short story reflects "an attitude of mind that is attracted by submerged population groups, whatever these may be at any given time. . . ."[32] O'Connor's emphasis on human loneliness endemic in submerged population groups rather than length as the primary characteristic of the short story represents a signal contribution to short story criticism that MacLaverty has employed often in his pared-down narratives of lonely members of submerged population groups who are often left out of official discussions of conditions in Northern Ireland, although he modifies O'Connor's focus on marginalized characters by showing their need for community.[33]

Examples of human loneliness in short fiction abound, but two important Irish examples come to mind that take as their themes variations on paralysis or imprisonment. For instance, the father of the modern Irish short story, George Moore, published a series of often bleak short stories in *The Untilled Field* (1903) that influenced James Joyce's realistic stories of *Dubliners* (1914). Although the influence of Joyce's *Dubliners* may seem slight on first reading MacLaverty's earliest work, it tends to accrue weight on subsequent readings. Joyce's resolve to shake Ireland out of its paralysis can be seen in the urge of MacLaverty's early short fiction to express and then shatter the paralysis of constrictive Northern Irish society. The lives of many of these characters seem circumscribed, even hopeless, as they move through a series of static environments at home, school, and through Belfast. However, while some of Joyce's stories end with epiphanies on the part of his main characters, MacLaverty's stories sometimes reject this essentially nineteenth-century, Romantic aspect of the form and conclude in the way Ian Reid has described as characteristic of many contemporary stories with no beginning or end, only a middle. "The character shows himself unable or unwilling to alter his situation; the movement is of a treadmill sort or suggests continuous transit. . . ."[34]

While forward-looking in this newer manifestation of the form, MacLaverty's stories are also formally backward-looking, clearly influenced by the long oral tradition of tale-telling from which modern and contemporary Irish short stories spring. Such stories often are told for sheer pleasure and do not illustrate a particular point. As William Trevor suggests, "It may be laid down that it [the modern short story] has to have a point, that it must be going somewhere, that it dare not be vague. But art has its own way of defying both definitions and rules, and neither offer[s] much help when examining, more particularly, the short stories of Ireland."[35] Some of MacLaverty's short fiction seems inert, not dynamic, but this seeming inertia may well be derived from his childhood immersion in the Irish oral tradition.

Thematically, MacLaverty returns time and again to the notion of imprisonment in his novels and short fiction. As a Belfast writer, MacLaverty is especially attuned to how, after the Troubles began, the province and notably Belfast itself became a kind of prison, especially in its ghetto areas, through the British Army's erection of "peace lines," high barricades separating flashpoints between homogenous areas of Catholics and Protestants, and through its vast array of surveillance apparatuses such as radar, recording devices, checkpoints, and cameras. Patrick Grant has argued that because of these tactics, "Northern Ireland has come to resemble a prison," and that Belfast especially, with its high population density and "geographical segregation" has been the effective epicenter of this prison.[36] MacLaverty often simulates this repressive atmosphere in his fiction. For example, Brother Benedict in *Lamb* kidnaps the boy Owen from what he perceives as the prison of the religious school where Benedict teaches and holds him virtual prisoner in a flight to London, then Northern Ireland and Donegal, before killing him. The title character of *Cal* is mentally imprisoned by the incessant recall of his role in the murder of Marcella's husband, and the novel concludes with his perverse anticipation of being beaten while jailed. Catherine McKenna in *Grace Notes* is imprisoned by her postpartum depression, her abusive boyfriend, and her abstraction of the Protestant community in Northern Ireland, yet finally experiences freedom in the soaring qualities of her creative work and life of her child. Finally, Martin Brennan in *The Anatomy School* feels trapped in his Catholic school and by his inability to express himself to girls.

Much as Joyce's protagonist Stephen Dedalus vows near the end of *A Portrait of the Artist as a Young Man* to escape the nets of Irish religion, family, and even personal relationships by becoming an artist, so will some of MacLaverty's later pro-tagonists, who can also be seen as budding writers and artists of other types, starting with Cal, who dreams of being a blues player, reaching an apogee with Catherine McKenna, and continuing with Martin Brennan, who may become a photographer. This urge toward freedom on the part of his protagonists typifies MacLaverty's own relatively exilic condition, proving the truth of Said's assertion that "The exile knows that in a secular and contingent world, homes are always provisional. Bor-ders and barriers, which enclose us within the safety of familiar territory, can also become prisons. . . . Exiles cross borders, break barriers of thought and experience."[37] The very lack of rootedness of these characters—one thinks of the Catholic Cal and his father being firebombed out of their home in a sectarian Protestant hous-ing estate and of Catherine's long search for literal and figurative homes—and their provisional homes enable them to escape the atavistic, enervating attitudes that result from such skewed perceptions of home by fictional members of the Provi-sional IRA such as Crilly in *Cal*. Georg Lukács's claim that the novel constitutes the form of "transcendental homelessness"[38] because of the unsettled nature of its authors' societies becomes particularly important for appreciating the inherently generic trajectory toward freedom from imprisonment experienced by leading char-acters in MacLaverty's novels.

If imprisonment constitutes a major theme of MacLaverty's work, then it is set in a dynamic dialectic with love, which is expressed on personal, national, and theological levels. The love between father and son has long been one of MacLaverty's major foci and is explored throughout *Lamb* through a variety of father-son rela-tionships, in "Father and Son" and "Life Drawing" from *A Time to Dance and Other Stories* (1982), and in Cal's and Shamie's relationship in *Cal*. The aching absence of the father in *Grace Notes* and *The Anatomy School* is a void that casts a pall over these novels despite their comic trajectories. *Lamb* obliquely and *Cal* more directly show how perversions of love of country lead to sectarian warfare and death. But the more positive love of Christ for believers in the Grunewald painting of the Cruci-fixion in *Cal*, Catherine McKenna's love for her child and her music in *Grace Notes*, and the embryonic love of Martin Brennan for a mystery girl in *The Anatomy School* suggest that MacLaverty views love, with its emphasis on freely choosing another and selflessly putting the beloved above oneself, as a sort of antidote to the determinism of virtual and actual imprisonment. Truly sacrificial love, in contrast to the negative sacrifices of Owen Kane in *Lamb* and the endeavors of Crilly and Skeffington in *Cal* for the Irish Republican Army, seeks the well-being of the other, revels in humility, and disdains glory. In MacLaverty's fiction, real sacrificial love points away from the petty concerns of self and country and toward an ideal wor-thy of our full pursuit.

Although Joyce's urban themes of paralysis and imprisonment were exemplary to MacLaverty, closer to our own time, Michael McLaverty's depictions of rural Catholics who immigrate to Belfast were also influential. John Cronin has pointed out that McLaverty's displaced Catholics do not fare very well in "the grime and smoke of Belfast. . . . The city is a place of menace, hatred and death."[39] MacLaverty's gritty depictions of bleak areas of Belfast demonstrate his concern to highlight the particular dislocations of citizens of Northern Ireland in general caused by their sometimes disabling identity as neither fully Irish nor British but as some amalgam of the two.[40] John Wilson Foster has noted that Belfast serves as the locus of this identity crisis, calling it "a city that symbolises the ambiguity of nationality suffered by Ulster people."[41]

As an example of his urge to show this "ambiguity of nationality," MacLaverty portrays the unease that middle-class Protestants experience in Belfast. He has thus modified the emphasis of his fellow Catholic Michael McLaverty's studies of Catholic characters on the margins of Belfast. In significant stories such as "A Happy Birthday," "Some Surrender," and Walking the Dog," which will be examined in this study, Protestant characters are portrayed as geographically and psychologically marginalized in Belfast. In his attention to characters from a community often thought diametrically opposed to his own, MacLaverty evinces a concern with depicting the frustrations of displaced members of a transnational, transcultural community of humanity.

His fiction fulfills this community-creating function. He has taken a genre suited to isolation, the short story, and transformed it to suggest his characters' longing for community, while his novels, particularly the gapped form of *Grace Notes* and *The Anatomy School*, display "all the fissures and rents which are inherent in the historical situation [that] must be drawn into the form-giving process" of that genre, as Lukács puts it, and show how societal wholeness might be imagined.[42] His humane characters working toward creating community are the best antidote to poisonous political categories.

MacLaverty's fiction about the cultural, religious, and political conditions in Northern Ireland exposes calcified notions of identity to his work's imaginative force, in the process creating new fictions that may become reality. In this regard, they accord with the radical nature of form articulated by Denis Donoghue: "Form transfigures what otherwise merely exists, and by that transfiguration it maintains the validity of freedom. . . . Form is content as imagined, not merely received: transfigured, not mimed."[43]

In its various forms, MacLaverty's fiction borrows from two major media—film and music. Although the fictional techniques of his exemplar, Joyce, anticipated the varying techniques of film,[44] MacLaverty—who has transformed his novels *Lamb* and *Cal* into film scripts and who has recently directed his own film short, *Bye-Child*, based on Seamus Heaney's poem "The Bye-Child"—is thoroughly familiar with cinematic techniques and incorporates them into his fiction through carefully presenting and rendering a series of searing and evocative images. He has noted in an interview that "I've loved the cinema since I was a little boy. My father worked as advertising manager in the Capitol Cinema in Belfast."[45] MacLaverty also has a keen musical ear. In 2000, he wrote and presented a monthly radio review program, "The Best of 3," for Radio 3 in the UK, and in 2000 and 2001, he wrote and presented "Grace Notes," a two-hour classical music radio show for BBC Scotland. MacLaverty's fiction, supremely in his masterpiece *Grace Notes*, can become nearly indistinguishable from music. Although both his cinematic and musical techniques compete for our attention in particular works, subsequent chapters delineate the use of these techniques according to three phases. The first phase builds toward a fully visual fiction in *Cal*, whereas the second, musical phase, reaches its apotheosis in *Grace Notes*. The final phase, which begins with *The Anatomy School*, retains sonic concerns, even as it returns to the cinematic, signaled by the emergence of the budding photographer and central character Martin Brennan, who sees and perceives with remarkable acuity. It would be difficult to think of another twentieth-century novelist and short story writer, besides Joyce, who is so fully conversant in techniques inherent in film and music and who deploys them so successfully. The comparison is purposeful.

Appearance Versus Reality
in *Secrets and Other Stories*

MACLAVERTY'S IMMENSE TALENT as a short story writer is evident in the mixture of light pieces and weightier fiction in this volume written in the 1960s and 1970s, which was released in Britain and Ireland in 1977 but not in America until 1984. The collection won an award from the Scottish Arts Council in 1978. This chapter examines the nuanced characters of *Secrets* and the ways in which their Northern Irish milieu shapes their motivations and desires. A full carnival of these characters is on display here, including drunks, priests, young children, and women. Although one theme does not unite the stories, many of them explore variations on the theme of appearance versus reality.

Most of the stories in this volume adhere to Poe's theory of compression in their brevity, although there are exceptions such as "Between Two Shores" and "Hugo," which share with the longer short story form of the tale what Weldon Thornton has termed the "rich, meandering" quality of that subgenre.[1] But like much of MacLaverty's short fiction, they generally reject two other qualities often thought essential to short fiction and derived from Poe: a gradual build to a crisis and a controlled plot—the so-called "symmetry of design" first identified by Brander Matthews in his 1901 study *The Philosophy of the Short Story*.[2] As Ian Reid has shown, however, despite the insistence of critics such as Matthews and later ones such as A. L. Bader, the importance of plot, particularly its Aristotelian components of "conflict, sequential action, and resolution" comprising a symmetrical design, is "patently not a property that belongs to that form in any distinctive indispensable way."[3] Indeed, some of the best stories in *Secrets* have no crisis or resolution; instead, they provide deep insights into a character's mind and show the vacillations within that mind, ending in a state of ambiguity.

Comparing these stories to those by William Trevor, a clear measure of his respect for MacLaverty's talent, Robert Hogan points out MacLaverty's similarly "detached observation of several kinds of people," then notes that "[u]nlike Trevor, however, MacLaverty has several kinds of stories which are written to produce different kinds of effects, ranging from the Trevorian study of accumulating failure of 'Hugo' to the jokey fantasy of 'The Miraculous Candidate.'"[4] Certainly more of the stories convey an impression that is gradually built up of failure or decline, but several of them more optimistically offer glimpses of an active fantasy life: along with the levitating schoolboy of "The Miraculous Candidate," there is the male protagonist of "A Pornographer Woos," writing out his sexual fantasies about his nearby wife; the recently bereaved young teacher of "Anodyne," who has a (Leopold) Bloomian fantasy of a fourteen-year-old girl he meets on a Donegal beach; and the narrator of "The Bull with the Hard Hat," who dreams of becoming the race car driver Emmerson Fittipaldi and acquiring a more organized and attractive wife. Yet even "Hugo" has an element of fantasy—Hugo's conviction, finally dashed by the narrator, that he is a writer. Again, such disparate stories are unified by the relationship between appearance and reality. Almost always, reality is introduced into a situation by a character from outside the fantasy. The ability to preserve a positive fantasy life marks some of the strongest stories, such as "The Exercise."

Although "Hugo" and "The Exercise" differ in their patterns and feel, they both explore the intensity of school life, as does "The Miraculous Candidate," the first story in the volume, and "The Deep End," the last story. Taken together, these four stories illustrate how fantasies and happiness can be shattered and only sometimes restored. They are stories of yearning—for manhood, more responsibility, greatness—that eschew the saccharine and sentimental in favor of the reality of lived experience.

"Hugo" is MacLaverty's first picture of an artist—two artists, in fact—and his first, tentative foray into metafiction when it is revealed halfway through the story that the main character is writing it. His experiments with metafiction would reach an apogee with the later collection *Walking the Dog*. The protagonist is quite taken with the older pharmacy student Hugo, a lodger along with another student named Paul, in his mother's house. Like Kevin Sweeny's father in "The Exercise," Hugo tutors the boy with his homework and becomes a figure of admiration for him. More important, he enables the narrator to overcome his stuttering through an inventive exercise that includes singing and the rhythmic beating out of the words on a table.

Although Hugo passes his pharmacy finals with high honors, he soon retreats to write the ultimate novel, an endeavor that eventually leads to his solipsistic withdrawal from society, his personal decline, and his fall from the narrator's idolization of him. After he finally convinces Hugo to let him read his masterpiece, the narrator realizes that [i]t was all too embarrassingly bad" and that [h]e had not even grasped the first principles of good writing" (*S* 89). Apparently, although the narrator, a budding writer at that time, is good at writing only and nothing else, Hugo, who excels at many subjects and only wants to be a writer, does not have the talent required for success. When he tells Hugo "possible ways to improve" (89) the novel, Hugo shuns him and the narrator only sees him twice more before Hugo kills himself as his own father had done.

The narrator's authorial aside to the reader in the middle of the story constitutes a valiant attempt to deal with his guilt over Hugo's suicide by casting the story as an episode of honestly rendered autobiography. He admits as much when he asks himself "why should I write it at all?" and then answers by saying "perhaps to show something of my respect, perhaps to assuage my guilt" (79–80). If this is an expiation, it is one cloaked with qualifications and justifications. For example, the narrator claims that his experience in writing the "biography of a sort" on Sir Aubrey de Vere has given him the expertise to write such a story (79). Apparently, the narrator, also an English professor, has never experienced writer's block before. Usually, he says, "When I sit down to write a critical article or a lecture the words seem to flow from my pen. Indeed my first job is to limit them" (79). The very difficulty he has in writing this particular story suggests not only his long refusal to deal with his guilt over discouraging Hugo, who had so greatly encouraged him, but also his refusal, probably stemming from that guilt, to deal with his own life generally, preferring to immerse himself in the lives of others rather than reflect on his own. His preference for fictions that reject sincerity (80) suggest his own emotional impoverishment and escape into literature, a very unflattering first portrait of an artist for MacLaverty. In his retreat into a world of words, the narrator has become something of a Hugo himself but without his generous, humanizing qualities. Perhaps in writing about this incident from the past, he will acquire such qualities, but the story is best seen as a "one-off" for him, an escape of a different sort—this time, from his academic work.

Kevin Sweeny, the young boy of "The Exercise," has an image of his father that anticipates the previous narrator's first view of Hugo and one that is nurtured by certain assumptions of his importance in the outside world. For example, when feeling in his father's pockets for a sixpence, he notices that the smell of porter emanating from his teetotaling barman father "mixed nicely with his grown up smell" (7). His father has been informally tutoring him at home in his school lessons, and Kevin has come to regard him as an expert, even though his parents did not go very far in school. One night, Kevin's father, after shaving and before going out, calls out the answers to the Latin exercise to his son. In the hands of a lesser writer, Kevin's immediate reaction might have been shown, but MacLaverty merely has the boy lower his head when his father stoops to kiss him on the way downstairs

(9). It is only when his father leaves that Kevin stands and stares into the basin where his father shaved and sees "the bottom . . . covered in short black hairs, shavings" (9). The combination of Kevin's seeming disdain for his father's affection and desire to be an adult, signified by the "shavings," subtly suggests his belief that when he is a man, he will literally and figuratively have all the answers.

But he is punished at school for having all the wrong answers and revealing to Waldo, the priest who teaches his Latin class, that his father gave him the answers. Waldo, as fearsome a priest as any from Joyce's *A Portrait of the Artist as a Young Man*, whips his hands with a cane in front of the class. This loss of innocence seemingly functions as an epiphanic crisis in the story. However, although Kevin is physically hurt and embarrassed, he learns a more important lesson than that his father does not have all the answers and that adulthood does not equal wisdom. Instead, by returning home, doing his lessons himself, meeting his father at the bus stop, and lying to him that his answers were correct, thus preserving his father's fantasy about his own intellectual ability, Kevin models responsibility and shows that he knows the value of maintaining fictions to spare others' feelings. His preservation of appearances to his father in the domestic sphere thus coexists with his recognition of reality in the external world: the former constitutes the real exercise, a sincere fiction, which he must now undertake when his father "helps" him with his school exercises.[5]

In a much more humorous story about the pressure of needing to have all the answers in school, "The Miraculous Candidate," a fourteen-year-old Catholic boy named John panics when given what turns out to be the wrong examination and prays for help from St. Joseph of Cupertino, who helps him apparently levitate above his desk.[6] When the irate invigilator accuses him of copying from the boy in front of him, John wants to tell him that St. Joseph has helped him to levitate but fearfully thinks he will not understand. "The man looked like a Protestant. The Ministry brought in teachers from other schools. Protestant schools. He wouldn't understand about Saints" (44). When John is finally threatened with disqualification, he still cannot return to his seat until he says "fuck the Pope" (45). Once John is back in his seat, the invigilator realizes that the levitating lad has been given, ironically, the advanced-level physics exam; the invigilator then hands him the junior-level science exam instead, which John can easily pass. The importance of having spiritual faith to pass a science test suggests how easily MacLaverty commingles the ineffable with the quotidian and highlights the significance of faith, another theme common to these schoolboy stories.

Paul, the main character of "The Deep End," also levitates, but purposely so, similarly drawing on his faith. His soaring flight at the local swimming pool and sense of accomplishment are quickly dashed, however, when the body of a boy is later discovered at the bottom of the pool. For Paul, this incident confirms that the pool functions as a site of danger; earlier, when he is changing into his swimming trunks, he sees the water still moving "from the previous session. It looked still enough on the surface but the black lane lines snaked too [*sic*] and fro continuously" (126). His mother has already hilariously warned him that he could contract polio from that particular pool and that threat, and the water's serpentine qualities, make the pool sinister. Before the boy drowns, Paul hears "a cry smothered by a dull explosion" and panics until he realizes that his friend Olly has just dived into the water (126). He blesses himself before he enters the water the first time and before jumping off the side of the pool, unable to jump from the end of the board. Paul's faith, like John's in "The Miraculous Candidate," is important to him but he uses it like a good-luck charm to achieve the appearance of courage and daring. And in the end, all the blessings in the world cannot ward off the intrusion of reality as the pool becomes a site of death when a young boy drowns in the deep end.

The sonic qualities of this story suggest MacLaverty was already experimenting with musical effects in his fiction, a practice that would reach its apogee in his novel *Grace Notes* twenty years later. More specifically, anticipating Catherine McKenna's positive reclamation of the Orangemen's lambeg drums from emblems of Protestant triumphalism to harbingers of joy in the second section of that novel, Paul tries to make over the negative sounds he hears about him in the pool. He is frightened by the "[s]plashing and slamming of dressing box doors mixed with a continuous jagged scream, which echoed and multiplied when flung back from the high glass roof" (128). Although this collective sound of boys screaming stays "at the same sawing pitch throughout," once "[t]he long whistle to end the session shrilled . . . the noise reached a crescendo as everybody plunged in for the last time" (128). Paul, however, refuses to get in the water again and, feeling safe and having survived the frenetic din of the pool, begins to undress again. As he ponders his pubic "wisps of hair," he reflects on whether "he would ever have a bush like the gym teachers" (128), a moment of pre-pubescent longing akin to Kevin Sweeney's perception of his father's shorn facial hair in the wash basin as the badge of confident adulthood. Then the sound of a different screaming and the siren of the ambulance coming for the drowned boy temporarily shatter all those hopes.

Paul has been given a deeper knowledge than Kevin, however, in his realization of the ubiquity of death, which MacLaverty conveys through images of prone bodies throughout the story. The story actually opens with its final scene, making what follows a flashback. The closing image of this first, but chronologically last scene features Paul lying on his bed, crying for the boy who died (123). When Paul is watching Olly diving, he sees "a boy at the bottom of his dive, alone in the pool," who is "flat, spread-eagled" (126), both an anticipation of the soon-to-be drowned boy, who is described as "a still figure lying on the bottom at the deep end" (129), and of Paul's own "drowned" body, with eyes full of tears, at the conclusion of the story. Paul's prone position on the bed, figuratively between the daring, living body of his friend Olly and the inanimate, dead body of the drowned boy is thus intermediate, halfway between life and death. The pool will undoubtedly continue to unnerve him in the future, although his newly discovered empathy for others' suffering may enable him to comfort others who fear the water.

The "bray of an ambulance" (129) that signals the approach of the emergency vehicle in "The Deep End," the aural image of the frenzied cries of the swimmers, and the visual image of the drowned body trapped in the hermetically sealed world of the glass-domed public pool symbolically function as a proleptic microcosm of the similarly closed world of Northern Ireland, with its attendant sectarian energies rebounding and echoing once its superficial calm would be shattered at the end of the 1960s. Indeed, the scenes at the public pool in which Paul feels he is being watched by everyone else, along with John's fear of his invigilator in "The Miraculous Candidate," and Kevin's fear of the authoritarian Waldo in "The Exercise" together display qualities that the Northern Irish poet and critic Tom Paulin have identified as "the negative, claustrophobic aspects" of Northern Ireland's "provincialism," such as "[t]he fear of being seen and judged, the continual sense of being watched, the slavish attitudes to authority."[7] Thus, while MacLaverty is committed to exploring the intersection of appearance and reality in the realm of personal relationships in these early stories about schoolboys, he also hints at the province's anxieties and fears beneath its outward face of unflappable confidence.

Only two of the stories of *Secrets* more directly demonstrate his interest in treating the Northern Irish conflict and the effect it has on its inhabitants, whom he often views sympathetically. Even in these stories, the exploration of the conflict is oblique, especially in "Between Two Shores," a story on which MacLaverty worked for more than two years.[8] This work is a penetrating psychological study of a man from County Donegal who has worked as an emigrant in England off and on for years and who is now coming home to his family riddled with the syphilis he has contracted from an affair with a nurse who tended him after an appendix operation. Despite being from Donegal, part of the Republic of Ireland, the nameless man is well acquainted with the sort of terrors that have been occurring in contemporary Northern Ireland. As he sits watching the passengers on the boat cross the Irish Sea to Belfast, he first sympathetically notices some British soldiers, "men and boys with short hair," and acknowledges their probable unease at having to return to the province during Easter holiday. "He thought how sick they must be having to go back to Ireland at Easter" (48, 49). Later he notices some young Catholic girls from Belfast who are interested in the soldiers but realizes, "The soldiers wanted nothing to do with them. Soldiers before them had chased it and ended up dead or maimed for life" (51).[9]

The soldiers' "sickness" becomes part of the metaphor of disease that runs through the story, representing the unhealthy, sectarian Northern Irish society and its infectious nature, which is epitomized by the protagonist's syphilis that is rending and tearing his body internally. When his lover, the nurse, first notices the sore on his body, she is alarmed for his sake and tells him how destructive the spirochetes' passage through his body will be if it goes untreated. "She explained to him how they were like minute corkscrews going through the whole body" (52). But he refuses treatment, fearing its violence more than the rending power of the disease itself. "He had listened to stories on the site of rods being inserted, burning needles and worst of all a thing which opened inside like an umbrella and was forcibly dragged out again" (53). Untreated, just as the unsolved conflict in the province will continue to ravage its citizens, the syphilis in the man's body will destroy him and his wife. "She had said they were like tiny corkscrews. He thought of them boring into his wife's womb" (54). Tortured by such thoughts of creeping destruction, the man finally rises from his prone position and roams the ship.

His vision grows increasingly nightmarish and indirectly suggests images of the Troubles as its horrors accrue. Viewing the sleepers in the lounge of the ship, he sees them as in a "graveyard," thinking that "[p]eople were meant to be straight, not tilted and angled like this" (57). Surrounded by these macabre bodies, he again tries to sleep but in a dream is drawn inexorably back to bodily decay and disease. As he touches the nurse's breasts, he unexpectedly "felt warm moistness, revolting to the touch. His hand was in her entrails" (58). After he wakes and contemplates suicide, he sees the land on both sides of the Belfast Lough and thinks the shore resembles dismembered body parts, "arms or legs" (59). The images of the disease gnawing at the bodies of the man, his lover, and potentially his wife, combined with his ghoulish perception of the sleepers on the ship and the Belfast shoreline, suggest syphilis as a metaphor for the sick society of Northern Ireland.

This metaphor represents one of the most subtle explorations of the collection's theme of the interaction between appearances and reality. Although the man's body seems outwardly healthy, inwardly, he is being destroyed and will become blind. Similarly, to the outside world, Northern Ireland seemed healthy and prosperous after Partition, but internally, sectarian sickness festered, finally breaking out in abject violence and figurative blindness to the detriment of the cross-cultural humanity of its divided inhabitants. If its sectarianism is left untreated, the story suggests, it will gradually strike everyone in the province. And indeed the modern Troubles have. Almost everyone living in the province has experienced the violence directly or indirectly by having loved ones or friends hurt or killed or by knowing such victims.

Additionally, the man's dislocation, although typical of the Irish emigrant who is homesick abroad and restless on returning home, symbolizes the liminal position of Northern Irish citizens, who are figuratively between two shores themselves, neither fully British nor Irish, but something stateless and in between. This peculiar dispossession, grounded in a lack of nationalism and its attendant, reassuring narratives of location, recalls Said's description of the condition of exile as "fundamentally a discontinuous state of being" in which "[e]xiles are cut off from their roots, their land, their past."[10] Although MacLaverty's protagonist is from Donegal and thus part of the Republic of Ireland, MacLaverty cleverly uses the peculiarity of this county, part of the traditional province of Ulster, now virtually cut off from the Republic except from the south and abutted by Northern Ireland, to express the alienation of the dispossessed of Northern Ireland: both Protestants originally from Scotland or England who are committed to their long-distance union with Great Britain and Catholics who long for union with Ireland.

To emphasize the bleakness and hopelessness of life in the province during the 1970s, MacLaverty closes "Between Two Shores" with disturbing visual and sonic images that recall those from "The Deep End." As the story concludes, the man is greeted with a cluttered vista from the Belfast Lough: "Gasometers, chimney-stacks, railway trucks. They looked washed out, a putty grey against the pale lump of the hills. Cars were moving and then he made out people hurrying to work" (59). Edna Longley has discussed how often the literary portraits of Belfast miss capturing the essence of the city, preferring to see it as a site of literal and figurative blackness, created by the industrial revolution and by its Protestant fundamentalists. Instead, she argues that "the North of Ireland has never been a 'black country' in the sense of producing iron, steel, coal or widespread smog."[11] She further holds, citing M. F. Caulfield's novel *The Black City*, that such depictions make for good melodrama but also "suggest the high degree of pathetic fallacy that obtains in writing about Belfast."[12] Yet the concluding view of Belfast in "Between Two Shores" is not so much black as grey, not so much smoky as smudged. Its urban industrial core is revealed as a site of bustling activity and determination.

To escape these busy, purposeful images for a few moments more, the listless protagonist closes his eyes and rests his head on his arms. MacLaverty's refusal to employ stereotypical images of black Belfast or employ the pathetic fallacy in his description makes the final sentence chilling in its mounting terror. "Indistinctly at first, but with growing clarity, he heard the sound of an ambulance" (59). Reading backward from this wailing siren, we see the aforementioned images of industrialism, "moving" vehicles, and "hurrying" people acquire a more sinister context, seeming grimly mechanical and increasing the protagonist's despair. His possibilities seemed more open on the boat, if ambiguous, between the two shores of Britain and Ireland; yet now, on his way home to Donegal, he appears about to be sucked back into the poisonous vortex of Northern Ireland, with its Protestant work ethic frenetically heightened by the imagined bodies about to be picked up by the ambulance.

The Troubles feature directly only in one well-crafted story from *Secrets,* the ironically titled "A Happy Birthday." The presumably Protestant Sammy lives at home with his mother while attempting to be a man about town. One morning, before he collects his welfare money, he reads of more explosions in the province and inwardly reviles the Irish Republican Army. "Nothing but bloody explosions and robberies again. Something would have to be done. The IRA was getting the run of the country without one to say boo to them. *Something* would have to be done" (28). Coming out of the pub that afternoon, he praises some British soldiers he runs into, but despite their shared politics, they are separated by the common language they speak. Sammy says to one of them, "Yis are doing a grand job," but the soldier, not understanding, merely says, "Wot?" Sammy rephrases the comment, exclaiming, "Yis are the boys," but is merely met again with the same response, and he moves off in disgust (28, 29).

Shortly afterward, he runs into a group of Catholic civil rights protesters, whom he assails, finally telling them, "Yis have never done a day's work in your lives. You don't know what you're talking about. So-called civil rights. Why don't yis go down south where yis belong?" (29). Drinking steadily throughout the afternoon, he boards a carnival ride and ends up vomiting on the heads of the assembled crowd, anticipating the vomit on the floor of the bathroom on the ship in "Between Two Shores." Sammy sprays his vomit in a particularly violent and enveloping manner. We are told "it came out of him like sparks from a catherine wheel. An emulsion of minestrone-stout. Spraying on the multi-coloured domes of the exhibition. Exclamation marks, yellow and buff bird-dung streaks flecking the canvas. Sparking off the tarmac paths, soaking spots in people's Sunday best. Children slipped and fell" (30). The trajectory of the vomit and its force recall a bomb explosion, yet there is a certain black humor in the children's falling and Sammy's own escape from being covered in vomit.

The story ends with Sammy fishing for his last pound and vowing to go for a drink because it is his birthday, suggesting his willingness to become sick again and hinting obliquely at the circularity of violence in the province. His hypocritical claim to the Catholic civil rights protesters that they have never worked a day in their lives reflects his own frustration and that of many Protestants at the time who were similarly unemployed and felt that Catholics could take their jobs and the privileges that they had held for many years. The story thus links self-destructiveness and subsequent violence to disaffected members of the Protestant population, while the Catholic student protesters are featured in a positive light. Yet the figurative effects of Sammy's sickness, like those of the syphilis of the man in "Between Two Shores," also symbolize the pervasive disease of violence in Northern Ireland. Despite Sammy's obnoxious, even repellent behavior, MacLaverty's evident sympathy for him in his drunken and poverty-stricken condition qualifies our own disdain for his actions.

The very real dangers lurking in the streets of the province's capital city at that time was a contributing factor in MacLaverty's decision to leave the province in 1975. Like his unnamed character in "Between Two Shores," he was repelled and frightened by the violence.[13] Living in Scotland undoubtedly enabled him to gain distance from and perspective on the conflict and begin to explore it tentatively through focusing on its personal devastation caused by such characters as Sammy who may never have fired a shot but nonetheless used angry invective against civil rights marchers and thus indirectly and tacitly supported the rise of Protestant paramilitaries against what they perceived as the danger of newly mobilized Catholics.

The title story of *Secrets* returns to the theme of appearance versus reality in its treatment of a young boy's relationship with his great-aunt, whose mien seems the epitome of Catholic respectability but who has lived another life in her past unknown to the boy until he reads her personal letters one day. She has always read stories to him and been the storyteller in the family, nurturing the child's latent penchant for adventure and excitement. When she has gone to devotions one Sunday evening, he reads many letters sent to her by her lover from the European trenches of World War I. Later letters suggest he has become a priest to sacrifice himself to God because of the battlefield sacrifices he has seen. Their passion and poignancy grip his imagination, and he reads on till it is too late: She returns immediately after he has hastily thrust the letters back into the desk and discovers he has read them. She slaps him, calls him "dirt" repeatedly, and vows, "I shall remember this till the day I die" (39), leaving him with his own secret that he must keep from his mother.

The story is framed by the great-aunt's death and its aftermath, which may lead the boy to speculate about the positive role of fantasy. Its tension, more obvious than any other tension in the collection besides "Between Two Shores," gathers its strength from the boy's fear that his great-aunt will tell of his betrayal of her on her deathbed. But when he questions his mother in the conclusion, she merely replies that "she was too far gone to speak, God rest her" (40). The outcome of this story remains ambiguous. What sort of lesson has the boy learned? Did his aunt ever forgive him? The silence on these issues is deafening. We find out in the beginning of the story that the boy has been studying for his A levels, but the emphasis on a formal examination, so clear in earlier stories like "The Miraculous Candidate," is downplayed here in favor of the emphasis on a life lesson, as it is in "The Exercise." If the boy remains attentive to the possibility that others older and different from him may have unknown, hidden lives that function to obviate some of the dreariness of their quotidian days, his own fantasy life may similarly and positively flourish.[14]

Critical praise for *Secrets* was generally strong in Britain and Ireland. In America, the collection was also widely acclaimed, although this praise was slower in coming because the volume was not published there until 1984. Perhaps the most sustained negative assessment of the collection occurs in Thomas Kelly's 1981 review that reads all the stories as either failed or successful variations on the anecdotal form. Kelly observes that "MacLaverty has obvious talent and discipline, but he often lacks the consciousness of the tradition and techniques within which he is working to achieve successfully the modern voice within anecdotal structures."[15] For example, Kelly argues that, although the concentration on character of "Between Two Shores" makes it more successful than many of the stories, it nevertheless "fails for lack of purpose, for lack of a specific point of view by which to direct the reader: it is more of an overwrought character sketch."[16] The present author feels that this story lays claim to being the best in the volume, precisely because of its deep psychological insights into the protagonist's character, coupled with its use of the man's symbolically and literally torn body as a metaphor for the increasingly divided province of Northern Ireland. Kelly's attempt to place the range of stories in *Secrets* into a pre-determined category fails in its inability to read these nuanced stories with the attention they deserve.

Additionally, Kelly's review also presumes that MacLaverty is working within the parameters of the modern short story as established by Poe, but as I have tried to demonstrate, while they generally conform to Poe's theory of compression, these stories often eschew both a crisis and symmetry of design. Even a story such as "Secrets" that does contain a crisis—the great-aunt's discovery that the boy has read her personal letters—diffuses this seeming climax by the crisis that the boy experiences in the present—that his great-aunt would reveal his betrayal on her deathbed. Stories such as "Between Two Shores" and others such as "St Paul Could Hit the Nail on the Head" and "Umberto Verdi, Chimney Sweep" represent another strand of the modern short story characterized by Ian Reid as "virtually without start or finish, representing only a state of affairs rather than a sequence of events."[17]

Robert Hogan, on the other hand, favorably compares MacLaverty's worldview with that of William Trevor, Aidan Higgins, and John McGahern in their short fiction, noting that MacLaverty's outlook can be "as gray as" theirs, but overall "is more balanced, less misanthropic, and finally more convincing."[18] In discussing MacLaverty's fictional technique, Hogan observes that he "tries for nothing ambitious or exceptional" and "writes observed, dramatized scenes, and . . . does them as well as Trevor or [James] Plunkett or Montague. He uses a lot of dialogue, and his descriptions and narrations do their tasks quickly and briskly."[19] The comparisons to such established, accomplished writers are telling, suggesting just how much MacLaverty achieves in this remarkable first collection. Hogan does not contextualize the stories in their Northern Irish milieu, however, which is a drawback in assessing the negative and positive aspects of the society that has helped produce these lonely, yearning characters with their desire for community and delight in language.

Anne Tyler's 1984 review of *Secrets* in the *New Republic* represents the most insightful contemporary reading of the collection. She praises it for its well-drawn characters and deep insights into the wellsprings of human motivation, along with commending its unobtrusive style, which she describes as "so apt and vivid and unstudied that you're not so much reading it as seeing it pass before you."[20] Tyler notes that MacLaverty's ability to portray a cross section of characters' lives makes "you feel you've been granted privileged information."[21] Although she observes that "[t]here are trite moments here and there . . . , they are saved by the stories' atmospheres—the richness of texture that comes across as truthfulness."[22] That richness of texture has become a salient feature of MacLaverty's writing in general and would enable him to continue grounding his stories and novels in the lived realities of Northern Irish life while suggestively evoking both its underlying despairs and joys through a range of skillfully drawn characters.

True and Distorted Fatherly Loves
in *Lamb*

MACLAVERTY ORIGINALLY CONCEIVED HIS 1980 NOVEL *Lamb* as a short story about a man and boy feeding gulls on the ferry between Larne, Northern Ireland, and Stranraer, Scotland, but he quickly realized that the arc of the characters' lives required the additional length of the novel form, as he told George Watson in conversation. Watson argues that "the decision to move from short story to novel form . . . contributes to one of the book's most powerful effects: the sense of relentless movement, of a grim process of inevitability. The sense of inevitability, to be convincing, clearly needs that wider development through time offered by the novel form."[1] As part of this "grim process of inevitability," MacLaverty at first sympathetically examines the disillusioned Brother Michael Lamb's escape to England with the epileptic boy Owen Kane, then more critically suggests how Lamb's urge to protect the child leads to the man's gradual, disturbing replacement of God with himself and his murder of Owen. Lamb's role as surrogate father is influenced by his filial relationship with a series of father figures, including Brother Benedict, the head of the school for boys where Lamb works; his own kindly father in rural Ulster; the Greek mythic father Daedalus; and God. Lamb, or Brother Sebastian as he is known in the religious industrial school in which he first meets Owen, is an unlikely source of evil actions in the novel, and thus his descent into despair and murder shocks all the more. This chapter assesses how Lamb's well-intentioned, fatherly actions result in disaster for his young charge and himself as their father-son relationship based on affection changes, negatively suggesting how a truly sacrificial love might work differently. The strength of these themes led *Lamb* to be awarded a prize from the Scottish Arts Council and the runner-up award for fiction from the *Guardian* in 1981.

Watson has observed that MacLaverty's long immersion in the short story form has created a tightly built narrative and a spare novelistic writing style. As he points out in his essay on *Lamb*, "Here, as in his later novel *Cal* (1983), are all the virtues of the good short story writer: tight narrative construction, clean and clear visualization, the ability to suggest more through the telling use of tiny detail (the pinball machine in Chapter 10, for example), the sharpness and ease of dialogue."[2] It is not the case, then, that *Lamb* is an extended, bloated short story; rather, it grew organically from an imagined short story and retains all of MacLaverty's mature style, resulting in a novel that unremittingly carries the reader into the repressive world of the Catholic boys' school where Michael Lamb and Owen Kane live and then into their frenetic flight across Britain and back to Ireland.

MacLaverty has termed the novel an oblique commentary on the situation in Northern Ireland. Although it opens at the school in western Ireland, most of the novel is set in London, and it concludes with a drive across Northern Ireland as man and boy journey into County Donegal. The subtle presence of the conflict is evoked through the repressive Brother Benedict's approval of the IRA, Lamb's recollections of his rearing in the North, conversations about the conflict, and this final, stark drive. The novel suggests that a seemingly noble sacrifice for an imagined good is ultimately evil: Lamb's murder of the boy symbolizes the way in which republican or, by extrapolation, loyalist violence in the province destroys the future of its children. At the same time, MacLaverty's realistic evocation of the restrictive milieus of Irish Catholicism and republicanism allows him to distance himself both from his own Catholic upbringing and from republicanism, and implicitly endorse other expressions of belief and a nationalism that desires a united Ireland without violence.

All of MacLaverty's novels explore the condition of exile set against a backdrop of imprisonment with the possibility for freedom. As his first novel, *Lamb* constitutes MacLaverty's first extended fictional foray into the contested psychic terrain of the self, a terrain filled with Biblical pitfalls such as pride that eventually leads to Lamb's delusional "sacrifice" of Owen to save him from returning to the oppressive atmosphere of the school and from his mother's hatred of him. Michael's growing pride is presaged by the myth of Daedalus and Icarus that he and Owen read in their London hotel on their second day in the city. The imprisoning labyrinth of the religious school that they have escaped in their flight to London, however, is merely replaced with a series of other dark mazes with their own monsters that they try to fly by: London itself, the series of cheap hotels they live in, the old house they squat in for a few days, and finally Ireland and Northern Ireland on their return to the island. The trajectory of the novel traces a deadly, labyrinthine circularity, starting by the ocean in western Ireland (Galway) and finishing in northwestern Ireland (Donegal).[3] Michael Lamb drowns Owen, who has become his sacrificial lamb, but is unable to drown himself as he had planned and is tormented by his growing realization of the evil inherent in his horrific act even as seagulls swoop down on the boy, presumably to peck out his eyes, in the final scene.

MacLaverty has long been interested in the relationship between fathers and sons and explores this dynamic often in his short and longer fiction. Partly because his own father died when MacLaverty was twelve, many of his male adolescent characters are portrayed searching for a father. Besides his autobiographical interest in the subject, he was likely influenced by a series of literary antecedents from Ireland and Northern Ireland who focused much of their work on the interaction of fathers and sons. As Declan Kiberd has shown, fictional Irish father figures are generally shown to be inadequate in classic works of the Irish Literary Revival by Synge, Joyce, and O'Casey. Kiberd even argues that "At the core of Joyce's art is the belief that fathers and sons are brought together more by genetic accident than by mutual understanding, and that most sons are compelled to rebel."[4] Additionally, fiction written by several prominent authors from Northern Ireland in the 1960s, such as Jack Wilson, Maurice Leitch, and John Montague, the time in which MacLaverty was learning his craft, also examines father/son relationships, as John Wilson Foster has shown. Foster holds that this relationship is so common in novels of the period because "the writers themselves are like sons confronting the ancestral sins of the land." In Foster's formulation, there is a "separation-initiation-return sequence"[5] observable across the decades of Northern Irish fiction he surveys. Characters in fiction written during the early years of the formation of the Northern Irish state leave the land for the city as a necessary break from the rural father figures "that never submitted to the outside world. Those who return to the land discover . . . that their maturity in the city has been an illusion and that coming to terms with the father and with the dark land is in fact their last initiation into manhood."[6]

To his great credit, MacLaverty departs from the negative fatherly models established by the Irish revival writers and novelists from the North such as Wilson, Leitch, and Montague in his lovely evocation of Michael Lamb's father, whose profound love for his wife and son anchors his family and provides them with deep emotional sustenance despite their modest living. Lamb instead rebels against a more traditionally repressive "father," Brother Benedict. But if the sons of the Irish literary revivalists and the Northern novelists of the 1960s are often relatively valorized in contrast to their distant or harsh fathers, MacLaverty's first novelistic son, Michael Lamb, turns out to be a monstrous father in his own right, despite his good intentions for his "adopted" son, Owen Kane.

The first father figure, Brother Benedict, who terrorizes the boys and likewise the adult teachers under him such as Sebastian (as Michael Lamb is then known), seems the likely antagonist when the novel opens. Although he invites the young teacher in for a drink, he chastises him for taking the whiskey with water

(*L* 8) and quickly points out Sebastian's lack of interest in books and languages. To twit Sebastian and demonstrate his own superior learning, Benedict observes that he speaks Latin, Greek, and Gaelic and has focused his book collection in these languages, noting finally, in one of his pet phrases, that "a man with one language is like a man with one eye" (8). Although he indirectly ascribes limited vision to Sebastian, Benedict actually possesses the narrower vision—in both his educational practices and his republican politics. He is the true Cyclops figure of the early chapters—one-eyed in his worldview and associated with destructive power like the mythic Cyclops who forged thunderbolts for Zeus.

Fearing that Sebastian is not conforming to the pedagogical agenda of the borstal, Benedict demonstrates his lack of fitness for running a reform school by clearly defining what he sees as his purpose. He tells him at the end of chapter 1, "If they do not conform, we thrash them. We teach them a little of God and a lot of fear. It is a combination that seems to work. At least we think so. There is no room here for your soft-centred, self-centred idealism" (14). In the third chapter, while Benedict and Sebastian talk on the beach, Benedict again remarks, "A man with one language is like a man with one eye" (25), and Sebastian pretends not to hear him. The observation is closely followed by Benedict's dictum, "They teach you young men nothing nowadays. . . . Too much useless psychology" (25). Benedict believes not in psychology, shorthand to him for trying to understand his charges, but in the tongue and the hand as punishing tools. Benedict fancies himself not only an intellectual, but also a man of action and finds both intellect and action lacking in Sebastian, whom he casts as "Educationally Sub-Normal" at one point (10).[7]

On the other hand, Benedict clearly believes that the young male members of the Provisional IRA, whom he praises to Sebastian in the beginning of the novel, are men of action with appropriate vision. His vitriolic rhetoric sounds astonishing in the mouth of a Christian Brother, one who is supposedly committed to peace, but accords with his hostility toward both his students and fellow teachers. The Cyclopean Benedict ironically terms the IRA "angry men with vision" and notes that "by God their anger is justified. Ireland has not much longer to suffer. Her misery will soon be over and we'll be a united country again" (9). Sebastian agrees that a united Ireland may be on the horizon but rejects "their methods" (9). Instead, he finally argues to Benedict that "human elements can't be kept out. Anger, hatred, spoil the purity of the vision and the result is evil. If you know anyone who was killed, then you know how evil it is" (9). The juxtaposition of Benedict's tacit support for republicanism with Sebastian's humanist pacifism in this passage shows clearly that Sebastian, although much the younger and less experienced of the two, nevertheless possesses more wisdom than his superior. If he could only know it at the

*anger & hatred
don't contaminate
nt - love does*

time, his description of the way in which "human elements" creep into such fraught situations perfectly foretells how his own relative purity of vision in caring for Owen will eventually become contaminated by anger and hatred and result in evil.[8]

Benedict's presence in the novel, however, finally underscores Sebastian's growing loss of faith and decision to leave the school after his father dies. Benedict should be a model of servant leadership for the school, but his petty, tyrannical rule over the teachers and boys suggests his own replacement of a loving yet just God with himself, a prideful distortion of God filled with hate and wrath and without forgiveness. Unfortunately, his negative leadership in this sense models an independent elevation of the self to divine status that Sebastian Lamb gradually adopts and copies while on the run with Owen. Although Lamb tells himself that he loves the boy and eventually kills him out of a misguided love, his self-worship results in something far worse than Owen would have had to endure in Benedict's school or at home with his mother.

By far the strongest and warmest bonds in the novel are those remembered by Lamb as inhering in his family when he was young. His mother was crippled from the waist down by a heifer when he was five, but she lived on for another six years. The father's devoted service to her almost repels the boy with its sincerity and integrity and functions as the only proper model of true love in the novel, contrasted as it is with Brother Benedict's lack of love for his charges; the courting of Owen by the homosexual Haddock in the condemned house; and finally Lamb's deadly "love" for Owen.

Recalling his father's love for his mother one sleepless night in London, Lamb remembers their nightly ritual that displayed his steadfast affection for her in an incredibly tender way. He recalls that "each night before the family rosary, his father would freshen her up, washing her face and hands with a damp face-cloth. Although she could do this herself, she always let her husband do it. It became a sort of ritual, when he would caress her face with the cloth, looking at it as if for the slightest speck of dust. Then she would put her head down and let her hair fall forward while he washed and massaged her neck" (85). This repeated loving act of physical and emotional caregiving precedes the family recitation of the rosary and thus places familial devotion to this earthly mother above that of even the heavenly Virgin Mary. Moreover, if some fictional Irish farmers were traditionally married to their land, as John McGahern's foreboding fictional father Moran is in his 1990 novel *Amongst Women*, much to the detriment of his neglected second wife Rose, Lamb's father values his marriage to his wife well above the farm, causing the boy to realize that "with the time taken up looking after her, the farm began to go down" (86). He even feels that his father "sacrificed his life for her" (86), suggesting the real, enduring power of such loving, years-long care and evoking a clear contrast between the unnatural sacrifice that he finally feels ineluctably led to perform with Owen.

The love of Lamb's parents for each other is best described as a type of love the Greeks called *eros*. C. S. Lewis has written of *eros* that, within it, "a Need, at its most intense, sees the object most intensely as a thing admirable in herself, important far beyond her relation to the lover's need. . . . *Eros* . . . is . . . about the Beloved. It becomes almost a mode of perception, entirely a mode of expression."[9] Michael Lamb's father so loves his wife that his active care for her becomes his primary way of perceiving and expressing this love, in utter neglect of himself and of any needs that she might fulfill for him.

The father's attitude toward his wife, furthermore, is part of his "respect for every living thing" (86). Lamb recalls him even killing rabbits sick with myxomatosis quickly and mercifully to prevent their suffering and doing the same with chickens (86). Tellingly, however, he hates the local seagulls and leads his son on expeditions among the cliffs to destroy their eggs. Gulls are associated, like Brother Benedict and the IRA, with a lack of vision. Literal blindness is thought to be caused by the birds, as the boy's father tells him that "they'll peck the eyes from a lamb before the ewe can get her born—aye, and the tongue too" (86). That horrific potential of sightlessness lies dormant in the boy's mind for many years but will resurface in the novel's final scene as the three seagulls bear down on the real lamb of the novel—the lifeless Owen Kane. The contrast in the horror prevented by the only act of killing Lamb's father would countenance and the horror created by Lamb's own selfish murder could not be clearer.

In fact, despite having had such a warm, loving father and thinking himself to be such a father to Owen, Lamb comes to stand for everything diametrically opposed to what his father held so dear, his stiff, artificial actions a grotesque parody of the natural ones performed by his father. When he recalls his father's care of him, he realizes that "never once had he thought of his role as a father. It came so naturally to him to communicate his enthusiasms, his warmth" (86). Thus his father's love flowed naturally for him, but his own sense of love for Owen is not rooted in anything biological, natural, or meaningful, and he has to constantly and consciously think how he should care for the boy. Whereas Lamb's father protected him from danger and is recalled as lifting "Michael bodily across white water" (87), Lamb exposes Owen to possible harm by taking him to the football match and finally drowning him in the salty water of the Atlantic.

Lamb's actions with Owen at the match exemplify his failed parody of his own father's actions with him that made him feel so safe and secure. Like his father had done for him at the football turnstile, he lifts Owen up "so that he could get a glimpse of the pitch," using the same phrase, "stiff elbows," as his father had with him (91). But he has not made allowances for the stress that the game will place on Owen, and the lad quickly becomes stiff in another way as he experiences an epileptic attack (92–94). To add insult to injury, Owen becomes a sort of side-show, viewed voyeuristically by "[a] line of faces on a level with the track [that] watched, stunned" (94). Because this incident is preceded almost immediately by Lamb's recollection of the violent aftermath of the football match he attended with his father in childhood, the contrast between the father figure's actions in each case stands out in bold relief.

He recalls his father protecting him on the train ride home from the many drunks: he goes with him to the bathroom with "a large hand on each shoulder" (87), covers him with his coat, and finally twists a man's wrist behind his back who tries to attack him with a bottle (88). All these actions seem to come naturally to him, and his father's ease and calmness in performing them put the boy's mind at rest, although he still cannot get to sleep on the train. This type of love, which the Greeks called *storge*, or affection of parents toward offspring, is termed by Lewis as "the humblest love," which "gives itself no airs."[10] After thinking of this memory and of his father's catching a seagull once on a pier by accident, which he then has to kill, Lamb fervently thinks that he wants "to be to Owen what his father had been to him" (89). The incident at the football match shows instead how he exposes the boy to danger repeatedly in an attempt to cater to his wants, not his needs, and also how his own pride increasingly renders his attempts at *storge* love useless.

For example, Lamb manages to get them places down by the crush barrier at the match, traditionally one of the most dangerous places in a football stadium because hooligans are drawn to the area, and fans sometimes attempt to rush the field, risking serious injury. Indeed, he notices the skinheads at the barrier, who are shown "oathing and making obscene gestures" (92). One even urinates into a beer can and tosses it "into the crowd" (92). While Lamb's father would not have led him down to the barrier in the first place and would surely have moved away from such violent fans, the child Owen finally leads them away, trying to save face for Lamb, who clearly is out of his depth, by saying, "I think we could see better from down there" (92). Once Owen's epileptic fit starts, the roar of the crowd prevents Lamb from calling a doctor, and he and a fan have to heave the boy over the barrier to get air (93). Although Owen finally recovers with the help of Lamb and some paramedics, as the father figure, Lamb should have monitored the boy's condition more closely and probably not brought him to the game at all. In Lamb's misguided efforts to please, not protect the child, Owen runs the risk of serious injury.

The disaster at the football match not only shows how Lamb fails to live up to the fatherly standards he wants so desperately to emulate, but also how he is beginning to act out the life of another, much more negative father—the Greek

CHAPTER 2 *Purnell argues that Michael turns into Daedalus*

Daedalus, who also thrusts his son into a life-threatening situation with deadly results. In the chapter before the one recalling Lamb's childhood football incident, he and Owen read the Daedalus and Icarus legend from Thomas Bulfinch's *Age of the Fable*. The myth is new to Owen, not to the adult, but both subside into a stunned silence on Lamb's reading of the conclusion of the tale: "The playful mood of a moment ago had disappeared completely and they sat, each knowing the other was depressed" (79). The feathers used by Icarus and Daedalus reinforce the image of the flight the two have taken from Ireland to London and enable our understanding that they have been acting out these two mythic roles for some time and are only just now temporarily made aware of them.

Reading backward from this scene, we realize that the western Irish borstal Owen and Lamb have escaped is their first labyrinth and Brother Benedict its Minotaur. The school is part of a complex of buildings around a former Anglo-Irish Big House, which has been added onto over the years and is surrounded by "various prefabs scattered around the house for classrooms"; the complex is surrounded by "a high wire fence which screamed and whistled in the constant wind from the sea" (18). The whole affair is on "a promontory jutting its forehead into the Atlantic wind" (18). Both in its isolated location on the peninsula and in its mazelike corridors and welter of buildings, the borstal recalls the labyrinth on the island of Crete from which Icarus and Daedalus literally fly. Although he is not compared explicitly to the Minotaur with its head of a bull and body of a man, Benedict is often likened to a monstrous bird: his head is described as "sharp, beakish, owl-like" (13) and as has been noted, he loves to attack both the students and the teachers.

Although understandable given the oppression at the school, Lamb's prideful assumption of the Daedalus role in spiriting Owen away from there—ostensibly to protect him, as the real Daedalus did for his son in the Greek myth—places the boy into a series of dangerous situations. Strengthening the avian imagery specific to this mythic intertext, seagulls accompany the ferry across from Belfast to Stranraer, Scotland. They are portrayed as having "hard yellow eyes" and are not so much "flying but gliding, occasionally shrugging their shoulders to keep pace" (27). Their effortless flight contrasts the labored flight of Owen and Lamb as they try on their new identities of son and father, Icarus and Daedalus, and flit from one place to another.

A whole series of mazes await them in the vast teeming metropolis of London. The city itself and its Underground are one large, confusing maze to the man and boy. When first faced with this urban maze, the narrator observes that "Michael did not like to admit it to the boy, but he was stunned by the Underground. The moving stairs that bore them down to the guts of the city, the stopping each time they came to a sign to interpret it as people rushed around them" (58). Soon they desert this maze and take taxis for longer trips within the city. Along with the London hotels they negotiate, with their long, labyrinthine corridors, the home stadium for Owen's favorite football team, Arsenal, also functions as a maze. Once he is launched into his brief flight over the crush barrier during his epileptic fit, he lies there gasping for air "like a fish as he arched and flapped on the track" (93). As the two try to leave the stadium after the boy has recovered, they quickly become lost in the winding corridors and tunnels, finally asking for directions. Lamb remarks "it's like a maze," seemingly oblivious to the role he is gradually assuming as danger-seeking Daedalus to Owen's Icarus (95).

The Daedalian and Icarian roles that these two characters increasingly act out may be their unconscious attempts to remake in a positive way the various negative avian images abounding in the novel. Along with Benedict's portrayal as a pecking bird, the watchful Christian Brothers at the borstal in western Ireland are described as moving "like crows, their black soutanes flapping" (19). The threat of seagulls pecking out lambs' eyes from Michael's childhood and the trapped seagull killed by his father, along with the staring seagulls that trail their ferry to Scotland and the particular gull that nips and bloodies Owen's fingers, coalesce with these other avian images to create a negative bird complex in both Lamb and Owen somewhat analogous to what Weldon Thornton has identified in the text of Joyce's *A Portrait of the Artist as a Young Man.* Thornton argues that Joyce's Stephen Dedalus, plagued by such a complex, eventually tries to remake this negative image "into an image of beauty and of his destiny" in embracing his role as the fabulous artificer signified by his last name.[11] And yet, as Thornton shows, Stephen implicitly identifies with Icarus in addressing Daedalus in the novel's conclusion as "old father, old artificer" and thus unconsciously expresses that "his flight to freedom is not so secure as he would like to believe."[12]

MacLaverty's characters, save for that one moment in the hotel reading Bulfinch's rendition of the Greek myth, seem largely unaware of their avian roles as Icarus and Daedalus yet nonetheless may be guided by them and thus unconsciously heading for a fall. In a twist on the Greek legend, however, MacLaverty's Icarus figure, Owen, has none of the pride associated with his archetypal forerunner, while his Daedalus figure, Michael Lamb, manifests the pride usually associated with Icarus. In increasingly attempting to fly away from the various entrapping mazes they encounter, they repeatedly enact these roles, confirming their identity as these mythic characters and thus narrowing their possibilities for true escape. Typical of "maze-treaders," their "vision ahead and behind is severely constricted and fragmented," and as a result, they often "suffer confusion."[13]

Having escaped the entrapping labyrinth of the old house containing the monstrous Haddock, who is gradually seducing Owen while Michael works on building sites during the day, Lamb resolves for them to fly metaphorically close to the sun and go back to Ireland. He risks discovery at the airport check-in, during the flight, and afterward, but these are small hindrances to the fulfillment of his plan, finally decided on after he realizes the risk Owen faces in the condemned house alone with Haddock. After he finds Haddock and Owen smoking pot together and the man's arm around the boy (130), Michael decides that "[t]he plan would have to become a reality. If he had the courage. Sacrifice was required. God knows, he had tried every way to avoid it. It was the only answer left" (132). This murderous sense of sacrifice diverges completely from his initial sense of self-denying sacrifice at the beginning of his flight with the boy. As he tenderly watches the sleeping boy on the ferry ride to Scotland, he eagerly anticipates "caring for the boy" and "[d]ressing him well, not prissily, buying him things he had never had before, taking him places. Teaching him. He knew there was more than enough time to salvage him, this piece of jetsam. Sacrifice was what was required" (34). Michael Lamb's changing notions of sacrifice are grounded in his evolving attitude toward God, perhaps the most important father figure of the novel.

After gazing at the boy on the ferry to Scotland, Lamb realizes that "he had never really felt this way before" (34) because his love had previously been "channeled toward Jesus and Mary," before whose pictures he would kneel in adoration, prayer, and worship. Michael's childhood picture of Jesus shows Him "walking on the water, His hand raised in benediction, His lightly bearded face full of love and pity" (34). Jesus reaches His hand out to Peter who is sinking in the Sea of Galilee because of his lack of faith. The picture of Mary represents her as iconic and elongated with her long, thin hands not so much holding the baby Jesus as being "placed against Him as He floated. Her face was turned to heaven and exuded a love that Michael had tried to imitate" (35). Significantly, both these pictures have as their focus divine, sustaining power. Jesus's loving, merciful gaze literally helps Peter float in the water, and Mary's caressing hands undergird the floating baby Jesus.

When he was a believer, Michael approached God as a friendly father accessible through his amicable relationship with Jesus. As he and Owen sit at eight o'clock morning mass in London, he recalls the "warmth and security of having in his mind a Christ figure that loved him, that he could talk to intimately and as he believed then, who would listen to him" (110). Asking forgiveness for his sins in Jesus's name would lead him to a tearful reconciliation with God. "Love. Jesus. Him. Imaginary companions. His loving father" (111). Singing the hymn "Blood of My Saviour" made him feel purified and holy, washed in Jesus's sacrificial blood shed for believers everywhere (111).

Yet as he loses his faith, Lamb retains a core belief in love and sacrifice that increasingly becomes prideful and egotistical. His new notion of love is severed from an outward, saving sacrifice and dependent on his work, not the work of Christ on the cross. Instead of believing that "God is love," he now feels strongly that "I am love" (112). He even believes that his father was a savior figure and that he is too. "Thousands of saviours like his father in any one lifetime would be sufficient fuel for the world. They must exist. He knew because he was one of them himself. He knew he was good. I am love. There was no pride or pomposity in this thought for him. He just knew that he wanted to help in whatever way he could the suffering of the world" (112–13). These lies ignore the lingering power of original sin in humanity and lead Michael into a delusional self-worship. He misunderstands his father's sacrificial love of him, rooted in a Christlike denial of self, a real storge love, and instead views himself as a savior capable of relieving the real and imagined suffering that he fears Owen will be exposed to if he returns him to Benedict's school or to his mother's care.

Stephen Watt notes that "even though Michael hopes to rescue Owen from Brother Benedict's cruelty, he also craves the emotional gratification his intervention will produce,"[14] an insight that suggests the inherent neediness of Michael's attempted storge love of Owen. C. S. Lewis argues that overly needy parents, like King Lear, "may be full of such ravenous love. But it works to their own misery and everyone else's. The situation becomes suffocating."[15] Michael's need to be loved by Owen shares Lear's insatiability for his daughters to quantify their love, but is more characterized by its perversion of love as a gift, a deviation from true storge love. Lewis suggests that this perversion is "one that needs to give; therefore needs to be needed. But the proper aim of giving is to put the recipient in a state where he no longer needs our gift. . . . Thus a heavy task is laid upon this Gift-love. It must work towards its own abdication. We must work at making ourselves superfluous."[16] Michael Lamb wants to constantly give Owen things (34) but always "needs to be needed" and finally exalts himself, in the process crippling Owen, not equipping him with life skills he truly needs to flourish as an independent human being. As Lewis notes, left unchecked, "The ravenous need to be needed will gratify itself either by keeping its objects needy or by inventing for them imaginary needs. It will do this all the more ruthlessly because it thinks . . . that it is a Gift-love and therefore regards itself as 'unselfish.'"[17] Michael keeps Owen dependent on him, choosing to view himself as a selfless giver, not the selfish needer that he is.

In this radical, prideful exaltation of his needy self and perversion of storge love, Michael sheds the identity of protector associated with his Christian name that recalls the archangel Michael, but retains, with tragic consequences, other elements of that identity, namely, his desire to bring judgment and his association with water. As his "angelic" identity is subsumed into his Daedalian identity, he becomes truly prideful and acquires an additional identity with another winged figure of pride—Lucifer. The night before the football match he will attend with Owen, Michael recalls the admonition of the Novice Master about the powerful allure of pride symbolized by Lucifer. This man observes, "pride, Brothers, is one of the worst sins of all. I see Lucifer on useless wings plummeting into the sea of Hell for all eternity because of it. It is only by subjugating your will to the will of others—and God—that you will find your true self" (90). Michael's attempts to follow this advice are finally frustrated because he is simply not capable of submitting his will fully to God. Only God can perform this act. Instead of patiently praying for his egotism to be crushed and to be sanctified by the Holy Spirit, Michael finally turns on God, effectively replacing Him with himself, copying Lucifer's rebellion. Just as Lucifer falls, bringing others down with him, so will Michael.

By the end of the novel, Michael Lamb feels he must not sustain Owen through a love based on that of Jesus for Peter, of Mary for the baby Jesus, or, most important, of Jesus for believers—a love that requires a self-abnegating sacrifice by the teaching or parental figure—but that he must save Owen by sacrificing the boy's life. Lamb's role of prideful Daedalus, careless of his son, leads him into active, Luciferian rebellion and to immerse the boy in water and drown him. MacLaverty himself has pointed out the conflation of mythic action and Christian sacrament in this scene, calling the act "the perverse baptism which takes place in" water, pointing out that Owen is "the Icarus figure who plunges into it."[18] Water, which had been associated with freedom,[19] is used finally with force, not sustaining power, to kill Owen at the end of the novel. Michael Lamb, previously the lamb figure of the novel by virtue of his seeming innocence and meekness, along with his sacrificial love of Owen, now kills the real lamb, Owen, whose name means "lamb" in Gaelic.[20] This helpless, epileptic lamb is sacrificed by a man who shamelessly prays to the Lamb of God to help Owen die quickly. "Dear Jesus, make it now" (150).

Michael's perversion of striking visual elements in the narrative of Christianity—baptism, Christ's sacrificial death on the cross for the sins of believers—shares certain salient features with the destructive power of extreme nationalism in the novel and anticipates the fuller development of this theme of nationalistic martyrdom through the subtle visual evocations of the republican hunger strikers in *Cal*. Just as Lamb realizes that "he had started with a pure loving simple ideal but it had gone foul on him, turned inevitably into something evil" (152), the rhetoric of the novel suggests that so has Irish republicanism become perverted and even evil as the contemporary Troubles turned increasingly violent and indiscriminate.[21] In this analogy, just as Michael Lamb moves from being the defender of the helpless boy Owen Kane to becoming his murderer, the IRA was transformed from a defender of marginalized Catholics in Northern Ireland to a destroyer of the Catholic community. Lamb feels that significant moments in his life have followed this same pattern. "It had been like this all his life, with the Brothers, with the very country he came from. The beautiful fly with the hook embedded" (152). The metaphor of the alluring fly, so closely following the reference to Northern Ireland, implies that the beautiful ideal of a united Ireland ensnares those who obsessively pursue it, and the novel clearly condemns such a misguided pursuit. The Owen Kanes always suffer as a result, as do all the innocent of the province.

More important, MacLaverty suggests great hope in his bleak criticism of this personal and ideological ideal. In the novel's conclusion, Michael Lamb's body is rendered analogous to a bombed-out building in Northern Ireland: he feels "gutted. It was as if his insides and his soul had been burned out. There was nothing left of him but the sound of his crying" (152). His crying and the final horrific vision of the novel—"the three gulls, their yellow beaks angled with screeching, descending slowly, with meticulous care" (152)—seem utterly hopeless. Yet in this tableau lie the seeds of personal and societal redemption. Gary Brienzo has articulated how MacLaverty's "bleak renderings" of Ireland and his characters are heightened "because of his commitment to a sympathetic inner vision and detailed realism as the sources of the awareness needed before any changes can occur."[22] In this sense, because Lamb recognizes his own evil, and by extension, we recognize how our own idealistic actions can lead to disaster, his emptiness and our own vicarious gutted feelings may produce a vacuum into which truly sacrificial love may enter and transform our lives and our societies.

Seasonal Communication
in *A Time to Dance and Other Stories*

IN 1982, MACLAVERTY RELEASED HIS SECOND VOLUME of short stories, *A Time to Dance*, which won an award from the Scottish Arts Council in 1982 and an arts award from the *Irish Sunday Independent* in 1983. These stories develop themes from earlier work, such as the father-son relationships central to *Lamb* and the motif of limited sight from that novel. Although there is no unifying theme in this collection, most of the stories are placed into the context of seasonal movement across the periods of human life. This concern is signaled by "A Time to Dance," which borrows its title from the famous words of the Old Testament prophet in Ecclesiastes and connotes a movement of timeless normality that contrasts the false normality in many nonworking-class areas of Northern Ireland at that time because of the continuing violence in its ghettos. Two of the most sympathetic pieces include the lengthiest and most-developed story, "My Dear Palestrina," a coming-of-age story about a young boy and his relationship with his unusual, outcast music teacher, and "The Daily Woman," which are early examples of MacLaverty's immense attention to female characters, an interest that reaches its apogee in *Grace Notes*. The best stories in the collection feature a range of artists, in an expansive sense of the term, who show the limitations of higher human language by conveying immutable human feelings such as pleasure and pain through primal sounds and physical actions.

Robert Hogan has argued that most of the pieces in *A Time to Dance* "are static sketches of character rather than stories."[1] This contention is not meant to denigrate them; indeed, Hogan holds that "as sketches, they are generally successful and provocatively contrasting both in subject and in tone."[2] The lack of movement and character development in the collection, with the significant exception of "My Dear Palestrina," may reflect the increasingly static society that Northern Ireland had become by the late 1970s and early 1980s because of the Troubles. One of the most insightful chroniclers of life in the province in the early to mid-1980s was the American journalist John Conroy. He has argued that the Provisional IRA's change of tactics in the late 1970s to "fight a very selective war, shooting and bombing soldiers . . . [and] policemen" along with the British Army's isolation of working-class Catholic ghettoes such as areas of west Belfast combined to effectively insulate "normal society from the conflict," while ensuring further frustration and violence in ghetto areas.[3] Conroy's formulation needs qualification. He seems to view "normal society" as the preserve of middle- and upper-class inhabitants of the province, a problematic notion, to say the least. Additionally, there were sectarian atrocities carried out separately from the operations of the IRA or the British Army that did occur in areas of Northern Ireland outside of the working-class districts—events that created lingering tensions and fears in the Northern psyche across classes. Yet Conroy's central point is incontrovertible: the poorest quarters of the province felt the brunt of the violence.[4]

A Time to Dance, on the other hand, inscribes an enduring, different kind of continuity—that of the movement of human life through its various stages from youth to old age. The portrayal of such lives reassures the reader that, despite the ongoing violence, the normal cycle of life and death also endures, as it would elsewhere in the world. Juxtaposing lives cut short by violence, as, for example, in the young man's murder in "Father and Son," with the looming death from geriatric cancer of the old woman in "Eels" heightens the lost potential of abbreviated lives, while still showing how the old have profound regrets about their own lives. Moreover, although stories about adolescent boys still dominate the collection, just as they did in *Secrets*, stories about middle age, such as "Language, Truth, and Lockjaw," and old age, such as "Eels," lend a voice of experience and wisdom that tempers the exuberance of youth in other stories.

MacLaverty's continuing concern with the often-strained relationships between fathers and sons is manifested in his first story directly about the Troubles, "Father and Son," and also in "Life Drawing." The father figure in the first story is seen as an old woman and in the second, as a tyrant, while the sons attempt to create their own separate identities from that of their fathers, often with debilitating results. "Father and Son," while criticized by Hogan as a "too-short" piece,[5] actually melds content and form admirably in its truncated form detailing a snuffed-out life. Not only does the terseness of its form convey the son's abbreviated life, but also its interior monologues, interspersed with moments of conversation between father and son, suggest their essential aloneness despite their love for each other. They cannot communicate except in short bursts of nagging by the father, who is dedicated to order—to his job and to domestic life—and in angry retorts by the son, who is dedicated increasingly to his chaotic vocation of violence. Much of the poignancy of the story is conveyed through the physical descriptions of their shaking hands: the father's from fear and the son's previously from exhaustion and the effects of drug use when he returned from London and now from hatred. The father's repeated desire to put his arms around his son, finally realized with the young man's murder at the conclusion of the story, similarly conveys a deep sorrow that blends emotion and an oblique Catholic venerational iconography.

Each plays a role for the other at odds with his actual outlook. The father pretends to be a guardian and rescuer of his son, but is actually a coward, while the son pretends to be an obedient child, but is secretly a man of violence seeking autonomy from his father. These roles have some grounding in reality. For example, the father has actually rescued his son from a life on the streets in London in the past (*TD* 12), and the son, who is forced to still live at home because of his lack of a job, tries to assuage his father's fears for him when he pretends to be asleep in the opening interior monologue (9).

Both men, however, increasingly have become something other than their ostensible roles they play for each other. The father annoys his son with his fearfulness, as the young man notes in one interior monologue. "You live in fear. Of your own death. Peeping behind curtains, the radio always loud enough to drown any noise that might frighten you, double locking doors. When you think I am not looking you hold your stomach. You undress in the dark for fear of your shadow falling on the window-blind" (12). The father's fear for his son and himself makes him a veritable prisoner in his own home when he is not at work, and the son, eager to fly the nest, increasingly chafes at his concern.

Father and son, if they could only know it, resemble each other physically, a likeness that is represented by their shaking hands. After his father tells him he shaves at night "because in the morning my hand shakes," the son links his shaking hands to his father's cowardice. "Your hand shakes in the morning, Da, because you're a coward. You think the world is waiting round the corner to blow your head off" (11). Yet this interior monologue is immediately followed by the father's recollection of his son's shaking hand when the exhausted young man returned from London. "Son, you are living on borrowed time. Your hand shook when you got home. . . . I fed you soup from a spoon when your own hand would have spilled it" (11). Shortly before the son is murdered on the doorstep of their house, the father realizes how "full of hatred" the boy is (13) and recognizes his hatred by his shrill, shouting voice and his shaking hands (13). Hands are one of the body parts that generate the highest amount of neural activity, and MacLaverty's use of them to such a degree in this story draws unconsciously on our heightened mental processes in making our own hands move, which in turn allows us to more easily generate a moving mental image of these particular hands.[6]

The relative compression of this story highlights the physicality of father and son in a manner that recalls Austin Wright's description of the effect of "recalcitrance" in short fiction. Wright argues that if form is "a work's unique principle of wholeness, its organizing, shaping, unifying principle," then recalcitrance "is simply the resistance offered by the materials to that form as it tries to shape them."[7] The recalcitrance of content achieved in "Father and Son" is consistent with what Wright terms "a general recalcitrance common to all short works, manifest in the intensity of detail that shortness confers. In general, the shorter the work, the more prominent the details."[8] The brevity of this story, especially in contrast to the other works in the volume, along with the compelling passages separated by white spaces on the page, work together to intensify the process by which the reader's attention is repeatedly focused on every passage and every image. We are especially drawn to the hands of the father and the son and the father's continual desire to embrace his son through a process that Wright terms "the arresting of notice at every significant point."[9]

Although father and son never really get to talk in the story as the father wishes, they are united finally by the son's death and the father's embrace of him, a moment that, on closer inspection, borrows its iconography from traditional Catholic artistic renderings of the Pieta. As he slowly realizes that his son is dead, shot through the head, the father silently tells him, "My son, let me put my arms around you" (14). Although this moment bespeaks father-son reconciliation on one level, on another, it also adumbrates an image that MacLaverty would explore again at the end of *Cal*—the Pieta of the suffering Mary holding the crucified Christ in her arms. The son has earlier linked his father to his dead mother and obliquely to the Virgin Mary by musing, "My mother is dead but I have another one in her place. He is an old woman. He has been crying. I know he prays for me all the time" (11–12). The son's description of his father as a mother continually practicing intercessory prayer for him and his father's feminized apprehension for his son's safety and his desire to embrace him show how reading this final scene from a Catholic iconic perspective imbues it with a sacrificial tone that deepens its emotional resonance. The danger in this reading, of course, lies in identifying the young man's death, presumably on behalf of the republican cause, as redemptive, even saintly. MacLaverty's description of the son's handgun from the father's perspective as "black and squat, dull like a garden slug" (13)[10] goes some way toward de-romanticizing the lad's death, however, as does the father's desperate attempt to lead a normal life in the midst of "[t]he sound of ambulances criss-cross[ing] the dark" (10). Overall, the story powerfully both demonstrates how the often-indiscriminate chaos of the Troubles could enter the domestic strongholds of citizens trying valiantly to carry on with normal life and suggests the allure of violence as vocation to the younger generation.

Visual images of physicality also permeate a later story about fathers and sons in the collection, "Life Drawing." The son, Liam Diamond, who is returning after twenty years of absence to be there for his dying father, is an artist who has been compared to Mondrian (79). As he travels home on the train, he sees the paintings of Viennese artist Egon Schiele and is taken by their graphic, visceral qualities. "All sinew and gristle and distortion. There was something decadent about them, like Soutine's pictures of hanging sides of beef" (69). These grotesque images of flesh, sinew, and gristle are indirectly linked with a graphic moment from Liam's past that he recalls as he sits with his father that night. When he was sixteen, his father was cooking sausages in a skillet and Liam tried to grab one, only to be jabbed with his father's fork in the back of his hand, causing "four bright beads of blood" to be raised. (74)

Indeed, the sheer physicality of both his brother and his father has led Liam to hate them. For example, recalling the game he played with his brother as children in which one child leaned his head back over the edge of the bed and the other one watched the head grow red "as the blood flooded into it" (77) makes him realize that "in adolescence he had come to hate his brother, could not stand the physical presence of him, just as when he was lying upside down on the bed" (77–8). Similarly, "It was the same with his father. He could not bear to touch him and yet for one whole winter he had to stay up late to rub him with oil of wintergreen" (78). Liam would stand there, "massaging the stinking stuff into the white flesh of his back. The smell, the way the blubbery skin moved under his fingers, made him want to be sick" (78).

Another incident he recalls with his father suggests how much Liam associates physicality, especially physical violence, with art. When he was painting his self-portrait late one night, his father had burst in and yelled at him, smacking "him full force with the flat of his hand on his bare back" (78). Liam leapt to his feet, ready to fight, and his father met him with cocked fists. After he retreated and his father left, Liam "looked over his shoulder into the mirror and saw the primitive daub of his father's hand, splayed fingers outlined across his back" (78). It is natural for his artist's mind to perceive the print of his father's hand on his back as a daub of paint, but its forcefulness and his brief conception of himself as a canvas, coupled with his father's immediately subsequent smashing of his self-portrait with a poker, renders him briefly without an identity, covered with his father's imprint. Further, the blood that is raised on his back by his father's slap is conflated with a potential image of spilled blood when the boy steps on the shards of the painting the next day. His father strangely, almost affectionately, warns him to "watch your feet in the morning," at the end of this passage (78).

Because of his hatred for the sheer physicality of his father's and brother's presence, Liam has become exceedingly unemotional and distant, even specializing in abstract art that has been criticized as "cold" and "formalist" (79). His relationships display the same qualities as his art. When he wonders whether he should blame his father for his failures with women, he observes, "He had married once and lived with two other women. At present he was on his own. Each relationship had ended in hate and bitterness, not because of drink or lack of money or any of the usual reasons but because of a mutual nauseating dislike" (80). Liam is probably a secular Gnostic, disdaining the life of the flesh because of the repulsion associated with flesh from his childhood that is manifested in his intensely abstract art. His father's death, however, gives him a renewed interest in physicality that may augur the recovery of Liam's potential to enter into emotionally and physically satisfying relationships.

Having viewed his sketches of hands in red pastel in his childhood sketchbook earlier that evening and remembered his potential in life drawing (76), Liam retrieves the sketchbook and begins drawing his father. The motif of hands connecting father and son, introduced in "Father and Son," is more fully explored here with the image of Liam's painted red hands figuratively connected to the red handprint his father left on his back years ago. Additionally, as he draws his father, Liam recalls how, earlier in the evening, "when he had held his hand it had been clean and dry and light like the hand of a girl" (79). As his father physically recedes from him, somehow Liam is inspired to more fully render him in his charcoal drawings; ironically, these "life drawings" are of a dead man, as Liam realizes at 5:30 that morning (80).

As he wonders what to do with his dead father, he has a Joycean epiphany, somewhat analogous to Gabriel Conroy's concluding revelation in "The Dead." Liam, too, has viewed the snow falling outside the house, occasionally hitting the windowpane (79) and has finally realized, like Gabriel, his own lack of emotion. "Then he saw himself in his hesitation, saw the lack of any emotion in his approach to the problem. He was aware of the deadness inside himself and felt helpless to do anything about it. It was why all his women had left him. One of them accused him of making love the way other people rodded drains" (81). This awareness of emotional coldness and his subsequent kneeling beside his father's deathbed and imagining his hard work on behalf of him and his brother lead Liam into a positive memory of his father, which is associated with the dead man's hands and his mouth lying open in death. His father always "megaphoned his hands to tell the story" of two ships passing in the night and the Cork captain's elaborate exaggeration of his city's name as "Cork a–lorka–lorio" to the other captain, who has told him he is bound for "Rio–de–Janeir–io" (81). Like Gabriel, Liam cries, his eyes filling with tears, and although he is not able "to keep them coming" (82), he nevertheless experiences remorse at his father's death and a new resolve to remember him, which is expressed in his desire to "work on the drawings later. Perhaps a charcoal series" (82). Connected now to the dead like Joyce's protagonist, Liam may be able to draw new connections with the living, a significant development for this previously frozen artist.

The connection between art and emotion is most fully explored in the longest story in the volume, "My Dear Palestrina." In an anticipation of *Grace Notes*, which would feature the composer Catherine McKenna realizing the fruits of two acts of creativity—the composition of a new symphony and the birth of her child—this story revolves around a Jewish immigrant to Northern Ireland, Miss Schwartz, a piano teacher who becomes pregnant in the course of the story and is ostracized by the rigid Catholic community, yet leaves her best pupil, Danny, with a lasting appreciation of how supremely personal art can precipitate emotion.

Danny has another teacher as well—the Marxist village blacksmith who pounds out his metalwork to a musical rhythm that Danny walks to as he passes the man's forge coming back from his music lessons. In a direct allusion to the famous opening line of Seamus Heaney's "The Forge" from the poet's second volume *Door into the Dark* (1969), the entrance to the forge is described as the "door into the dark," and MacLaverty also invokes Heaney's comparison between making metal and making art as he describes "the high pinging of the blacksmith's hammer" (31). Both the poet and the smith make their own distinctive music, according to Heaney, through a mystical process that involves reverence and receptivity.[11] MacLaverty too seems to adopt this model of creativity, portraying "the rhythmic sound of hammering" (36) coming from his smith's forge as he portrays yet another artist in the making, the young Danny, who blossoms into a talented musician during the course of the story.

The link between the ephemeral, delicate Miss Schwartz and the stolid, big-boned blacksmith is subtly evoked in both these music teachers' efforts to try and convey to Danny their belief in equal rights and tolerance while teaching him their respective crafts. Miss Schwartz is a Jewish refugee, having left Poland as a young girl when she was around Danny's age (50). She tells Danny of her feelings of desolation because of her deracination, musing, "to be an exile, to be cut off from your country is a terrible thing" (50). In the local Catholic community's eventual rejection of her because of her out-of-wedlock pregnancy, she is displaced again, cut off from her source of income when her pupils' parents pull them out of lessons. The irony is profound: as MacLaverty implies, it is exactly these characters, fictional analogs for actual Catholics living in the Protestant-dominated Northern

Ireland of the late 1950s who have been systematically discriminated against, that should be most receptive to Miss Schwartz.

Both Schwartz and the blacksmith, however, despite their despair over present conditions—she, for her new state of exile, he, for the divisions between the working-class Catholics and Protestants in the province—evince great hope in the future, when they believe a revolution will occur. For her, the revolution will be symbolized by music. As she tells Danny on his last visit to her house, "It will come. I'm sure it will come. People are like the beasts of the field. They know nothing of music or tenderness. Anyone whom music has spoken to—really spoken to—must be gentle, must be kind—could not be guilty of a cruelty" (64). Her exemplar of the coming revolution is the composer Palestrina, who reportedly was told by one of the popes, according to Schwartz, "The law, my dear Palestrina, ought to employ your music to lead hardened criminals to repentance" (64–65). She cannot imagine the town would ruin her financially "if they had truly heard one bar of Palestrina" (65). As she plays a Palestrina piece for Danny at full volume on her old gramophone, she has him close his eyes and feel the music. Although she has wanted him to cry from the "sheer beauty of it," (64) he cries mostly because of his great regret for leaving her, although he does recognize the great beauty of the "stairs of sound ascending and yet descending at the same instant" (65). Believing that he is crying because of the music's beauty, she abruptly stops the record and hugs him on her knees (65), "the tears streaming down her face, wetting her chin" (66). He responds by putting his arms around her neck, but when she kisses his head repeatedly, "moving towards his mouth," he wrenches "his head to the side, not knowing what to do" (66).

MacLaverty deploys a virtually unrecognizable image of the Pieta in his depiction of Schwartz's maternal, then sexualized embrace of Danny, whom she seems to perceive as both son and lover. She sees Danny as pure and, knowing he is soon to be virtually dead to her through his absence, weeps over his living body like the Virgin Mary did over her crucified son. Yet instead of recalling the Jewish Mary as the chaste, heavenly-impregnated mother who will see her son taken from her all too soon, MacLaverty gives us a contemporary Jew, impregnated by an unknown lover, who laments her adopted son even as she tries to finally kiss him on the mouth. Nevertheless, Schwartz's posture profoundly conveys her wrenching loss of her best student even as it ironically and playfully suggests the failure of the local Catholic community to recognize a woman whose situation, in significant secular ways, is remarkably similar to "Our Blessed Lady" (66) who they venerate.

Just as Danny learns from Miss Schwartz the importance of personally feeling music and how music, and by extension, art, might unite human beings living in a chaotic world who feel their beauty and order, he learns from the blacksmith the radical similarity between people. In a classic Marxist critique of the divisions in Northern Ireland, the man tells Danny at one point that the upper class has purposely set "one side against the other. Divide and conquer. It's an old ploy and the Fenians and Orangemen of this godforsaken country have fallen for it again" (51). While Schwartz predicts a revolution of thought and feeling later in the story, the smith argues that "a change is coming, Danny Boy. We must be positive. Prepare the ground. Educate the people. Look to the future the way Connolly and Larkin did in 1913" (51). The smith perceives the potential unity across sectarian division that inheres in the common interest of the working-class to advance economically. His practical blacksmithing lessons to Danny that show him how to make beautiful shapes of order out of the messy, molten metal echo his political sentiments that class unity and order can arise from chaos and opposition.

Ordered by his parents not to see either of these teachers anymore, probably out of their misguided fears that they will somehow infect Danny with their pernicious mentalities, the boy fights with his parents after returning from his last music lesson and retreats to his hut in the garden after being beaten by his father. As he crouches in the hut, Danny seems to wrap himself in its "darkness," hugging himself and resting "his wet cheek on his knees" (67). He thus recreates the ideal condition for artistic creativity, as shown him by both Miss Schwartz and the blacksmith. Both teachers like to work in the darkness, which functions as a correlative to the receptive, unconscious mind: Danny's last lesson even ends in darkness, partly so Schwartz can attune his ears to the music. While the snow in "Life Drawing" paradoxically highlights the frozen Liam's awakening into a new appreciation of his father and possibly into a new emotional warmth for himself, the snow surrounding Danny's hut at the end of "My Dear Palestrina" symbolically preserves the warmth of his memories under the tutelage of both teachers. Even though his mother finally retrieves the physically numb boy, imploring him to "come into the heat, love, . . . come in from the night. Join us" (67), Danny has found a warmth outside of his parents' love in the knowledge of the beauty and order of art and its ability to connect seemingly disparate human beings, a message that would become increasingly prominent in MacLaverty's later fiction—most supremely so in *Grace Notes*.[12]

The boy Nelson in "A Time to Dance" seems worlds removed from the violent young man of "Father and Son," and indeed he is in some ways. Yet he, too, is aimless and a drifter of sorts, skipping classes in his Catholic school in Edinburgh when he can. His father's absence and his mother's Irishness mark him as different from the other boys in school, as does his lack of money. Compounding his isolation from the other boys is the eye patch he is forced to wear so that he will not go blind. Whereas in *Lamb*, Brother Benedict's monocular vision and that of

Lamb himself showed their metaphorical blindness to the needs of others, Nelson's eye patch symbolizes his relative innocence and shelters him from the degrading aspects of life such as his mother's nude dancing at a men's club.

When he is caught skipping school one day by his mother, she is forced to bring him to the club where she works, potentially exposing him to the sordid side of her profession. She forces him to cover both his eyes with patches so he cannot see her perform, but he takes them off, and, standing on some crates, sees "a crowd of men standing in a semicircle," who are watching his mother dance (23). She dances for them three times, and they cheer loudly. When she returns, she is panting and he accidentally hits her belly with his hand and feels "her bare stomach, hot and damp with sweat" (23–24). If he had not realized it before, Nelson now at least knows his mother dances for a living. Her dancing in this context renders her a perverse, distorted symbol of the artist. Unlike the son in "Life Drawing" or the artist figures in "My Dear Palestrina," she has no choice about when she must "create," and she must do it not to please herself, but to please others.

Yet her continual sacrifice of herself onstage for her son and the sexual performance she likely will give for Nelson's housemaster, Mr. MacDermot, so that he can stay in school are ultimately heroic, self-abnegating acts to further his education so that he can have a real profession. After Nelson leaves the conference with his mother and Mr. MacDermot, the housemaster tells him "I have some more things to say to your mother." As he leaves, Nelson sees that "his mother had put her knee up against the Housemaster's desk and was swaying back in her chair, as she took out another cigarette" (27, 28). Although his mother may well enjoy the acts she will perform for the housemaster, she nonetheless knows she is incapable of doing otherwise: a trapped dancer, she works hard for her shiftless son, who seems unappreciative of what she goes through for him.

When Nelson goes into the classroom and hears his teacher read from Ecclesiastes, he seems oblivious to the language, but the reader realizes that the seasonal thrust of the verses suggests a lovely rhythm to our lives. "There is an appointed time for everything, and a time for every affair under the heavens. A time to be born and a time to die; a time to plant and a time to uproot. . . . A time to kill and a time to heal; a time to wear down and a time to build. A time to weep and a time to laugh; and a time to mourn and a time to dance" (28). If Nelson and his mother can enjoy the time they have in their current seasons of life, they may recognize that this time of dancing can be a joyful one that will steel them for times of mourning later. While Nelson's mother recognizes the necessity of her degrading dancing and performing, Nelson seems to fail to see how his time in school will help prepare him for a fruitful future. As the story concludes, he rips off his remaining eye patch and stares closely at the passage from Ecclesiastes, "thinking that if he was going to become blind then the sooner it happened the better" (29). Despite its negative language, this passage may suggest his determination to concentrate more fully on his lessons, a potentially liberating move that will allow him to quit using his lazy eye as an excuse to be a bad student.

Physical affliction as a precipitator of self-knowledge also drives the action of the last story in the collection, "Language, Truth, and Lockjaw," about a university lecturer in philosophy on holiday whose jaw locks during a visit to his dentist and later in his lovemaking with his wife. Just as the painful jolt of Liam's seeing the open jaw of his newly dead father in "Life Drawing" leads him to a pleasurable memory of his father's humor and into an emotional awakening, so does the pain of Norman's lockjaw in the midst of pleasure show him his connection to humanity and the folly of his vanity. Despite Norman's disdain for the mentally retarded men who are staying next door on their own holiday, after his jaw locks during lovemaking with his wife, he eerily resembles them physically and linguistically. Ironically, they have gone on holiday to better communicate, his wife having told him earlier in the story, "You don't talk to me any more" (167). Norman's locked jaw and his subsequent temporary inability to communicate actually lead to a deeper communication beyond words, rendering him humbler and making his wife more tender toward him.

The close juxtaposition between the sexual pleasure and bodily pain Norman experiences contradicts the subject of the paper that he is writing, which has been "sparked off by [Gilbert] Ryle's distinction between pleasure and pain—that they were not elements on the same spectrum, that positive quantities of one did not lead to minus quantities of the other" (165). The inadequacy of Ryle's position and the falsity of Norman's own argument to his wife that "if you can't put a thing into language, it doesn't exist" (168) are exposed by the bodily knowledge of his wife he enjoys and his realization of the inarticulacy of language to express the feeling of love for his wife and children. After Patricia fixes his jaw, they snuggle together in bed, and Norman ponders what has happened and why she has laughed so hysterically at him, realizing how mysterious she remains to him. Newly connected to his family and more obliquely to the retarded men next door, whose facial expressions he has briefly copied, Norman drifts off to sleep hearing his wife's laughter shaking the bed "in the same way as shudders remain after a long bout of crying," (174) a passage that underscores the close connection of pleasure and pain again. He has escaped the straitjacket of a type of academic Gnosticism that disdains the body and its knowledge in favor of mental "experience"; his lovemaking and his lockjaw have restored the balance between mind and body necessary for his functioning as a fully human being.[13]

Both "Language, Truth, and Lockjaw" and "Phonefun Limited," an earlier story in the volume about an elderly lesbian couple who run a phone-sex service, brim with humor and generally favor elemental language and physicality over more elevated diction. Indeed, the simulated sounds of oral sex that Agnes makes over the phone to one client by moving her finger against her lips in "Phonefun Limited" (91–92) suggest the primal sources of pleasure in our quotidian lives. MacLaverty shows how near-wordless communication, like the physical "spooning" of Agnes and Sadie at the end of the story and the concluding embrace of Norman and Patricia, more closely articulates love than spoken words ever can. In a similar vein, the iconic embraces of Miss Schwartz and Danny in "My Dear Palestrina" and the father and his dead son in "Father and Son" more fully express their pain than mere words could. The juxtaposition of hilarious stories such as "Language, Truth, and Lockjaw" and "Phonefun Limited" with such depressing ones as "Father and Son" and "Eels," about an old woman's dawning realization of the futility of her life while dying from cancer, demonstrates how MacLaverty's zaniness and zest for life are linked to his full recognition of bleakness and depression, suggesting how the cycles of such deep emotions run across the seasons of our lives. By linguistically expressing how inarticulate feelings can be best conveyed through basic sounds and actions, *A Time to Dance* subtly evokes our deeply spiritual humanity and connectedness to one another, a theme MacLaverty would develop more fully in the pictorial scenes of *Cal.*

Perception, Confession, and Community
in *Cal*

$\mathbf{T}$HE RICHEST, MOST PROFOUND LITERARY WORK of MacLaverty's early career is *Cal*, which features a nineteen-year-old Roman Catholic protagonist, Cal McCluskey, who lives with his father, Shamie, in an otherwise Protestant housing estate near Magherafelt in County Derry, Northern Ireland. Despite his unwillingness to be caught up in sectarianism, Cal drives the getaway car when his friend Crilly, acting for the Irish Republican Army, murders an off-duty Protestant Royal Ulster Constabulary (RUC) reserve officer, Robert Morton, at his home. Cal pursues love with the murdered man's widow, Marcella, and is captured in the conclusion by the RUC. *Cal* serves in many ways as a summa of the themes treated in earlier chapters and brings to a close the first installment of MacLaverty's career. Symbolic, threatened, and finally imminently proleptic, imprisonment functions as one of the two major themes of the novel, in dialectic with various manifestations of love. Perhaps drawing his inspiration from the restricted lives of the paramilitary prisoners in Northern Ireland's Long Kesh jail, MacLaverty explores the cloistered life of a young Catholic male in the province who is on the dole,[1] rejects a job at the local slaughterhouse, and thus is made an easy target for recruitment by the local branch of the IRA. His absence of a vocation is heightened by the relationship between nagging father and petulant son, as it was in *Lamb* and in "Father and Son." The title characters in the latter provide important models for Shamie and Cal, although Shamie's relationship with Cal is much more affectionate.[2] But the importance of this relationship fades as this protagonist, who is older than many of MacLaverty's young adolescent male characters already discussed, finds romance with an older woman.

Additionally, in the most sustained development of his visual motif of physicality, explored most fully to this point in the stories of *A Time to Dance*, his characters' physical postures speaks volumes about their motivations and desires. The

novel centers on the religious image represented by the murdered RUC man's genuflection when he is murdered by Crilly and is framed by the erotic image on the
cover of the first American edition, Edward Munch's *The Kiss*, which represents Cal
and Marcella, and by the description of Grunewald's gruesome painting of Christ's
crucifixion in the novel's conclusion. Marcella holds a copy of this last painting in
front of her body, thereby creating a Pieta scene, an image that may be extended
imaginatively into the future as a soon-to-be beaten and bruised Cal will remember being held during the last night of his freedom by Marcella. The sincerity and
intimacy of these artistic tableaus contrast Cal's penchant for fixing other scenes
in his mind by pretending he is taking pictures, a process that renders the subjects
of these snapshots fragmented, inanimate, and two-dimensional, while distancing
Cal from feeling for them.[3]

MacLaverty's increasing emphasis on the visual in this pared-down novel
accords with several strikingly pictorial events that had recently taken place in the
province, particularly the graphic protests by IRA members in Long Kesh prison
of the British government's new policy criminalizing paramilitary prisoners, who
formerly had been considered political inmates. These protests began with republican prisoners' refusal in 1976 to wear prison-issued uniforms; these inmates donned
plain wool blankets instead. The movement escalated to the so-called "dirty protests"
beginning in late 1977 in which fecal and later, menstrual matter from female prisoners was smeared on cell walls. The situation culminated in the devastating hunger
strikes of 1981, during the course of which ten young men died, including most
famously Bobby Sands, who was elected a Member of Parliament from Fermanagh-
South Tyrone a month before he passed. Images of republican prisoners wearing
blankets and of the dirty protests quickly led to graffiti and then found their way
onto the nascent republican murals springing up in working-class areas across the
province. Soon the stark, gaunt representations of the hunger strikers came to occupy
many of these murals and sometimes gave a religious thrust to the self-inflicted
suffering of these prisoners through their implicit and more explicit Christian
connotations.[4]

One of the most acclaimed republican muralists in the 1980s was Gerard
Kelly, who told Bill Rolston in an interview that "people would stand and look at a
mural before they would read a paper," suggesting the powerful visual appeal of such
images.[5] MacLaverty, although certainly not a propagandist or a republican, chose
to focus his audience's attention on arresting physical images in *Cal*, perhaps partially in the hopes of attracting readers who had been increasingly trained to view
their recent history pictorially.[6] The defiance associated with such republican murals,
however, is absent from the rhetoric of the novel, which consistently rejects hatred,
violence, and intolerance in favor of three types of love: storge, the affectionate love

between parents and their offspring that we have already observed in the love of Michael Lamb's father for him in *Lamb*; the eros love between Cal and Marcella; and the *agape* Christian love expressed in God the Father's love for His Son, in Mary's love for Jesus, and in Jesus's love for believers. Caught between images of symbolic imprisonment such as the loyalist curbstones and flags of his street (*C* 9) and literal ones like the republican wood-burned plaque from Long Kesh and the brass image of a mother paired with Patrick Pearse's poem "A Mother" (58), Cal soon chooses to surround himself with positive images religious in nature such as the sanitized crucifixion hanging in the Catholic church in Magherafelt and the horrific Grunewald crucifixion in the book of that artist's work he buys for Marcella.

Love is one of the oldest and most universal themes in human history, but it has been relatively absent as an alternative to the deterministic pressures of history and politics in writing by male Irish authors during the period 1965–1990. John Wilson Foster has suggested that "It is odd . . . that Irish male writers have hardly considered it worth exploring love and sex as avenues of escape from history and politics (Bernard MacLaverty's *Cal* is an uncommon exception and exhibits the difficulties), even if they are subsequently rejected."[7] MacLaverty consistently uses Christian artwork to signify truly sacrificial, freeing love in the novel—Jesus's selfless sacrifice—which is contrasted with the somewhat selfish sacrifices of the republican hunger strikers, who deprived their families of sons. If this religiously inspired sacrificial love bears secular fruit, such as Cal's partly expiatory love for Marcella and her more selfless love for him, and spreads through increased dialogue between members of opposed communities and especially between criminals and their victims, much reconciliation might occur. Yet Cal's inability to confess his sin of enabling the murder of her husband to Marcella and the continued penchant for secrets and silence generally in the novel render that outcome unlikely. Her shock and horror at the revelation that he drove the getaway car for Robert's killer will probably destroy their relationship. There are hopeful signs of a thaw in sectarian relations in the conclusion, however, as Cal calls the confidential telephone number to report the bomb Crilly has placed in the library (151) and then welcomes the chance to confess to the RUC and even to be beaten during his forthcoming interrogation (154).

The cumulative weight of the republican prisoners' protests and the corresponding, sharply increased tension on the streets of the province may have finally led MacLaverty into an artistic conviction that he must treat the violence directly. His decision accords with what Seamus Deane, writing in the mid-1980s, has termed "the effects of the Northern crisis and its increasing demands on the writer as it prolongs itself from their youth into their middle age."[8] Besides "Father and Son," none of MacLaverty's fictional works so far had explored sectarianism so directly, and even that story is relatively restrained, focusing as it does on one father and son. *Cal*, however, places the father-son relationship in the wider martial, political, religious, and cultural conflict then occurring, attempting to give an insider's account of the republican movement and the alternately restrained and violent reactions of Orangemen like Cyril Dunlop and loyalists such as those on Cal's street, respectively, to that movement.[9]

Cal McCluskey's feeling of imprisonment and deracination stems from his living in majority-Protestant Northern Ireland, a feeling that leaves him temporarily, only to quickly return once he crosses the border to Clones and attends a football match. "Once over the Border he experienced the feeling of freedom he always got. This was Ireland—the real Ireland. He felt he had come out from under the weight and darkness of Protestant Ulster, with its neat stifled Sabbath towns. On top of a tree a green, white and gold tricolour flickered in the wind. . . . But the thing he had done was now a background to his life, permanently there, like the hiss that echoed from the event which began the Universe" (39).[10] His sense of confinement and dislocation even in the Republic as he recalls his role in the murder of Robert Morton is compounded by his particular living situations in the novel—as a member of the only Catholic family in a loyalist, Protestant street; then, after he and his father are burned out of their house, as a temporary squatter in his father's cousin's home; finally, as a more permanent squatter in the cottage on the Morton estate, the last of which recalls how Catholics squatted in abandoned flats in Derry to claim them in the run-up to the civil rights marches of the late 1960s.

The novel form, which Lukács sees as inherently dissonant among all the other genres, renders it "as something in process of becoming,"[11] an ideal form for portraying both Cal's fluid character and the dynamic society of Northern Ireland. Lukács observes that such aberrant behavior as crime and madness are either missing, offset by equitable punishment, or purely symbolic in the epic and tragedy, and thus only properly found in the novel because they are "objectivations of transcendental homelessness—the homelessness of an action in the human order of social relations, the homelessness of a soul in the ideal order of a supra-personal system of values."[12] Cal's crimes committed as driver for Crilly thus conform to their typical appearance in this genre because of its formal properties of unsettledness and searching restlessness.

If the novel as genre is well suited for portraying the fluid, sometimes deviant nature of its leading characters, its form—particularly in a realistic novel such as *Cal*—also ideally expresses the rapid changes that a society such as Northern Ireland experiences. Somewhat surprisingly, the novel at first mimics the static plots of the over-used Northern Irish thriller subgenre that has been employed by many bad writers to "exploit" the conflict "for authorial fame and financial gain,"[13] only to explode this subgenre and subtly critique the problems endemic in Northern Irish society through its dynamic form.[14] Bakhtin has trenchantly observed that "The novel is the only developing genre and therefore it reflects more deeply, more essentially, more sensitively and rapidly, reality itself in the process of its unfolding. Only that which is itself developing can comprehend development as a process."[15] The fluidity of the novel form itself then, in a sense, keeps pace with the unfolding events in society, although of course those events are mediated through imagination and memory, which prevent the form from sinking into mere journalism.

As Luckás puts it, the novel's form allows memory full creative play in such a way as to transform the subject and dissolve his separation from society if he perceives the wholeness of his entire life. "Only in the novel and in certain epic forms resembling the novel does memory occur as a creative force affecting the object and transforming it. . . . The duality of interiority and the outside world can be abolished for the subject if he (the subject) glimpses the organic unity of his whole life through the process by which his living present has grown from the stream of his past life dammed up within his memory."[16] As we will see, Cal's memory is triggered by his inherently human desire to confess his sins, especially his crime of enabling the murder of Marcella's husband. Only when he truly confesses—in a proleptic moment in the RUC station where he will be taken after the conclusion of the novel—will he be free of his solipsism and integrated into society. Yet that moment of integration and homecoming can only be imagined because its achievement is alien to the very homelessness inherent in the novelistic form. Ironically, Cal's prison home will actually become a site of personal freedom, because he will be able to pay his debt and reject the sectarian shibboleths of his society, imagining a new society opposed to hostility and founded in frank, open dialogue. Part of that society is extratextual, implicitly including the reading audience of the novel and viewing audience of the film because "confession is the deliberate, self-conscious attempt of an individual to explain his nature to the audience who represents the kind of community he needs to exist in and to confirm him."[17]

Because of its grounding in the evolving culture of Northern Ireland, the novel consistently courts parallels to the 1981 republican hunger strikers in establishing the physicality of its protagonist, while also resisting such comparisons at times. Cal, like the majority of the hunger strikers, is very young, just on the cusp of manhood; increasingly gaunt; and, after being burnt out of his house, has long hair, like many of the hunger strikers. Additionally, the labyrinthine streets of his village and the small house where he lives with his father, Shamie, symbolically function as a prison for him, while his freedom is literally restricted to the margins of town by the security gates around the city center.[18] But differences between Cal and the strikers also abound. For example, despite believing in a united Ireland, he repeatedly rejects violence, and he purposely tries not to draw attention to himself. And as Stephen Watt has argued, once the relationship between Cal and Marcella becomes sexual, the cottage Cal comes to occupy on the Morton estate becomes a site of freedom, "transformed . . . into an alternative space for both of them."[19] Most significantly, his obsession with his body, his refusal to eat very much while at home with his father, and his increasing predilection for imagined and actual mortification suggest similarities to truly religiously inspired figures that use mortification for expiation of sins.

This process of self-denial, as we will see, leads him closer to confession. Already accustomed to denying himself and inflicting violence on himself, Cal, despite his seeming disbelief, soon becomes fascinated with the suffering of others including that of Ireland; Robert Morton; the Catholic penitent Matt Talbot; the Morton family, especially Marcella; Shamie; and Christ. By nearly continuously dwelling on these imagined and glimpsed images of national and personal suffering, Cal is convicted of his sinfulness and desires to confess as a first step in the expiation of his sin of murder. His relationship with Marcella, a figure of the confessor to him, makes him desire to confess, but he cannot do so except to the readers.

The central and most troubling image of the novel occurs for the first time in the middle of Cal's long mental recollection to himself, a "confession" that is inefficacious within the plenum of the novel because he has no fictional confessor, especially Marcella, hearing his story, save the readers of the novel. Yet our reading of this scene starts the development of a new, extratextual community for Cal, as we sympathetically view the pain he has caused. As Cal remembers watching, Robert Morton dies at Crilly's hands, reminding Cal of genuflecting in front of the altar. "Cal saw the man smile. Then he looked confused. Crilly pulled the gun from his pocket and the man froze. . . . Crilly shot him twice in the chest. The gun sounded unreal—like a child's cap gun. The man very slowly genuflected. He shouted as if he'd been punched in the stomach, 'Mar-cell-a.' It was a kind of animal roar. . . . Then Crilly fired a shot through his head, the gun only inches from it. Stuff came out on the wallpaper behind him" (87). Of all the attempts at ekphrasis in the novel, this one is the most successful in its verbal representation of the visual. As W. J. T. Mitchell has argued, a moment of such "ekphrastic hope" occurs in all ekphrastic literature, in which "the impossibility of ekphrasis is overcome in imagination or metaphor, when we discover a 'sense' in which language can do what so many writers have wanted it to do: 'to make us see.'"[20] This central vision of the novel becomes the dynamic force driving Cal's actions thenceforth.

Even back at the town hall where he and Crilly return to the dance they had attended earlier in the evening, the alcohol Cal drinks and the body of the girl with whom he dances cannot erase the vision of Morton genuflecting. As he dances with her, "He saw the man genuflect again, his heel coming away from his slipper, the astonishment in his eyes" (89). The very ordinariness of Morton's heel coming out of his slipper, combined with his extraordinary genuflection, make an indelible image in Cal's mind.[21]

Besides inwardly being tormented by this vision, Cal feels "that he had a brand stamped in blood in the middle of his forehead which would take him the rest of his life to purge" (89). Surrounded by red images throughout the novel, Cal, believing his sin calls for his own blood, values the marks on his body he increasingly acquires as a perverse Christ-figure.

For example, while stacking the wood for Mrs. Morton, he realizes, "His hands were so sore now that he used only his fingers to make the stack of wood. It was as if his palms had been scalded" (45). That night, when some loyalist youths jump him on his home street and pummel him, he stares at himself in the mirror, enjoying having swollen lips, spits "blood and saliva into the washbasin," and sees his "skinned and bleeding knuckles." Now his hands are marked on both sides, something that amuses him. He is portrayed turning "his hands over, looking at the blisters on one side and the scars on the other" (47). When he awakes the next day, he stares at his naked body in the mirror, seeing that "the lower half of his body was covered in blue-black bruises. . . . They were on his buttocks and thighs, distinct marks the size of toe-caps, and on the fleshy parts of his shoulders there were longer welts" (48). After returning the next day to the Morton farm and splitting some of the larger blocks of wood, Cal's untied bootlaces that have been dragged through the muddy yard mark his hands again. We are told, "tying them up left black welts all over his hands" (54). Later, when the soldiers kick open the door of the cottage and assault Cal by kicking him "on the side of the head," placing him "spread-eagled against the wall" and using their hands to "probe . . . his body from top to bottom" (93), his body is bloodied again. With his repeatedly marked body, specifically the welts on his shoulder, his torn and bleeding hands, and his bleeding scalp, Cal somewhat resembles the crucified Christ, yet his "martyrdom" without confession cannot obtain forgiveness for his part in the murder, whereas Christ's death and resurrection purchased the salvation of believers.

In addition to this physical, largely self-inflicted torture, Cal often cannot help but remember what happened the night of Robert Morton's murder, as he must in order to confess and experience any expiation for the role he played in it. After over a year of forgetting his part in Morton's murder, Cal now is painfully and unavoidably remembering it through a series of physical and verbal associations.[22]

His process of remembering is inherently confessional. For him not only to face responsibility for his sins and receive forgiveness for them, but also to become a fully functioning member of his community again, he must undergo the process of remembering through confessional storytelling. As Peter Brooks has remarked, confessions are essentially moral acts of rehabilitation that help reinstitute the confessor into the community he has been ostracized from. "Confession of wrongdoing is considered fundamental to morality because it constitutes a verbal act of self-recognition as wrongdoer and hence provides the basis of rehabilitation. It is the precondition of the end to ostracism, reentry into one's desired place in the human community."[23] Brooks's emphasis on confession as necessary for rejoining "the human community" is revelatory for understanding Cal's "confession" to the readers of the novel about Morton's dying genuflection and his proleptic confession to the security forces. His gradual move away from nationalism in the novel and toward the embrace of a wider, imagined community through his confessions invalidates one commentator's argument that "*Cal* must be read as a narrative act of nationalist contrition whereby the Catholic nationalist guiltily offers himself up as a sacrifice to the proper authority of the Northern Irish state against which he has offended."[24]

Cal's slowly enters society by virtue of his realistic memory of Morton's physical posture when he is killed, which later gives way to a fascination with Marcella's body and with Christ's. His lingering vision of Morton's genuflection that deadly night stands in stark contrast to the moments he captures like fast camera shots in other passages in the novel: when he drives the getaway car for Crilly to rob the off-license (61), when he sees Marcella in the library (71), and when he spies on Marcella undressing in preparation for her bath (92). In these "shots," the subjects are rendered as two-dimensional objects and lack any agency. Additionally, Cal as viewer competes for our attention by his conscious reference to these perceptions as snapshots. As Alan Spiegel has argued in his discussion of fiction and the camera eye, perception through a camera is simultaneously objective, "for it can neither think nor feel," and subjective, because the camera is always self-referential in a sense. Spiegel observes, "the camera is a subjective medium, for it cannot show us any object without at the same time revealing its own physical position—its angle and distance from the object—as part of what is shown. This means that the images produced . . . will only allow us to experience the object through a series of perspectives; that the ontology of the image itself will never allow for an apprehension of the object as a whole."[25] Cal's two perceptions of the robbery of the off-license exemplify Spiegel's argument. In both views, the door of the shop acts like the shutter of a camera. When Crilly first enters the building, Cal sees the fear of two customers but cannot feel it. "The door swung shut after him on its spring but in the instant that it was open, as if it was the shutter of a camera, Cal saw two women customers look up in fright" (61). Similarly, when Crilly leaves after the robbery, Cal again feels distanced by seeing the same customers, now prone. "Suddenly the door sprang open and in its shutter-instant Cal saw the two women lying face down on the floor" (61).

Although these are striking images, all they really manage to do is objectify the women and render them dehumanized in their partial perspectives, which in turn is compounded by Cal's self-insertion into the shot. More disturbingly, these "photographic" shots partake of the consumption of fragments that Walter Benjamin has identified in *Illuminations* as characteristic of viewing photography and film, and the static quality of real pictures, which offer, as Susan Sontag has argued, only "imaginary possession of a past that is unreal."[26] Karen Jacobs argues, based on her reading of Sontag's *On Photography*, "that the photograph serves, finally, as a *memento mori* associated with mortality and loss,"[27] a reading of the photograph that is particularly apposite to Cal's failed attempts to preserve fleeting moments of dangerous intensity through this figurative filter.

Direct perception through the naked eye, however, has been described by Rudolf Arnheim as inherently dynamic. "In looking for an object, we reach out for it. . . . Perceiving shapes is an eminently active occupation."[28] Morton's genuflection, seen directly by Cal, obtains a three-dimensional and active quality that serves virtually to exclude Cal as viewer yet personalize the perception and precipitate his deep sympathy for Morton by perceiving what Spiegel terms "an apprehension of the object as a whole." Seeing Morton without the filter of a "lens" creates a searingly intimate vision, unlike those earlier, more mechanical perceptions that are inherently voyeuristic and passive. This self-abnegating mode of perception also creates a seemingly continual movement to Morton's collapsing body, proving the truth of Elaine Scarry's contention in her study of how we generate mental pictures when reading that "suppressing the sense of one's own agency appears to be crucial in achieving vivacity."[29]

Unlike his objective, controlled perception of those other "frames," Cal cannot help but witness Morton's body collapse and his lack of deliberateness, along with the profound emotion engendered by this vision, makes him unable to control its reappearance, especially when he is in similarly intense personal situations. For example, late in the novel he tries to make love to Marcella, but suddenly, "he saw her husband genuflect and the sudden soiling of the wallpaper behind him," and he cannot have an erection and is shamed by it (138). Eventually, however, "the shame of his weakness blotted out the sickening visions of her genuflecting husband" and by taking an interest in Marcella's body, not the body of Robert Morton, Cal can sustain an erection and successfully makes love to her (139). Their lovemaking that night and the next crucially changes Cal's focus from Robert to both Marcella Morton and to the crucified Christ in the early sixteenth-century Matthias Grunewald painting *The Crucifixion*.[30]

At the end of the novel, MacLaverty skillfully juxtaposes the two central events in Christ's life—the Nativity and the Crucifixion—with Cal's pending beating in jail the next day, Christmas Eve, and presumed confession and "rebirth" that will occur as a result. Cal's life will thus soon stand in a chiastic relationship to that of Christ as he moves from a crucifixion of sorts to a new life freed from his sin of murder. When Cal gives Marcella a book of Grunewald's paintings including *The Crucifixion* after they make love on the evening of December 23, she opens this present and the other, a bottle of perfume, completely naked, kisses him, and then holds up the plate of the painting in front of her body, creating a mixed-media Pieta as it were:

> The weight of the Christ figure bent the cross down like a bow; the hands were cupped to heaven like nailed starfish; the body with its taut ribcage was pulled to the shape of an eggtimer by the weight of the lower body; the flesh was diseased with sores from the knotted scourges, the mouth open and gasping for breath. She was sitting on the floor with her back to the couch, her legs open in a yoga position and the book facing him, just below her breasts. Cal looked at the flesh of Christ spotted and torn, bubonic almost, and then behind it at the smoothness of Marcella's body and it became a permanent picture in his mind. (153)

Richard Haslam has argued that this image is consistent with "the photographic motif" MacLaverty has developed throughout the novel, but notes that while those earlier attempts to freeze particular moments are unsuccessful, Cal's viewing of Marcella's embrace of the print of the Grunewald painting is successful because of its permanence, making it "an icon which allows him to look forward with masochistic gratitude to being beaten 'to within an inch of his life.'"[31] Haslam's analysis of the lasting quality of this "picture" is compelling; I would add that another part of the reason even Cal thinks this picture will achieve permanency is because of both Marcella's intimacy and the intimacy of the painting itself, which places this composition in the context of Robert Morton's genuflection rather than the detached "photographic" images in Cal's mind of other scenes. Yet just as the image of Morton's genuflection has become replaced in Cal's mind's eye with this "picture," it too is destined for a sort of replacement through alteration and insertion. In a sense, this image is already morphing into another one featuring Cal as a Christ, a role for which his repeatedly marked body earlier in the novel has prepared him.

Marcella's kissing of Cal at the start of the passage incorporates him into this scene, and her subsequent embrace of this painting conflates in miniature the first American edition's cover of Edward Munch's *The Kiss* with Grunewald's *The*

Crucifixion into a mingled image of erotic, worshipful sorrow, a Pieta that recalls the posture taken by Miss Schwartz with Danny in their erotic/worshipful Pieta posture at the end of "A Time to Dance." Marcella, to a lesser degree than Miss Schwartz, functions as the Mary figure, while Cal, much more so than Danny, functions proleptically as the Christ figure, soon to be beaten by the RUC policemen after his arrest the next day on Christmas Eve. At the moment of arrest Cal is "grateful that at last someone was going to beat him to within an inch of his life" (154). In the near future, in his mind if not in reality, he will leave behind his identity as passive voyeur and substitute his own bruised body for Grunewald's spotted Christ, seeing himself clutched erotically by Marcella.

Even this perverse vision of himself as a martyr will be thankfully short-lived, however, replaced by a personal and possible societal resurrection. Cal's confession to the police will forever cut him off from the community of his republican friends and once he confesses to Marcella, as he claims he will do (154), more than likely from her love. MacLaverty suggests, however, that his new community, first in jail and later outside, promises to be free from deception and sectarianism, and grounded in frank dialogue. Throughout the novel, Cal immerses himself in different identities, for example, cursing himself in pidgeon French and immersing himself in blues music, suggesting that he has already been experimenting with imagining a new community.[32] Cal's existing fascination with other cultures and movement away from Irish republicanism suggest that he has seen through the use of force to achieve a long-range political end. Therefore, despite his proleptic, temporary submission to the security forces of the Northern Irish state to acquire the beating he feels he deserves, he will quickly reject that ideology as well. Joe Cleary's contention that the novel is caught between these violent binaries and that it "is utterly unable to imagine" any kind of "alternative political resolution" to the conflict rather misses the point—which is that Cal will become apolitical and explore and embrace a true multiculturalism.[33]

Of all genres, the novel, as Bakhtin reminds us, "best . . . reflects the tendencies of a new world still in the making."[34] Moreover, the best novels like *Cal* also help to create that world imaginatively. Although it is a tragedy, the novel accords with Theodor Adorno's description of art's relationship with the empirical world and art's subsequent creation of another world. "Artworks detach themselves from the empirical world and bring forth another world, one opposed to the empirical world as if this other world too were an autonomous entity. Thus, however tragic they appear, artworks tend *a priori* toward affirmation."[35] Adorno rejects art as sheer escape, however, claiming that "by virtue of its rejection of the empirical world— a rejection that inheres in art's concept and thus is no mere escape, but a law immanent to it—art sanctions the primacy of reality."[36] Works of art like *Cal* can achieve this sanction only through virtue of their dynamic form, because "through the ages by means of its form, art has turned against the status quo and what merely exists just as much as it has come to its aid by giving form to its elements."[37] Thus, only in *Cal*'s specific grounding in the immediate realities of war-torn Northern Ireland can it formally suggest an imagined, yet still somewhat ambiguous, alternative to that world.

This affirmative other world implied by the novel is also created by its confessional trajectory. The reading audience of the novel and the viewing audience of the 1984 film act as joint confessors to Cal and are bound together with him in another type of community, a humane one that transcends religion, politics, and culture. "Confession," as Terrence Doody has argued, "is always an act of community."[38] This community may ground its reaction to the perpetrators of atrocities in the Troubles and to their victims in Christ's Crucifixion, images of which have always blended "compassion as well as judgment."[39] If violence, as Patrick Grant has argued, drawing on the insights of Simone Weil, "congeals, hardening and turning the other to stone,"[40] *Cal*, through its dynamic novelistic form and evolving protagonist, renders temporarily and illuminatingly softened and animated the once and future victims of violence such as the genuflecting Robert Morton and Cal himself by showing that even men of violence and, by extension, their societies can change.

Hearing the Other:
Sounds of Connection and Community
in *The Great Profundo and Other Stories*

AFTER THE PERVERSIONS OF SACRIFICIAL personal and national love in *Lamb* and *Cal* and the explorations of often literal imprisonment in those novels, *The Great Profundo and Other Stories*, published in 1987, examines a series of isolated, mostly older characters on the margins of society and their journeys toward real love, which are usually dashed by societal expectations (in the case of Mary in "End of Season") or by their own refusals to accept such a gift late in life (in the case of the nameless illustrator in "Words the Happy Say"). Its style is typically spare and un-adorned, yet acutely penetrating in its insights into humanity. Brief moments of connection between characters normally separated by generations, distance, or voca-tions are subtly established and offered with characteristic compassion and irony. Unfortunately, there is a dearth of academic criticism on this collection, probably because of its departure from the intense exploration of religious, cultural, and polit-ical binaries in Northern Ireland found in *Cal*. Nevertheless, the collection won an award from the Scottish Arts Council in 1988 and caused MacLaverty to be named a joint winner of Scottish Writer of the Year, 1988; he also won the *Irish Post* Award for 1989.

MacLaverty continues to explore aspects of Catholicism, as for example in "The Break" and "Death of a Parish Priest," and elements of the political situation in Northern Ireland, in the lovely short story "Some Surrender." But images of vio-lence in personal and political contexts are largely occluded, literally so in the title story, and more obliquely in Linden's references to her body in "In the Hills above Lugano" (*GP* 64) and in Mary's references to the Troubles in "End of Season" (69), only fully emerging in the images of two different razor blades in "Across the Street." MacLaverty also widens his geographic scope in the title story about an aging sword swallower and in other stories, such as "The Drapery Man," set in Portugal; "In the Hills Above Lugano," set in Switzerland; and in "End of Season," set in a coastal village in Northern Ireland but given an exotic feel by the peninsula named "The Spanish Point" and the town's remoteness. The intense concentration on human lives typical of his earlier work is thus expanded geographically and suggests the inadequacy of assessing his fiction solely as a response to the continuing conflict in Northern Ireland as some reviewers did after the success of *Cal.* Instead, MacLaverty chronicles the human condition across a range of nationalities, beliefs, and ages.

Although many of the stories feature an artistic intertext, such as the illustrator's work in "Words the Happy Say," the narrator's and Jordan Fitzgerald's art in "The Drapery Man," Linden's novel and attempt at a movie script in "In the Hills above Lugano," the Matisse drawing of "The Great Profundo," and the griffito of "Some Surrender," these artworks are not employed ekphrastically as Cal's "photographs" of particular moments, his memory of Robert Morton genuflecting, or Grunewald's *The Crucifixion* are in *Cal.* In the first place, many of them are not visual representations of the verbal: The illustrator in this first story embellishes words, rather than replacing them with art, and the nameless narrator of "The Drapery Man" mechanically paints the often-abstract works Jordan dictates to him. Additionally, these artworks seem static in contrast to the shifting genuflections of Morton or the dynamic, concluding multimedia work featuring Marcella and the Grunewald painting and Cal's proleptic insertion of himself into that tableau.

Despite their consistent appearances in the collection, these visually oriented artworks fade into the background, while sounds—such as those broadcast by the radio in "Words the Happy Say" (12, 17), the Christmas tape playing carols in "Remote" (107–8), and silences—such as Mary's proleptic non-reply to Mr. Maguire's letters in "End of Season" after his first letter (89)—move into the foreground. MacLaverty had begun exploring soundscapes in "My Dear Palestrina" from *A Time to Dance,* and he does so more fully in these narratives, thereby beginning the second, aural stage of his fiction, the apogee of which is reached in *Grace Notes* with its aspiration toward the Paterian dictum that all art approaches the condition of music.

There is a Beckettian trajectory toward minimalism, closure, and silence in many of these stories featuring nameless Beckettian narrators that is nicely counterbalanced by an urge toward expansiveness, openness, and conversation in other ones, most supremely in "Some Surrender." Sometimes, for example, in the dialogue then silence between the illustrator and the woman in "Words the Happy Say" and between Mr. Maguire and Mary in "End of Season," this tension between these binaries is manifested within one story. This dialectic may stem from MacLaverty's immersion in a Northern Irish society that simultaneously values reticence and talk, silence and expressiveness. Generally speaking, the human silence that prevails in many of the stories bespeaks a lost opportunity to establish a relationship. On the other hand, the continuation of natural sounds, such as the geese's squawking at the end of "Remote" or human conversation such as that between father and son in "Some Surrender," suggests a moment in which a relationship may be established or reborn.

Formally, this collection ostensibly features some of MacLaverty's most traditional stories in its seeming adherence to Poe's conception of the short story as organically building to a crisis. Many of the stories end dramatically, with a situation between two characters that demands a decisive response, such as the woman's desire for a relationship with the illustrator of "Words the Happy Say" or Mr. Maguire's proposal to Mary in "End of Season." These clear moments of crisis, however, quickly dissipate as the central characters, such as the illustrator and Mary, respectively, reject the proffered relationship through their own inertia and passivity. Other stories such as "More than Just the Disease," "Some Surrender," and "Remote," which have no crisis per se, offer optimistic outlooks for their more active central characters. MacLaverty's use of character withdrawal to weaken the structural climax of certain stories in this collection suggests he views such so-called "typical" short stories as reductive in the binary responses they demand from both character and reader. Moreover, his use of wandering, longer stories such as "Some Surrender" to richly contextualize personal and cultural conflicts implies that he prefers employing nontraditional short story structures because the variety of form possible in this more expansive definition of the short story is more appropriate to the intricacies of human relationships.

The title story, the weakest in the collection, deftly encapsulates themes common to the volume. Its protagonist is struggling with the problems of growing old, and he struggles to fulfill the expectations of his audiences, finally resulting in his death while having swallowed a Claymore sword at the meeting of the Eccentrics Genuine Club. His attempt to meet his largely uncaring audience's desire for entertainment is shared with many characters in other stories who deal with their own and others' expectations, only either to frustrate them or be frustrated. The seemingly medieval opening of the story, which turns out to be false, also shares a predilection for the exotic in a number of stories, which are set abroad, often on the continent of Europe.

The Great Profundo's name suggests not only magnificence but also something performatively profound, yet his failure to match his appellation and his living situation in near-poverty shares aspects with other characters from the collection who perform work that is impressive and appealing to the public, such as the illustrator in "Words the Happy Say" or the schoolteacher Mary in "End of Season," but who live quotidian lives shot through with loneliness. When offered a chance for a real companion, the illustrator rejects it, settling for the impersonal companionship of his radio. "He turned up the volume and filled the flat with the noise of voices he could not put a face to" (17). Similarly, when Mr. Maguire proposes to Mary, she flirts with the idea of marriage, but does not want to disturb her domestic routine, which includes watching the best television shows of the year on Christmas Day with her sister. "She thought of herself and Kathleen in new dresses, full of turkey and sprouts and mince pies, dozing in armchairs and watching television for most of the day. The Christmas programmes were always the best of the year" (88). The illustrator and Mary settle for the simulacra of reality, symbolized by machine culture, rather than the real thing, and thus lose their last chances for human companionship with a member of the opposite sex.

As highly as he values it, MacLaverty does not valorize human companionship and, indeed, shows how perverse relationships can be just as disabling as solipsism. The nameless narrator of "In the Hills above Lugano" is a loner, generally eschewing relationships, but he is lured toward Linden, his friend Brendan's girlfriend. Despite finding her incredibly beautiful (64) and making love tenderly to her toward the conclusion, he is repulsed by her sadistic sexual relationship with Brendan. Brendan's predilection for inflicting pain on Linden, using "things" that he "brings . . . home from the hospital" (64), and her willingness to stay with him over eighteen months while professing a desire to go away with the narrator, makes the narrator realize he is healthier on his own. The rhyming names "Brendan" and "Linden" evoke a symmetrical relationship of co-dependency both are unable to break out of, despite their distrust of each other.

The relationship between yet another nameless narrator, the protagonist of "The Drapery Man," and his lover, the Irish artist Jordan Fitzgerald, also is co-dependent and conveys despondency, even despair, a condition that is echoed in the mechanical artwork produced by the two of them. Formerly lovers, the first-person narrator and Fitzgerald now are mere companions who have stayed with each other out of emotional dependency more than anything else. The narrator's identity is so entangled in Fitzgerald's that he wonders "what I will do when Jordan dies. I have given up my career and my life for him" (34). Although the narrator feels like a mere appendage of Jordan in his "translation of his vision on to canvas" (34), Jordan himself has become disconnected from his creative muse, reduced to having the narrator reproduce the pyramid of medals on the bottle of Irish Black Bush whiskey with tennis balls (37). Fitzgerald's move toward a Warholian pop art is a desperate attempt to stay abreast of artistic trends, but he seems only to be going through the motions in an attempt to convince the narrator that he is still needed and himself that he can still paint.

This couple, like Brendan and Linden, have a tendency for inflicting hurt on each other both verbally and physically. Jordan tells the narrator at one point that "you have a Reader's Digest grasp of the world" and delights in making him feel stupid. In response, the narrator imagines himself asking Jordan if he "wants his tears kept. If he wants a phial of them put in one of his paintings" when Jordan gets drunk that night, fully realizing that "the one thing he cannot stand is to have his work ridiculed—even by me" (39). Despite their nastiness to each other, the narrator and Jordan seem unable to be apart. The narrator even admits that "there is now a kind of unspoken acceptance that I am here until he dies" (39).

These characters, taken together, evince a Beckettian co-dependency akin to that of Vladimir and Estragon in *Waiting for Godot* and Clov and Hamm in *Endgame*. Moreover, the repetitive nature of these Beckettian relationships drives these circular stories with their trapped characters. And yet, like Beckett's characters, some of whom desire oblivion, Linden and Brendan, Jordan and the narrator go on, doggedly continuing their circumscribed lives. MacLaverty even playfully has the narrator criticize Beckett in "The Drapery Man" when he muses, "I have become involved in painting but am useless at it—as useless as Beckett's secretary is at writing, if he has one—as useless as Beckett is, come to think of it" (34). The passage suggests both the dependency of MacLaverty's narrator on Jordan Fitzgerald and MacLaverty's own reliance on earlier writers such as Beckett. In a sense, MacLaverty admits his own dependence on such famous authors and confesses his imitation of their techniques, characters, and themes. He shares with Beckett a dogged commitment to his own art, but his talent, unlike the narrator's or Fitzgerald's, is undeniable.

The trio of short stories "More than Just the Disease," "Remote," and "Some Surrender" together illustrate MacLaverty's continuing preference for a meandering story structure with little development and no real crisis. They collectively show how acceptance and honesty, broadly speaking, make human relationships meaningful and worth pursuing. The boy Neil in "More than Just the Disease" learns from an older woman, Mrs. Wan, not to be embarrassed about his psoriasis, which has kept him from swimming at the beach with his friend Michael and his family on holiday. The one time it has crept "above his collar line" his mother "had kept him off school," essentially reinforcing Neil's insecurity (42). Mrs. Wan, on asking to see his psoriasis, tells him that she has worked with lepers in Africa and assures him she is not bothered by his appearance. More important, she tells him, "watch that you don't suffer from more than just the disease. . . . It's bad enough having it without being shy about it as well" (50). When Michael appears and sees Neil's chest, Neil buttons his shirt and silence reigns between them; we are told, "neither boy said a word" (51). But unlike the defeated silences into which characters withdraw in other stories in the volume, this silence speaks volumes: Michael surely is chastened for his earlier teasing of Neil for not swimming, and Neil is finally forced into an honesty with his friend he did not have previously.

Crucially, the story ends not in silence, but in dialogue and laughter as Michael reaches out to Neil at supper, speaking to him in a friendly fashion, and then, later that night, Neil convinces him to go swimming (51). Even though Neil finally stops swimming in the water and lets Michael yell and ride "the breakers" further out while he sits in the "warmer shallows," Neil has successfully ventured out of himself and toward another, a process that has been enabled by his continual interaction with relative strangers—Michael's family and especially Mrs. Wan—throughout the holiday. Neil's voluntary immersion in water, unlike Owen's involuntary, perverse "baptism" at the end of *Lamb*, signals new life for him in his pursuit of healthy friendships, both with friends his own age and others older than him. It is only when he leaves the constricting confines of home and stops hearing his mother's well-meaning admonitions that he can accept his condition and jettison the corresponding psychological dis-ease that it has previously engendered in him.

Neil's trip to the beach functions as one of many literal journeys in the collection that has a figurative dimension of freedom available to characters, like Mr. Maguire in "End of Season," who pursues the freedom of marriage with Mary on his return to her village for the first time since his honeymoon with his recently deceased wife, only to be spurned. The nameless widow of "Remote" also is portrayed as going on a journey, but it is a recurring one that takes her out of her isolated home and into the life of the town and contact with other people. Although Neil has just learned the importance of honesty, this woman is habituated to it, as she gives the bird-watcher who offers her a monthly ride in his Land Rover an unexpected response to his question about her husband. "What did he do?" he asks. She replies, "He drowned himself. In the loch." The man, disturbed by such a gruesome detail, especially one concerning the water where his precious birds often cavort, quickly retreats, saying, "I'm sorry, I didn't mean that." But the woman persists, saying, "On Christmas Day. He was mad in the skull—away with the fairies" (107).

After she goes about her shopping in a Christmas season far removed from that deadly one in the past, the woman stops at a café and listens to Christmas carols on the speaker. But listening to the tape playing does not prevent her from remembering a chilling detail from her husband's suicide. "When they dredged him up on Boxing Day he had two car batteries tied to his wrist" (108). To cope with the discovery of his body, she remembers that "all that day the radio had been on to get rid of the dread," a similar strategy to that employed by the nameless illustrator in "Words the Happy Say" to block out the intimate contact he has had with the woman who has commissioned an Emily Dickinson poem to be reproduced and decorated by him. But where that earlier story ends in retreat, with the man turning up the volume of the radio to lose himself in a babble of voices, "Remote" concludes with the woman leaving the café when "Silent Night" comes on the tape and stopping the mailman for a ride home (108). As she waits for him, looking down at the loch where her husband had drowned himself, she gives herself an early Christmas gift, choosing not to remember the sight of his waterlogged body and the batteries he used to submerge himself but to hear instead in the present the lovely music of her bird-watching friend's geese, who "were returning for the night, filling the air with their squawking. They sounded like a dance-hall full of people laughing and enjoying themselves, heard from a distance on the night wind" (109).

This taciturn woman has learned to enjoy living on her own, buoyed by her monthly journeys into town to mail letters to herself and the sounds of nature around her. Comfortable with herself, she has earlier thought of visiting her friend Mary but realizes that she herself is not very good at conversation now and that talking to Mary might embarrass the girl. "Chat was a thing you got out of the habit of when you were on your own all the time and, besides, Mary was shy" (108). "Remote" is a supremely rendered story of old age and its solitude, although it is not so much about its loneliness and despair, as is the earlier, bleak "Eels" about an old woman dying from cancer in *A Time to Dance*. In its narrator's relative silence, "Remote" offers sonic proofs of our community with nature and the comforts of home.

The titular theme of "Some Surrender" draws on and qualifies an intransigent mantra of Northern Irish Protestant loyalists, no surrender, commonly invoked during a series of crises in the North, dating back to the city of Derry's refusal to surrender to Jacobite forces in 1689. It is a sectarian slogan, often extended to become "no Pope, no priests, no surrender." The story shows both MacLaverty's continuing interest in sympathetically portraying Northern Irish Protestants and his disgust with the resistance of some of them to perceiving and treating Catholics equally.

In the story, an estranged Protestant father and son climb Cave Hill overlooking Belfast and discuss their relationship in the context of their family and Northern Irish politics. Irish fiction often employs the family as a barometer of politics in the Republic, as in John McGahern's *Amongst Women*. Similarly, this fictional family's divisions, rancor, and possible reconciliation are analogous to both the broader fissures and potential for rapprochement in larger Northern Irish society.

Their geographic isolation from the bustle of the city emphasizes their personal isolation. We are soon told that the son has not seen his mother in twenty years and has seen his father only rarely—at rugby matches. As they climb, they soon start arguing, and the father's bigotry against Catholics is made clear. He finds out that his son has married and divorced a Catholic woman, who left the Church but insisted on sending their son to a Catholic school (121).

When they find the slogan No Surrender painted on a concrete beacon at the top, another argument ensues. Roy, the son, tells his father, "This was the place the United Irishmen took an oath to overthrow the English. They were all Prods as well." The irony of this Protestant organization dedicated, in part, to achieving Catholic civil rights in the 1790s is lost on his father, who answers, "History, Roy. It's not the way things are now" (123). Finally Roy tells his father, "I'd like to see a new slogan, 'Some Surrender'" (124). His father replies, "What matters is our identity. We've been here from the sixteenth century." Roy replies, "A minute ago you dismissed history. History in Ireland is what the other side have done to you. People have got to stop killing each other and talk" (124).

MacLaverty's portrayal of middle-class Protestants experiencing or discussing sectarianism is all the more striking because the impact of the Troubles on this cultural class rarely has been depicted, even by their fellow authors. "Some Surrender" draws on an increasing sense of isolation on the part of Northern Irish Protestants. This sense of isolation has burgeoned since the suspension of the province's Protestant-dominated government at the height of the Troubles in 1972 and the civil rights gains of Catholics in the province. As local, gerrymandered Protestant city councils have been forced to allow more Catholic representation, Protestants in Northern Ireland have felt marginalized in what they have viewed traditionally as their own corner of Ireland. Protestants in the province have traditionally looked to England or Scotland for their identity, but with the gradual withdrawal of British troops and the reduced flying of the Union Jack over government buildings, they are rapidly losing symbols of their British identity and being forced to examine or reimagine their identity.

For example, the fundamentalist Presbyterian preacher Ian Paisley and his henchmen have occasionally threatened a Unilateral Declaration of Independence from Britain. Paisley's extreme Calvinism is still shared by many Protestants in the province who see themselves as God's chosen people. But Northern Irish Protestantism is far from the monolithic, rigid entity the world has come to see it as, partly because of the well-publicized pictures of stiff Orangemen parading in sectarian strongholds like Portadown.[1] Although Protestants comprise the majority in Northern Ireland, there are many more young Catholics than Protestants. Many Northern Irish Protestants fear becoming what Frank O'Connor terms a "submerged population group," the focus of the typical short story, as he notes in *The Lonely Voice*, a claim explored in the introduction to this study.

Despite his father's bigoted intransigence, the son's attitude represents a thaw in sectarian tensions in the province that is even more evident two decades later. A full 71 percent of citizens in Northern Ireland voted for the Good Friday Agreement in 1998, which has already implemented a power-sharing executive and North-South bodies to facilitate increased communication between the province and the Repub-lic of Ireland. Although the executive has been repeatedly suspended over recent years before its implementation in May of 2007, there has been no return to the level of violence experienced in the 1970s, 1980s, or early 1990s despite a worri-some trend of hidden violence endemic in the remaining paramilitary groups. MacLaverty's story suggests that hope for the province's future lies in the younger generations, but it also provides a model of reconciliation on a familial level that could be applied more broadly across cultural groups. Roy's father's question to him near the story's end about visiting his mother could apply to reconciliation in the province as well: "But you might come round to it—some day?" (128).

The conclusion of the story is intensely personal and emotional in its evo-cation of a striking tactile image. As they start down Cave Hill together, Roy's father says, "That's when you know your age." Roy asks him "what?" in response, and the older man says, "When going down is harder than coming up." The concluding sentences of exposition and their moving image are startling after several pages of conversation and relatively belligerent talk. "Roy goes in front and offers his hand as they come down the steep, stepped part of the path. The old man ignores it and instead leans his weight on Roy's shoulder. Guiding him between two rocks the son puts his hand on his father's back and is startled to feel his shoulder-blades, the shape of butterfly wings, through the thin material of his jacket" (129).

The sublime delicateness of his father's body shocks the son and hopefully the reader into realizing the fragility of human beings generally and the need for reconciliation on personal and provincial levels. This tactile image's hopefulness is reinforced by the story's expansive setting on Cave Hill with its prospect of the city, from which the son is able to imagine a more unlimited cultural and political hori-zon in which frozen sectarian relations might thaw across the province. Finally, their alternately bellicose and tender dialogue suggests the possibilities for more ecu-menical conditions in the North based on conversation, not physical violence. This story's refusal of structural closure, signified in part by its use of present tense, which is particularly striking in its conclusion, enables its ideological openness.[2]

"Across the Street," the concluding story in the collection, continues the theme of cross-generational connection established in "No Surrender" in its depic-tion of the friendship of Mr. Keogh, a timid, retired policeman, with a lonely girl, Una, who is given to playing her flute in her flat across the street from his. In an analogous maneuver to that of the son from "No Surrender," Mr. Keogh leaves his comfortable solitude and establishes a somewhat uncomfortable relationship with the prickly Una founded in part on their joint love of music (he has previously played the cornet in a policemen's band). When Keogh finds out that Una has tried to kill herself, he forces himself to go across the street and comfort her landlady.

More uncomfortable still is his cleaning of the bathroom. His worst memory of his time on the force involved his confrontation with an old man threatening to cut his own testicles off with a razor. Keogh responded well by seeming to disdain the man, then wrapping him in a coat (138). After Keogh cleans the blood from the bathtub and throws the razor Una used away, he surveys her room and is struck later that night, drinking brandy to steady himself back in his bedroom, by the fact that "if he had ever married and had children, she would have been the age of his grandchild." He even prays "to God that she wasn't dead" (108).

In a drunken, early-morning tribute to Una and as part of his silent commitment to live life more fully, he digs out his cornet from the bottom of his cupboard and plays it tentatively, then more loudly. After playing a march tune, he recalls a jazz number, which he plays, "hearing the voice [of his friend Brian Goodall], knowing the words" (143). Despite being confronted by his enraged landlady, Mrs. O'Hagan, and waking up at noon the next day with a pounding headache, Mr. Keogh has made his life matter, both in his vocation, and now, more significantly, in his retirement. His reemergence as a musician signals his rejection of societal conventions and his determination to enjoy himself while reaching out to others who are hurting. Playing the freewheeling melodies of jazz, he recovers some measure of freedom in his own life, a freedom gained by a simple journey across the street to confront his fear of blood and death. Mr. Keogh's cornet soars above and fills the silence left in the wake of the mechanical ambulance taking Una to hospital (140), pregnant with playful possibilities and serving as a living, meandering antidote to her possibly deadly, precise act.

Framing the collection with the "static crackle" and babble of voices from the radio in "Words the Happy Say" and the wavering flute and joyful cornet played by Una and Mr. Keogh, respectively, enables MacLaverty to suggest that music and, by extension, art itself ineluctably lead to relationships because there must always be a listener, a reader, or a viewer. Although the narrator of the first story rejects the relationship offered to him by the woman who has been led to him by an admiration for his artwork, Mr. Keogh pursues a relationship with Una through first, a memory of his own "art," and then later, a recovery of it. Whether or not she lives is beside the point. Art—especially art created for the sheer joy of it, just as in "Life Drawing" from *A Time to Dance*—can establish, often unconsciously, communities of acceptance across the boundaries of sex and age and between even the living and the dead.

Ontological Encounters
with Others
in *Walking the Dog*

THIS COLLECTION CONCENTRATES on a range of lonely characters across national boundaries, while also retaining MacLaverty's focus on communities in Northern Ireland; published in 1994, it is his most formally interesting. *Walking the Dog* was shortlisted for the prestigious Saltire Society Scottish Book of the Year in 1994. The volume's nine "traditional" short stories explore relationships within the family and community in Northern Ireland and abroad within the context of personal, familial, and national identity. These characters are caught in peculiar dilemmas and struggle to balance their needs with the expectations of their communities and themselves. Interspersed between the longer, more traditional stories are very short, often wryly humorous sketches that feature "your man," the quintessential Irish subject of pub stories. Many of these are metafictional, dealing with the nature of the short story and writing generally.

The movement away from the visual and toward the sonic first adumbrated in *The Great Profundo* is accelerated here as listening takes on a greater emphasis— even as appeals to seeing continue—and becomes the foundation of relationships and of recentering the self, as Jimmy and Maureen discover in "At the Beach," the volume's longest and best story and indeed one of the best in MacLaverty's ouevre. Love and loneliness are the major themes of the collection. Although imprisonment remains a powerful theme, it is rendered more subtly than in previous works through stories such as "A Silent Retreat" and "In the Bed," and more directly in "A Foreign Dignitary." Love in its various manifestations becomes more positively defined in contrast to its perversions in earlier works. Positive examples of love include the deep friendship Ben has for his dying older friend Paddy in "Just Visiting" and the active caring about other people that Maureen discovers is the essence of her soul in her solitary time at the church atrium in "At the Beach."

In the titular and initial story in the volume, MacLaverty portrays the abduction of a man named "John Shields" walking his dog on the outskirts of Belfast and the subsequent identity confusion. They walk, as is typical for MacLaverty characters, in a liminal area between the country and the city, symbolizing the man's marginalization. "It was a country road lined by hedges and ditches. Beyond the housing estate were green fields as far as Lisburn. The city had grown out to here within the last couple of years" (*WD* 3). The loyalist gunmen, who are looking for a Catholic to murder, interrogate Shields about his cultural and religious identity until they discover he is from their community and disgustedly release him. It is simultaneously one of MacLaverty's funniest and scariest stories. The gunmen are caricatures, yet utterly believable. One of them hilariously says after getting the dog and Shields into the car, "There's something not right about it. Bringing a dog," and then quickly announces, "We're from the IRA," as if anyone from the IRA would actually announce themselves (5). Shields is so nonsectarian that even this announcement and their use of the phrase "Roman Catholic" (7), which is usually only applied to Catholics by Protestants, do not tip him off that they are Protestant.

After he tells them his name is John Shields, they query him, "What sort of a name is that?" (6) Finally, one gunman asks him directly, "Are you a Protestant or a Roman Catholic?" Shields says, "I'm . . . I don't believe in any of that crap. I suppose I'm nothing." They ask him then, "What was your parents?" He replies, "The same. In our house nobody believed in anything" (7). Finally, his kidnappers make him say the alphabet. Catholics pronounce the letter "h" as "haitch" and Protestants as "aitch," and the kidnappers are conducting a simple and simplistic linguistic test of the narrator. Shields covers his bases, pronouncing the letter both ways. They also make him tell them what he thinks of the IRA. After the man, thinking they are the IRA, denounces the organization anyway, they turn out to be thugs from a Protestant paramilitary group and they release him, having noted disgustedly, "Another one of our persuasion" (10).

The story concludes with an ominous image of "the clinking of the dog's identity disk as it padded along beside him" (12), which suggests the degree to which Northern Irish identity remains tied to prescribed labels, yet is incapable of fitting everyone, despite the paramilitaries' insistence otherwise. Even though John Shields is only very nominally Protestant, the gunmen still feel that he is "another one of our persuasion" (10). The resonance of the title becomes more apparent here with this final image. "Walking the dog" is a move performed by yo-yoers who attempt to keep the yo-yo spinning in one place for an extended time. Rigid identities have become analogous to this image, MacLaverty implies. They have become static and increasingly irrelevant to all but the die-hard ideologues but are still manipulated by those who wish to maintain conditions of cultural inertia. Yet the quotidian activity of literally walking a dog suggests that the continuation of normal activities is the best, even the most courageous response to terrorism's desire to instill fear in ordinary citizens.

The identities of both the loyalist gunmen and John Shields himself in the story have proved to be elusive to several reviewers, suggesting the difficulty, especially for outsiders, of negotiating the elaborate web of cultural and religious affiliations that comprises daily life in Northern Ireland. For example, Mark Wormald, writing in the *Times Literary Supplement*, wrongly holds that "Shields and dog are picked up at gunpoint by two IRA men."[1] Michael L. Storey's analysis is more sophisticated, especially when he intriguingly suggests that "the Irish violence that has been fueled by cultural identity may effectively eliminate all cultural identity. MacLaverty's protagonist, a cultural nonentity, may be the future citizen of Belfast."[2] As we will see, however, MacLaverty's ideal future citizen of the province, not just Belfast, is Catherine McKenna of *Grace Notes*, who, unlike Shields, still believes in something—the power of music and, by extension, art in general to connect human beings. Storey also misunderstands Shields's reticence about his Protestant cultural identity, even though it is nominal, and suggests that "the irony of the story is that, although we fully experience the man's terror, we never learn his identity: we do not know whether he is Catholic or Protestant, nationalist or unionist, or if what he says is true—that he has no allegiance, and therefore no cultural identity."[3] Shields is clearly Protestant at least in heritage, but so unattached from a cultural or religious community as to be a bland cipher, even saying "I'm nothing" (7). MacLaverty surely does not valorize characters that are utterly solipsistic and so completely detached from community.

If "Walking the Dog" confounds the categorically deterministic imposition of identities, the third major story in the volume, the pre-Troubles story "A Silent Retreat" also does so by establishing a cross-generational connection between a young Catholic boy, Declan, on a silent religious retreat and a Protestant B-Special policeman, a member of a sectarian force that was disbanded early in the Troubles (in 1970) only to be replaced by the mostly Protestant Ulster Defense Regiment. Yet this tentative, even wistful relationship is quickly dashed in the story's conclusion by a resort to calcified identities, which is spurred by the B-Special's increasingly hostile attacks on God, Catholicism, priests, and then Declan himself.

Shy Declan adumbrates the character of Martin Brennan in *The Anatomy School*, just as his imprisoning Catholic school anticipates Martin's school in that novel. Declan is considering becoming a priest, like Martin will later, and intends, like Martin does later, to find out if this vocation is God's intention for him on a silent retreat. Although Martin gets a definitive, negative answer, Declan re-encounters the B-Special he has met the previous day, who patrols the prison that abuts the back of the school playing fields and who interrogates him about his faith and about republican politics.

Their conversation during the silent retreat offers them both temporary respite and freedom from their respective prisons, and despite his occasional antagonism toward Catholics and republicans, the guard seems genuinely interested in learning more about Declan and "the other side." He even tells Declan at one point that "You're the first Roman Catholic I've ever talked to—apart from one guy at work" (53). Through Special Constable Irvine Todd's discussion of his mother's hatred of Catholics and his morning milk round, he becomes less abstracted as a fearful, nameless B-Special and more like an individual to Declan. Similarly, through Declan's tentative discussions of his own faith and admissions of his fear of the priests and dean at the school, he becomes a complex human being to Todd, not another unknown Catholic. After Declan tells Todd that he has an inferiority complex, however, the story takes a dark turn and the man aims his Sten gun at him (57–58). Todd purposely resorts to the stereotype Declan has briefly suggested and uses his gun to reassert his authority over the boy. This pre-Troubles story offers a glimpse of the hope of reconciliation offered through face-to-face dialogue, but ends ominously with the guard shouting to the retreating Declan in a preview of the subsequent slide into violent sectarianism of the province, "Fuck the future" (59).

The issue of personal identity in the context of a relationship is explored more satisfyingly in "At the Beach," the volume's strongest and most resonant story, which features a meandering plot that eventually leads the characters and readers into profound revelations. This story returns, not only in its titular setting but also in its thematic solitude and potential rebirth, to a favorite locale that MacLaverty has explored in earlier stories such as "Anodyne" in *Secrets*, in the novel *Lamb*, in "Language, Truth, and Lockjaw" from *A Time to Dance*, and in "End of Season" from *The Great Profundo*. It is as if the elimination of the intricacies of cultural, religious, and political identities endemic to Northern Ireland enables the elements of wind, water, and earth (sand) to bulk larger than they do in his urban narratives, which in turn creates a greater concentration of focus on the basics of a relationship. But whereas the earlier works are set at local beaches, this story is located in exotic territory—in Spain, on the occasion of a Northern Irish couple's twenty-fifth wedding anniversary. The story's controlling metaphor concerns temperature—both the literal heat wave Jimmy and Maureen endure daily, broken occasionally by air conditioning in the supermarket and cold beers, and the temperature of their relationship, at times smoldering with sexual desire (65, 73) and other times full of frigidity, especially when Jimmy keeps pressing Maureen to tell him about her sexual experiences before their marriage (70–72). Being around the tanned, topless Mediterranean women on the beach makes Jimmy acutely aware of his white skin and his added weight. Because of this near-constant visual stimulation on the beach—a sort of endless soft pornography movie—Jimmy is also aroused by Maureen and cannot simply enjoy being with her, as she wants to do without often being sexually intimate. When they shower together after their day on the beach, the water, significantly, is "luke-warm" (73). After they make love for the second time that day, Maureen even tells him, "Today is lovely but I don't want you—y'know—every time we close that door. We need our own space" (74).

Maureen's last sentence in this passage is prescient and applies not just to their time together on their holiday but to their marriage during the rest of their lives. Their daughters have grown up and recently left home, giving Maureen extra time on her hands. Her identity as a mother is in flux and she wants to test the waters of the job market. She expresses this desire to Jimmy the last night of their trip but he discourages her, replying both that she is too old to train for a job and that he is "just being realistic" (95). Her response suggests both the level of her intelligence and how much things have changed in Northern Irish society. "I got three distinctions in A levels. I held a good job in the photo works up until you came along. . . . They were the days when they sacked you for being pregnant" (95). Maureen will most likely start a career outside the home after their return, based both on her rediscovery of herself on this trip through her earlier visit to the sun-filled atrium and on the final image of an old man teaching his wife to swim, the latter of which suggests a pending change in Jimmy's attitude toward his wife.

Her silent visit to the atrium occurs because she is on her own that particular day, Jimmy having drunk himself into a stupor the night before after having barraged her with questions about her sexual experiences before their relationship. The contrast between the Beckettian silence of Maureen and the voluble babbling of Jimmy could not be stronger. As she moves down the colonnade next to an ancient church in the village, and then sits in the atrium, she is suddenly "aware of the absolute silence—aware that outside this cloister was the quietness of a town in *siesta*. Inside, everything was intensified" (91). MacLaverty employs a double Heaneyean intertext in this scene, obliquely referencing the poet's early poem "Personal Helicon," and a later work "The Toome Road." Heaney's autobiographical "Personal Helicon" grants us a look back at the adolescent boy's narcissistic fascination with literal wells and his reflection in their surface and his now-adult, metaphorical use of himself as a sound chamber for poems. "I rhyme / To see myself, to set the darkness echoing."[4] Maureen, however, cannot see herself in the surface of this deep well: she sees it as a "white disc" (91) and a "disc of light" (92). Nevertheless, her gaze is both a beginning entry into the depths of herself that she has not plumbed since her marriage to Jimmy and the birth of their girls and a deeply moving experience that confirms her place in the world as a spiritual being.

Her return to conceiving of herself as a "soul" (93) instead of merely as a bodily creature who has birthed two girls and fills Jimmy's sexual needs is precipitated by her listening deeply to the sounds of two 25 peseta coins she drops into the well. After she drops the first one, "Nothing happened and she was amazed at the silence" (91). As her mind races, wondering, "How could there be nothing? Where was the sound of the coin dropping into the water below—," her thoughts are interrupted by a "spluck!" (92). Incredulous, she takes out another coin and, using the skills learned from developing film in a camera shop before she met Jimmy, she counts "as if making an exposure" (92). At three-and-a-half seconds, the "spluck!" interrupts her counting, confirming the great depth of the well (92). Feeling the effects of the atrium and the well first in her body, Maureen's "knees began to tremble" and she has to sit and "lean her back against the font" (92). In this position, she draws on both visual and sonic properties of the atrium and well to confirm her spirituality as centered and whole by recalling the image of the omphalos Heaney uses in "The Toome Road."

After she sits absorbing the sunlight and the sacred atmosphere of the place for the better part of an hour and walks a bit through the cloisters, she realizes that the condition of solitude that she has desired throughout the trip is something positive and life-affirming. "The place emphasized her aloneness. It felt as if it had been made for her and she should share it with no one. The cloister was a well for light—the cloister was a well for water. The word *Omphalos* came into her head. She connected the word to a poem of Heaney's she'd read somewhere. The stone that marked the centre of the world. The navel" (92). Her perception of the double image of the atrium as a well of both light and water connects Maureen to the elemental, empirical world even as this image blurs the boundaries of the physical and spiritual and leads her into a perception of the unseen order of things. The passing reference to "a poem of Heaney's" containing "the word *Omphalos*" suggests the intertextual presence of "The Toome Road," a poem in which the speaker sees a "convoy" of "armoured cars" with "headphoned soldiers standing up in turrets" approaching down a quiet country road.[5] Although he feels threatened by their advance and attitude of watchful listening and seeing from their "turrets," the speaker takes comfort in a type of nonempirical, invisible power. "It stands here still, stands vibrant as you pass, / The invisible, untoppled omphalos."[6] MacLaverty's Maureen occupies a somewhat analogous position to that of the speaker in Heaney's poem. Although she feels somewhat threatened by the vigilant attempts of her husband to discover her past sexual history before their relationship began, she revels in the mysterious, secret power of this hidden space she has discovered that seems to connect her to the "centre of the world."

For the ancient Greeks and other people groups, the omphalos, a navel-shaped stone, symbolized birth and the interconnectedness of all life. The most famous of these stones was at the Oracle of Delphi and supposedly marked the center of the earth. Daniel Tobin, citing A.V.C. Schmidt's work on the omphalos, notes that "the sacral aura of the term *omphalos* 'raises acutely the issue of the cognitive validity of mythopoeic expression,' its value to human thought."[7] Taken together, these connotations suggest that Maureen's being seated at such a conduit enables an ontological rebirth in her in which she realizes how she is connected to all other life on earth, a sacred knowledge that will lead her to be more loving from now on as she embraces her new identity. The additional connotation of the omphalos in the Buddhist tradition as a "cord linking up the generations of mankind"[8] implicitly contrasted with John Shields's rejection of family and community in "Walking the Dog" suggests that MacLaverty values a sacred approach to life that recognizes humane values across the generations of human history.

As Maureen reflects back on her life, aided by the metaphorical "lens which made her see herself with more precision," which is formed by "the sunlight and the clarity of the air squeezed into such a small space by the surrounding roofs" (92–93, 92), she perceives the continuity of herself through the space-time continuum, realizing "she was still the same person she had been all her life. . . . She *felt* the same" (93; MacLaverty's emphasis). Musing in this manner, she realizes that the continuity of self she senses inheres in her soul, not her body. She defines her soul as "herself—it was the way she treated other people, it was the love for her children, for the people around her and for people she had never seen but felt responsible for. Her soul was the way she treated the world—ants and all" (93). Perceiving the soul as her loving actions toward others, including the ants she has helped Jimmy poison and kill earlier, Maureen recovers a true selflessness that will stand her in good stead spiritually and, perhaps, vocationally as she moves into the workforce in the future.

Having affirmed her new spiritual orientation, symbolized by the atrium and well, she thus rejects Jimmy's further questions about her sexual history the next night at their evening meal. MacLaverty casts their conversation epistemologically, as Jimmy whines that the second or third date in a relationship should be a time of revelation: "That was a time of finding out . . . of knowing everything there is to know . . . There must be no privacy between people in love." Maureen wisely responds that "there can never be a situation where you know *everything* about another person. It's harder to know one thing *for sure*. . . . When there's nothing left to know there's no mystery. We would all be so utterly predictable" (97; MacLaverty's emphases). Paradoxically, the abstract, sacred knowledge that her soul is defined by active loving, received when she sat by the atrium earlier that day, enables her to realize how hard it has been to "know one thing for sure" and how much harder and even soul-numbing it would be to know too much about another, even her husband.

MacLaverty's privileging of Maureen's new sacred ontology over Jimmy's epistemology of her body suggests not a move toward Gnosticism on the author's part, but a positive affirmation of the sacred qualities of quotidian life in our relationships with the least of creatures such as the ants and our relationships with our life partners. Maureen has told Jimmy early in the story that he "is just stirring up poison" by asking about her early sexual experiences (71), and she now links that charge to her realization that she should not have bought the poison and thus aided him in killing the harmless ants. "Her soul was the way she treated the world—ants and all" (93). Some things, ants and previous sexual behavior, are best ignored, while other things, such as a vital marriage, should be attended to deeply.

Although the solitariness that Maureen experienced in her moments of revelation in the atrium is clearly valued in the story, solipsism is not, and gradually, she moves back toward Jimmy and resolves to make the marriage work even as she assumes her new identity. On their last night, he has gotten drunk again and besieged her with the same old questions about her previous sexual activity, which finally enrages her and inspires her to tell him off (102). After he comes to bed and awakens her with loud apologies, she retreats to the sofa in the outer room but feels "alone on the narrow rectangle of foam—lonely even—a very different feeling to the wonderful solitariness she had experienced in the cloisters" (103). Although she muses about leaving him, she realizes, "It seemed so much simpler to stay as they were. The status quo. People stayed together because it was the best arrangement" (103). If the story had ended here, Maureen's solitary recovery of her soul would be rendered moot, but thankfully the story continues.

In a resonant final scene, Jimmy and Maureen watch a much older couple act out a prolepsis of their own new relationship. The old man is teaching his frightened but determined wife how to swim. She is supported by her husband but displays real initiative of her own. "She kept her face out of the water. The old man reached out from where he stood and cupped his hand under her chin. She began to make the breast-stroke motions with her arms, this time *in* the water. The old man shouted encouragement to her. She swam about ten or twelve strokes unaided until she swallowed sea water, coughed and threshed to her feet. The old man yelled and flung his damp cigar out to sea" (107; MacLaverty's emphasis). This realistic snapshot of a moving relationship between an old couple, who despite their frustrations with each other still actively love one another, augurs well for the future relationship of Jimmy and Maureen. As they watch them, Jimmy says, "Jesus—he's teaching her to swim," and as he stares at Maureen, who is "somewhere between laughing and crying," she exclaims, "That's magic. . . . What a bloody magic thing to do" (107). The old couple's relationship models the way in which Jimmy and Maureen must explore their new identities now that their children have grown up. If Maureen steps out in faith into a new job, Jimmy should use his own experience to support her in this endeavor or other ones she tries.

This positive aquatic image of baptism suggests that both Maureen and Jimmy have been born into a new life on this trip. Jimmy has cited the character Pozzo's despairing dictum from Beckett's *Waiting for Godot* on their first day of the trip in support of his own claim that life's pleasures such as food are fleeting and must be grasped quickly. Jimmy exclaims, *"we give birth astride the grave"* (65; MacLaverty's emphasis).[9] But Maureen's new ontology and Jimmy's shared appreciation of this old couple's actions suggests that they now see life more positively—unlike Beckett's characters in that play—not as time that must be passed in loneliness or boredom. Instead, probably unconsciously drawing on Beckett's own convictions to press on in determination and enjoy the seeming absurdities of life, they now value those ordinary and, at times, extraordinary moments that make up the bulk of our lives. More closely connected now in love than ever, Jimmy and Maureen will continue to need solitude but not solipsism in the rest of their marriage as they love each other and all things with an increased appreciation for life in its many vagaries.

In its presentation of the reorientation of Maureen and, to a lesser degree, that of Jimmy, "At the Beach" demonstrates the truth of Charles E. May's claim that short fiction "breaks up the familiar life-world of the everyday, defamiliarizes our assumption that reality is simply the conceptual construct we take it to be, and throws into doubt that our propositional and categorical mode of perceiving can be applied to human beings as well as objects."[10] Maureen's epiphany at the atrium and well would have been occluded in a novel, particularly a realistic one, because, as Percy Lubbock has noted, novels tend to recede in our memories even as we read.[11]

MacLaverty is clearly concerned in *Walking the Dog* with exploring how the short story form enables our ontological encounters with the other, whatever shape that other might take. In several of the collection's pieces, the other is audaciously represented by insects, such as the ants in "At the Beach," the crickets in "The Grandmaster," which is also set in Spain, and the flea from "In Bed." The endurance of these creatures becomes pleasing and even inspiring to the characters. Before Jimmy and Maureen poison the ants, he marvels, "Maybe they've been on this route for ten million years. . . . Somebody just built this place in their way fifty years ago" (74). "The Grandmaster" concludes with Isobel and Gillian sitting silently and listening to "the night filled with the sound of crickets" (37), a resonant moment of reconciliation marked by the harmony of the insects, whose persistent chirping has accompanied much of the story. Finally, the flea's refusal to die at the end of "In the Bed"—a story whose bedbound title character may be inspired by MacLaverty's own daughter Ciara's struggles with chronic fatigue disorder—engenders a moment of joy between mother and invalid daughter and suggests how persistence, hope, and joy are necessary to surviving and even flourishing in such a condition.

Most reviewers have chuckled at but largely dismissed the short short stories of *Walking the Dog*, yet their presence confirms the collection's desire to explore the ontological in a different, more self-referential manner than the longer stories do. A typical response comes from Tom Adair, who argues, "these pieces earn— and deserve—little more than fleeting attention. They are doodles, the dandiest of which present thoughts aspiring to be ideas, but which lack the roots from which to grow, or to tap our complicity."[12] But these humorous sketches have at least a twofold aim. They give us breaks from the longer, thematically weightier stories, and some of them, such as the opening vignette, "On the Art of the Short Story," and "The Fountain-Pen Shop Woman," "O'Donnell v. Your Man," "St. Mungo's Mansion," and "Looking out the Window—II," probe the nature of fiction itself.

Patricia Waugh has defined metafiction as "fictional writing which self-consciously and systemically draws attention to its status as an artifact in order to pose questions about the relationship between fiction and reality."[13] Much contemporary metafictional writing purports that all "reality or history is provisional: no longer a world of eternal verities but a series of constructions, artifices, impermanent structures. The materialist, positivist, and empiricist world-view on which realistic fiction is premised no longer exists," except as a way in which to foreground the fictional experiment being conducted.[14]

MacLaverty's embrace of a fundamentally religious worldview—i.e., one that recognizes the sacred dimension of another existence of reality outside what can be perceived through our five senses—in stories such as "At the Beach" and others, shares with metafiction this relative disdain for an "empiricist world-view," yet differs from metafiction's postmodernist trajectory. Where "traditional" metafiction takes as a given the position that everything is a construct, MacLaverty's fiction, as we have seen, rises above the empirical world and creates an imagined, but nonetheless real, world in which true verities like love flourish. His work thus reclaims such truths and attempts to instantiate them into the material world. The sketches of *Walking the Dog* fruitfully complicate this task through their hilarious send-ups of a writer, who often is beset by frustrations and insecurities. If imaginative writing generally is rendered somehow less "magical," MacLaverty has achieved part of his purpose. Creating alternate worlds is hard work and even the tools of one's trade, like the author's fountain pen in "The Fountain-Pen Shop Woman," are apt to let one down. More important, these vignettes critique the credulity given by Irish audiences conditioned by oral tale-telling even as they enchant us with their spells and affirm alternate realities to those simply empirically perceived.

William Trevor has articulated how modern Irish short story writers drew on "the heritage of an audience for whom fiction of brief duration—irrespective of how it was offered—was the established thing." As he goes on to argue, the "receptive nature of this audience—a willingness to believe rather than find instant virtues in skepticism—allowed the modern story to thrive, as the old-fashioned tale had." For Trevor, "Stories, far more than novels, cast spells, and spells have been nurtured in Ireland for as long as imperial greed has been attempting to hammer its people into a subject class."[15] MacLaverty's sketches cast this spell on their readers in several ways, but particularly through their written iteration as oral stories told in a pub in a heightened Hiberno-English by the quintessential Irishman, "Your man." This narrator gains our confidence through his instant familiarity to us, especially to Irish audiences, which is then heightened through the confessional nature of his hardships. In these ways, the sketches establish what Waugh calls the "'control' in metafictional texts, the norm or background against which the experimental strategies can foreground themselves" and thus create a "stable level of readerly familiarity."[16]

"Your man" is an author suffering from writer's block, a subject first broached in the story "Hugo" from *Secrets*. This condition results in these attenuated fictions, none of which are shorter than "On the Art of the Short Story." "'This is a story with a trick beginning.' Your man put down his pen and considered the possibility that if he left this as the only sentence then his story would also have a trick ending" (1). And yet this is paradoxically the one story in which "your man" writes precisely too much for his purposes.

"Your man" is also a lazy voyeur who enjoys seeing others frustrated in the act of reading or writing, as in "The Voyeur." "To see the reader or the writer interrupted—for the man or woman to be absorbed in what they're doing and be disturbed by their partner or spouse or friend—that, for him, is something special" (13). When he sends his fountain pen away to be repaired, he feels he cannot write with another implement and is thus hilariously "relieved that the responsibility of serious writing was removed from him for the best part of a fortnight" (39). His hope that the lifetime-guaranteed pen would be replaced for free is dashed when the fountain-pen shop woman says to him in the story's last sentence, "How can anything to do with writing be guaranteed for life?" (39). This telling comment on the nature of writing itself suggests its impermanence and Beckettian tendency toward failure.

From the terseness of "On the Art of the Short Story" to the convoluted, nested stories within stories of "By Train," these vignettes suggest the range possible within short story metafiction, a subgenre that is usually neglected in favor of novelistic metafiction. Through both these short short stories and the longer ones in the volume, MacLaverty evinces his concern to help create other worlds as viable alternatives to the ones that press in on us daily. Like many other practitioners of metafiction, he is "anxious to assert that, although literary fiction is only a verbal reality, it constructs through language an imaginative world that has, within its own terms, full referential status as an alternative to the world in which we live."[17] Published a few months before the first IRA cease-fire on August 31, 1994, which was followed on October 13 by the Combined Loyalist Military Command cease-fire, *Walking the Dog* uncannily arrived right on time, as the populace of Northern Ireland, especially its working class, was beginning to conceive the possibility of such an alternate world: a life not marked by serious violence.

The Beauties
of *Grace Notes*

WHILE MACLAVERTY'S BEST-KNOWN NOVEL, *Cal,* is a direct critique of the violence and destruction associated with the Troubles, his third novel, *Grace Notes* (1997), explores the birth of his protagonist Catherine McKenna's two new creations: her child and the symphony she has just written. Yet these creations are often threatened by Catherine's deep postpartum depression, which leads her at times to hate her child, have murderous thoughts about her, and despair of ever writing music again. *Grace Notes* won the Saltire Scottish Book of the Year Award in 1997 and was a short-listed favorite for the Booker Prize, although it did not win.

In the first section of the novel, set in the present, Catherine returns home to Northern Ireland for her father's funeral, reflects back on her childhood, and attempts to negotiate a better relationship with her mother, from whom she has been estranged for five years. The second section, set in the past, charts Catherine's life after she leaves home: her university and postgraduate years; her brief study in Kiev, Ukraine, with the composer Anatoli Melnichuck; her relationship on the inner Hebridean island of Islay in Scotland (where MacLaverty and his family lived for a time) with the Englishman Dave; the birth of her child, Anna; and the successful performance of her composition *Vernicle* in Glasgow. MacLaverty's gifts of stylistic reticence, colloquial dialogue, and penetrating insight into human character all are manifested here. Additionally, his often unrecognized use of humor is displayed brilliantly. This novel is one of the outstanding fictional explorations of the female psyche—it can be compared to Molly Bloom's monologue in Joyce's *Ulysses*—and is threaded through with moments of hope and transcendence that seem rare in much contemporary fiction.

Although the novel focuses on Catherine's development as an artist and human being, it also obliquely suggests a number of enabling strategies for dealing with the cultural and political problems of contemporary Northern Ireland. *Grace*

Notes autobiographically evokes MacLaverty's cultural hybridity and fluid ability to function as a British citizen and as a member of the Irish Catholic minority in Northern Ireland living first in Belfast, then Scotland, even as it suggests the importance of such a liminal position for understanding and starting to resolve binary thinking about identity in the province. The grace granted Catherine is not so much religious as aesthetic and biological and surprises us, as grace always does, with its delightful unexpectedness, another quality necessary for cultural dialogue and forgiveness. Finally, it is grounded in a conception of beauty that exerts aesthetic pressure to redress great wrong.

Despite MacLaverty's characteristic realism, the novel is leavened by some of the most hilarious moments in his fiction, such as when the Kiev composer Anatoli Melnichuck's large dog attempts to mount Catherine from behind when she is playing for the great man (*GN*71). Additionally, the conclusions of each section are positive, even joyful, as Catherine's love for her child and music, respectively, are confirmed. But this joy is achieved only through Catherine's journey into the abyss of herself, just as, the novel suggests, the hopeful Good Friday Agreement, approved at Easter 1998, was made sweeter by its emergence from the dark old days of bombings and killings in the province. Marilynn Richtarik suggests that *Grace Notes* "stands as one of the first literary fruits of the [1994 IRA and Combined Loyalist] ceasefire[s]," while cautioning that "the end of the novel, however, is not the end of the story, and in this way MacLaverty cautions against the belief in miraculous solutions to deep-seated problems."[1] If *Walking the Dog* cautiously welcomed the changed political climate in the province while acknowledging the perpetuation of binary identities like those the loyalists attempt to foist on the hapless victim in the title story, *Grace Notes* shows how individual triumphs emerge from the wreckage of particular lives in a more cosmopolitan conception of the cross-cultural traffic between the province and the British mainland.

In an interview with the present author, MacLaverty discussed how he began the novel intending to explore the unfair imprisonment of a number of people, but then concentrated on the mental imprisonment of Catherine. He recalls "writing half a dozen pages about an Irish woman who had been wrongfully imprisoned because she was in the wrong place at the wrong time. At that point, there was something like seventeen people who were imprisoned for something they had never done. And I just wondered how awful that would be. When I went back to work on the book, I subtracted the prison and the political elements, focusing on mental imprisonment instead."[2] Whereas earlier novels such as *Lamb* and *Cal* focused on physical confinement, present and proleptic, respectively, *Grace Notes* focuses on Catherine's confinement in the dark world of postpartum depression for many months after the birth of her baby, Anna. This imprisonment is placed in dialectic, once again, with the free will associated with love—both the deep storge love of Catherine for her baby and her love for her music. Only her deep, joyous creative love for Anna and her composing work can lead her out of this depression and enable her to live a fuller, healthier life. Catherine learns to actively love Anna, her music, and finally herself, a joyful process that stems from MacLaverty's comic conception of life, which is echoed by the comic trajectory of the novel. This loving transpires despite the societal and personal tragedies out of which Catherine arises and finally flourishes.

Comedy springs from a trajectory away from disorder toward order, toward a restoration of things as they ought to be. R. B. Gill has argued that comedy is an inherently creative reaction by the individual to this chaos. "Humor and comedy are active, creative responses by the self to the disorder of its world. In these happy structures, the psychological needs that give rise to humor translate into the narratives of comedy."[3] By using his creative powers to respond affirmatively to the sadness and despair of her life, MacLaverty writes a new narrative of hope and meaning out of the rubble of Catherine's personal life and the political life of the province. The beauty associated with this story and localized particularly in her music and child contrasts the atrocities of suffering given in several micronarratives in the novel and proves the truth of Elaine Scarry's apologia for beauty as "actually assist[ing] us in the work of addressing injustice, . . . by requiring of us constant perceptual acuity—high dives of seeing, hearing, touching."[4] Demanding the highest acts of perception from readers accustomed to his narratives of extreme perception epitomized by the genuflecting body of Robert Morton in the murder scene from *Cal*, MacLaverty asks us to heighten our sensory perception by seeing, hearing, and feeling Catherine's creations as deeply as she does. Only then, he suggests, will our own reawakened senses lead us toward pondering beauty more regularly in our own lives, allowing us to instantiate order into a very disordered modern world through our careful protection of that beauty.

One of beauty's foremost properties is pattern, and the patterned structure of the novel is particularly beautiful in its symmetrical shape, a point to which I will return. Within this symmetrical novelistic structure, beautiful objects abound. The most interesting of these in terms of considering beauty and its implications for beginning to redress the disorder endemic to Catherine's life and that of Northern Ireland's recent violent history is the shell. In one sense, the shell signifies her vocation, which she perceives as the most enduring part of herself and to which she retreats during the bleakest times of her depression. When she is home for her father's funeral and despairing, she forces herself to think about her work. Although she does not consider work in terms of a shell, her vocation is so much a part of herself that its function as a metaphorically auricular shell is nonetheless implicit

in this passage: "Work—she must think about her work. That was the most important thing of all. If anything was going to save her it would be that. She must hold
on to a sense of herself, of who she was, and how it could be told in terms of
sound" (31). She then remembers a scene from her childhood where she claps out
her name for Miss Bingham.

Catherine may even associate her depression with the image of a closed,
spiraling shell, not the open scallop shell she thinks of when terming her symphony
Vernicle. The image of a spiral has often been used to describe a descent into mental
illness or depression. MacLaverty himself has called Catherine's postnatal depression
"this spiral of despair that hits her out of the blue."[5] Associating Catherine with
shells enables MacLaverty to elicit our deep sympathy for her, much as descriptions of the beauty of her symphony and baby, as we shall see, lead us to want to
protect those fragile creations. In his classic study of intimate places, *The Poetics of
Space,* Gaston Bachelard devotes an entire chapter to the study of shells, concluding that "whenever life seeks to shelter, protect, cover, or hide itself, the imagination sympathizes with the being that inhabits the protected space."[6] By portraying
Catherine as moving in the intimate space of her shell and by surrounding her with
images of shells, MacLaverty suggests that her tough outward demeanor hides a
creature who needs protection from forces that would crush her.

She is surrounded by actual shells on Islay once she moves there, and she
collects them for display in her cottage; however, it is only when she thinks of herself as figuratively wearing a shell and being comfortable in her peregrinations across
Northern Ireland, Islay, Glasgow, and back again to Northern Ireland and finally
Glasgow that Catherine can come up with a different credo about her art that is
less disabling than the one that considers her creative abilities to lie safely yet ten-
uously within her own darkness. In the meantime, while peering at a wetsuit hung
on the clothesline to dry, Catherine sees her pregnant body at the beginning of the
second section as "a shell of a thing—just as she was an envelope for this baby. That
was her only function and when it was born she would be hung out on the line.
That would be her finished" (142). Empty, vacuous, and shell-like, Catherine feels
robbed of her identity and operates in a purely biological mode. Dave, her live-in
boyfriend, is also associated with shells, scallops in particular, which he dives for
and sells for a living. As Dave becomes more and more a shell of the man he used
to be, drinking himself to death, Catherine retreats into the shell of herself, finally
leaving Islay to have Anna in a charity hospital in Glasgow.

The turning point in her emergence from her subsequent postpartum
depression occurs the day after Dave hits her for the first time, and she walks on
the beach, surrounded by shells, with Anna. MacLaverty's penchant for portraying
moments of revelation at the shore, as in *Lamb* and the final scene of "At the Beach"

from *Walking the Dog*, is exemplified by this scene. The rhythm of the sea figures prominently in Catherine's reawakened love for her child, the arrival of a new piece of music in her head that will become *Vernicle*, and her renewed sense of optimism. As she walks the shore, she strides in the shallows, which seem "to cushion the impact—each heel breaking the skin of the tepid water before touching the sand a millimeter beneath. Repetitively. Splashing" (206). Somehow, immersing herself in the rhythm of the waves in this manner helps her to rise above the repetitive rhythm of her life as she cares for Anna day after day with no help from Dave. Thinking about this stultifying rhythm, she recalls, "No one had told her of the regularity of a baby's crying. The repetitiveness of it. Again and again" (210). Out of the blue, however, Catherine gets a sense, much as she will later in the taxi going back to Liz's flat in Glasgow after being home for her father's funeral, that things are going to work out: "Suddenly from nowhere Catherine felt good. . . . Whatever it was she hadn't felt like this since the baby was born" (211). Stripping her clothes off, she gradually moves into the cold water and dandles Anna in it, finally returning them both to the warm shallows. At this moment, Catherine feels so good "that she was overcome by a fierce joy and tears sprang into her eyes. They brimmed over and she was aware of weeping salt into the sea" (212). This is one of her three primary epiphanies in the novel—the others occur when she looks in the mirror holding Anna at the conclusion of the first section (138) and when she weeps on hearing the finale of her symphony at the end of the second section (276). Each is associated with tears that function as a sort of baptism—Catherine cries here and at the end of the second section and Anna cries shortly before the end of the first section (136). These are tears of joy, however, in contrast to the mournful, despairing tears that Catherine has cried during much of the novel during her postnatal depression.

After washing herself in tears while on the beach, Catherine hears the sounds of the symphony that will become *Vernicle*. After vowing to dedicate this music to Anna, she has her second revelation of the day, turning to find Anna "standing waiting for her. Bow legged and wavering, but standing none the less" (214–15). Just as Catherine will rise at the conclusion of this section to acknowledge the wild applause of the audience for her symphony, Anna stands here to acknowledge her mother as creator, giver of life to her.

This pilgrimage to the beach that sunny day enables Catherine to leave Dave, who has become increasingly alcoholic and abusive, and she conceives of herself increasingly as a contemporary pilgrim. Naming her musical piece first conceived at the shore *Vernicle* instead of *By the Sea's Edge* confirms her in this vacillating, yet comfortable identity. She gets the name *Vernicle* from a book called *The Scallop* she finds at an Oxfam bookstore one day. The book tells her that "medieval pilgrims

101

who had been to the shrine of Santiago de Compostela in Spain wore a scallop-shaped badge on their caps. To prove they had been where they said" (245). Additionally, she reads that "each important shrine in Europe produced its own badge—a vernicle." Having been on a journey into the heart of despair and depression and now beginning to emerge on the other side of it, Catherine is taken with the idea of calling her symphony Vernicle because it signifies her own long pilgrimage. She muses, "The word appealed to her—it had a good ring to it. Proof that you'd been there. In a land of devastation. At the bottom of the world. And come through it—just. She'd brought back evidence in the shape of a piece of music. *Vernicle*. A feather in her cap—for full orchestra. From the shrine of desolation" (245). Catherine's badge of proof, her talisman signifying her eventual recovery, comes in the shape of her scallop-shaped symphony, a piece of music that mirrors itself in content but not in context. And context is all. Remaking the often negative, spiraling, and constricting image of the shell she has associated with it before, Catherine opens herself to new experiences musically and personally rather than shutting herself off from the world.

MacLaverty's conception of cultural relationships in the province within an archipelagic context in *Grace Notes* constitutes a signal contribution to Northern Irish culture and literature. Catherine McKenna, in short, is a proleptic model of the kind of citizen who may emerge out of the context of the hope generated by the Good Friday Agreement in 1998. Such a citizen, no matter whether she is resident in the province or not, emigrates to other parts of the Atlantic archipelago and returns to the province when necessary. Catherine's shuttling back and forth between Northern Ireland, the Hebridean Islands, Glasgow, and Northern Ireland signifies not an abstracted globalism, but a fluid identity that should transcend calcified, binary notions of political and religious identity that linger on in the province. In this way, the character-based trajectory of the novel is somewhat consistent with what Joe Cleary has identified as the openness of 1990s narratives from Northern Ireland. Cleary observes that "in these narratives the future . . . remains open to transformation; a sense of the North simply as an atlas of atrocity gives way to a sense that new social forces are on the move."[7]

Formally, *Grace Notes*, like Catherine's symphony *Vernicle*, borrows its shape from a scallop shell, with each half of almost exactly similar length reflecting the other, starting tentatively and quietly, but ending affirmatively and resonantly, especially in the second half of the novel, which is chronologically the earlier section. The first half opens with the beginning of Catherine's journey home to Northern Ireland for her father's funeral, and her depression is signaled by the purposely repetitive, static openings of several of the sentences in the first paragraph. "She went down the front steps and walked along the street to the main road. . . . She tucked her hair back and put her collar up as far as it would go. . . . She made her way to the bus station on foot carrying a small hold-all" (3). Catherine's individuality is diminished by this structural maneuver at the sentence level, and her agency is further denied by the use of the past tense.

It is only in the last seven pages of this first section, which has been primarily concerned to convey Catherine's depression, that the narrative moves into the present tense when Catherine's plane lands in Glasgow. The effect is liberating, as her urgency to see her baby leads her literally forward at a frantic pace that suggests an end, at least for now, to her immobilizing depression. Now the repetitive sentence openings highlight her animation. "She has no baggage to collect so she moves quickly past the carousel, while others have to stand and wait. She is in such a hurry that she forgets to go to the toilet" (131). This driving rhythm that heightens our own awareness of Catherine's desire to see Anna replaces the repetitive thoughts that blacken Catherine's mind earlier in this section. The change in pace of this rhythm achieves what E. M. Forster claims rhythm generally in the novel does. As Forster observes, "By its lovely waxing and waning . . . [it] fill[s] us with surprise and freshness and hope."[8]

Spurred on by her need to see her daughter, Catherine is caught up in a near-breathless rhythm that subsides temporarily in the taxi ride from the airport to her friend's flat in Glasgow as she finally starts to believe she is going to recover from her disabling depression. This belief stems from her listening to the rhythm of the taxi, which moves in the fast lane, and which in turn leads her to hear the rapid "first section of something. Leading the way. A symphony. Called Symphony. . . . Then she knows with certainty what it is. The *Credo*. Her *Credo*. The linchpin of the mass she is writing" (132). The seven syllables she hears confirm her in her identity as she begins creating again. "Seven in all. That was her. A mythic number. Seven little claps in all. Catherine Anne McKenna. Mysterious" (133). Earlier in this section, she has recalled being told by Miss Bingham, her childhood piano teacher, to clap her name, which she does perfectly. "Seven little claps in all—spaced out as her name was spoken. That was her" (31). As she retrieves the rhythm of her mass in the speedy taxi drive home this day, Catherine recovers herself and realizes that in the patterned music of her name, she is wholly herself, that "she is being carried home" (133). Just as "she feels good about this," about beginning to write her mass, she realizes that order is returning to her life as well and that she will survive, even flourish. "And suddenly she feels good about herself. Someday she will be better. Wellness was inside her, waiting, on the edge of its seat. Like the Rose of Jericho. Ready to flower however long it has been dormant. She has to believe it. She will see her daughter again and together they will advance" (133–34). The repetition of several of the phrases in this passage such as "she feels good," along with the beginning of the last two sentences, varies the concluding rhythm of this section again, slowing the pace temporarily by force of its decisive, even joyful tone.

After this rhythmic epiphany, the driving rhythm of the earlier passages of this concluding section returns and does not slow until Catherine sees and holds Anna. Shocked, she cannot at first credit the changes that have occurred to her daughter in five days, just as she could not believe how her mother had aged in five years on her return home. In both cases, Catherine thinks daughter and mother, respectively, to be "changeling[s]" (136, 12), as if fairies had substituted one of their own for her family members, then she accepts the changed person. This section concludes with Catherine's delighted discovery that Anna has talked for the first time while she was gone, a development that suggests her daughter is becoming more creative in her acquisition of language. After Catherine uses the toilet holding her child, she is portrayed in a lovely passage that signifies just how much they resemble each other yet are uniquely different. "They look at themselves and each other. The child smiles at what it sees. So does Catherine. *Credo*" (138). This literal reflection of her creation makes Catherine believe even more strongly in herself as a competent mother who is capable of caring for the life she has helped create. Despite her re-immersion in depression earlier in this first section, this joyful vision also affirms her belief that she is getting better mentally and is able to create music again, as it recalls the title of her new mass.

This final moment in the present anticipates the concluding moment of the novel, where Catherine sits listening to her symphony *Vernicle* being performed in the past. Although she has not yet heard Anna talk in the present, hearing a new creation in her head and seeing her child's joy reflected back at her suggests her happiness, whereas in this seminal scene from her recent past, she revels in what she hears—the music of her creation. Paradoxically, the uniqueness of her humanity is sonically proclaimed by the orchestra's many musicians, confirming her in her identity as artist and creator of human life. "All this conformity was to express the individuality and uniqueness of one human being. Catherine Anne's vision. A joy that celebrates being human. A joy that celebrates its own reflection, its own ability to make joy. To reproduce" (276). This passage mirrors the concluding scene from the first section in Catherine's response to seeing her creation reproduced in front of her eyes. And yet each "work" is unique: Anna is certainly not her mother and will act in a manner inimitably her own, while Catherine's symphony will be played differently each time it is performed. Change, then, is built into these "reproductions" and becomes the great hope of literal and figurative advancement in this highly patterned novel. Its last sentence, "She rose," suggests that change embraces life in all its variety and, conversely, that stasis leads to death (277). Catherine is "[l]ike the Rose of Jericho" (133) she bought in Kiev: Without water, the plant stays shriveled and dry, but when it is watered, it blooms beautifully, just as Catherine does in this concluding moment of tearful joy.

Catherine's beauty, the beauty of her child, and that of her symphony together suggest that *Grace Notes* has achieved a beauty of its own that resonates with its beautiful content. Forster argues that music offers an exemplary type of beauty that the novel alone of all the literary genres might strive to emulate. He suggests that "Music, though it does not employ human beings, though it is governed by intricate laws, nevertheless does offer in its final expression a type of beauty which fiction might achieve in its own way. Expansion. That is the idea the novelist must cling to. Not completion. Not rounding off but opening out. When the symphony is over we feel that the notes and tunes composing it have been liberated, they have found in the rhythm of the whole their individual freedom. Cannot the novel be like that?"[9] MacLaverty's musical novel eschews completion and easy solutions and instead offers expansiveness. Indeed, music and literature generally are "constantly in a state of becoming," whereas the fine arts "stand as completed entities, wholly observable in space."[10] MacLaverty, having realized that music's expansiveness is even more appropriate to the human condition than the static paintings that appear in a novel like *Cal*, turned to this aesthetic structure because it, like literature, "share[s] with human experience" the process of "becoming without attaining closed form."[11] Catherine rises at the end of the second section, but as the first section set at a later time tells us, she is not quite fully back on her feet, but well on the way to recovery. Forster's conception of aesthetic beauty as signified by music's openness resulting in individual freedom perfectly captures Catherine's emergence from the constricting narratives of her past and entrance into an open-ended future narrative that she and Anna still have to write. By extension, Northern Irish society continues to expand and foster new narratives about itself in all its cultural, religious, and political complexity that are increasingly replacing the ugly, more closed stories of suffering in its past.

The question of art's relationship to suffering is raised several times in *Grace Notes*, but most prominently in its discussion of the Holocaust and the contemporary Troubles. While in Kiev, Catherine is told by her mentor Melnichuck about the new openness in Russian society after the collapse of communism. He surprises her by his deep Christian Orthodox faith, which is expressed in the title of his new work, "A Hymn to the Mother of God Seated on the Throne of Heaven" (126). Olga, Melnichuck's wife, relates to Catherine Shostakovich's bravery in calling one of his symphonies *Babi Yar*. Babi Yar was the site at which all the Jews in Kiev (almost 34,000) were massacred by the Nazis, other German units, local collaborators, and Ukrainian police on September 29 and 30, 1941. Catherine, recalling this moment as she flies back to Glasgow after her father's funeral, remembers "the geography of the places of death in her own country. . . . Cornmarket, Claudy, Tee-bane Crossroads, Six Mile Water, the Bogside, Greysteel, the Shankill Road, Long Kesh, Dublin, Darkley, Enniskillen, Loughinisland, Armagh, Monaghan town. And of places of multiple deaths further to the east—Birmingham, Guildford, Warring-ton. It was like the Litany. Horse Guards Parade. Pray for us. Tower of London. Pray for us" (127). Drawing on both the Marian litany from her Catholic upbringing and the tradition of *dinnseanchas*, or place-lore in Gaelic Ireland, Catherine com-poses a litany of contemporary *dinnseanchas* of the Troubles, each site with its own sad story to tell. In despair, she thinks "if she wrote the most profound music in the history of the world it would have no effect on this litany—it would go on and on adding place names" (127). However, her recitation of these atrocities and incorporation of them into a litany ensure that they will not be forgotten, much as physical memorials to such horrors across Northern Ireland have enabled remem-brance and continue to do so. In inscribing this litany of horrors, Catherine is per-forming a private, but inherently ethical act, because remembering, as Susan Sontag has argued, "has ethical value in and of itself. Memory is, achingly, the only rela-tion we can have with the dead."[12] The rhetoric of the novel confirms Catherine's sense that music and, by extension, art commemorates and questions, refusing to settle for easy answers. This type of insistently challenging repetition, in contrast to the constrictingly repetitive nature of her own depression, creates the condition in which penitence might be offered and answered with forgiveness, which does not mean forgetting.[13]

As an example of both the disabling and enabling characteristics of repeti-tion, the lambeg drums in her symphony *Vernicle* function both to iterate the hatreds of the province's past and suggest an avenue for a more harmonious future. When they first enter, their sound nearly overwhelms the rest of the orchestra, and their din is described as "almost like machine-gun fire" (271). After a brief pause of utter silence by all instruments, the drummers let loose with two more, increasingly sus-tained bursts, each followed by silence. This last drumming sounds destructive and chaotic, and achieves a brief synesthesia. The narrator tells us, "The black blood of hatred stains every ear" (272). Finally, the rest of the orchestra is silenced by their blattering, and their black sound reminds Catherine of her own depression: "the candle flames snuffing out beneath the invisible tide of suffocating gas" (272).

Traditionally viewed by Northern Irish Catholics as instruments symboliz-ing Protestant triumphalism, these drums, like shells, have always both repelled and attracted Catherine, as a scene rendered in a flashback early in the novel shows. When the child Catherine and her father see and hear some Protestant Orangemen practicing their drumming, her father tells her, "They practice out here above the town to let the Catholics know they're in charge. This is their way of saying the

Prods rule the roost" (8). Catherine's immediate reaction, however, is joyous. She remembers being "thrilled by the sound, could distinguish the left hand's rhythm from the right. She tried to keep time with her toes inside her shoes. . . . It didn't exactly make her want to dance, more to sway" (8–9). Only after thrilling to the complex rhythms and deep vibrations of the drums does she feel "an edge as well— of fear, of tribal war drumming" (9). Now, in the present, drawing on her post-partum depression, she evokes in the audience the reverse of the feeling she first felt when hearing them. "When the drums stopped on a signal from Randal the only thing that remained was a feeling of depression and darkness. Utter despair" (273).

The second half of the program similarly concludes with lambeg drumming, but because of a change in the preceding music, their sound is now joyful. Catherine draws on the crystalline sound of the church bells she heard in Kiev to impart a sense of clarity, order, and progression that gradually sweeps away the memory of the drums' dissonance, chaos, and stasis. As the seven notes of the bells are played, recalling Catherine clapping out the seven syllables of her name in her past and her future hearing of the seven-note first section of her *Credo*, all the instruments in the orchestra take up the repetitions of the bells and "gradually the horror of the first movement falls away, is forgotten. There is a new feeling in the air. It is urgent and hopeful and the tempo quickens. Things are possible. Work can be done—good work, at that. Love is not lost or wasted" (274–75).

This graceful tintinnabulation and its repetitions prepare for the second, triumphal entrance of the lambeg drummers. Catherine learned to be fond of word with dual meanings like "safe" from her father, and she draws on this knowledge to convey two differing tones from the drums in admitting both the harshness and hopefulness of their sound. Now, because of the sprightly, lilting melody begun by the bells and picked up by the orchestra, "the drumming has a fierce joy about it. Exhilaration comes from nowhere. The bell-beat, the slabs of brass, the whooping of the horns, the battering of the drums. Sheer fucking unadulterated joy" (276). In the full expansiveness of sound that emanates from the lambeg drums and the entire orchestra, *Vernicle*, and by implication, the novel itself, achieve that openness common to both the novel and music so aptly described by Forster, signifying their formal abilities to express both suffering and the triumph of the individual, creative spirit over calamity.[14]

On another level, *Vernicle* represents an impressive artistic and political recognition and appreciation of the culture of others with specific resonances for Northern Ireland. When Catherine muses about a title for her symphony before settling on *Vernicle*, she briefly considers calling it *Metamorphoses* or *Reconciliation*, but rejects these as hated "Latinate words that thrust into her head" (214). Nevertheless, the flux and change implicit in both titles offer insight into her embryonic hopes for the piece. When she is home for her father's funeral and visiting her former piano teacher Miss Bingham, both of them seem to dismiss the cultural implications for the symphony. Her former teacher mentions that the English papers covered it because it involved "A Roman Catholic using Protestant drums. The Lambeg angle," and rolls her eyes. Catherine responds, "They wanted to make a whole thing of it. . . . I said I just liked the sounds." Catherine does argue to her, however, "They *are* a great sound—they inspire intense feelings. Really complicated rhythms," and finally notes that she told the press that "it's the kind of drum a child would play" (105; MacLaverty's emphasis). These statements not only recapitulate her childhood feelings of both awed fear and joy at the booming sound and complexity of the drums, but also, read in the context of the symphony performance itself featured in the second half of the novel, they emphasize the "complicated rhythms" of the music, suggesting by implication that Protestant culture is far from monolithic and that recovering such rhythmic complexities are symbolically a necessary part of the cultural discourse needed in the province to quell old hatreds and kindle new alignments between Protestants and Catholics, among other groups. Finally, her noting that a child would play such drums should not be read as dismissive, but rather as a statement of the need for such childlike wonder as a precondition for listening to subtle nuances of performance, whether expressed in such drumming or in cultural politics.[15]

After recalling the revelation of the atrocity at Babi Yar to her by the Melnichucks and her own mental litany of the Troubles, Catherine faces the possibility of endless, worldwide suffering on a massive scale from now to the end of time, but nonetheless is cheered by her creative powers' ability to singularly inscribe the importance of the individual. She now knows "that her act of creation, whether it was making another person or a symphonic work, defined her as human, defined her as an individual. And defined all individuals as important" (128).[16] Her claim to the uniqueness of her created art and, correspondingly, of her own singularity is surely consonant with MacLaverty's own view of art's relationship to suffering, particularly in the novel's affirmation of the importance of the minor moments, the grace notes of our lives, to our development. This perception contrasts a view of the self and history that still prevails in some quarters as only consisting of major events, which, for all its positive ethical connotations, is negatively represented by Catherine's litany of the Troubles.

In a series of works, most famously in *Cal*, MacLaverty has considered it sufficient to portray the individual so intensely that characters such as Cal assume a luminous presence in our minds, particularly when they are conflated with the suffering they cause and will endure themselves. Catherine McKenna's mental sufferings are no less memorable for their absence of truly searing pictorial images.

And despite her own relative distance from the atrocities committed in Northern Ireland, her remembrance of them, mediated as it probably is by newspaper accounts and television and video footage, is no less powerful. It is tempting to claim that her amazing powers of musical and biological creativity stand as aesthetic and bodily bulwarks against chaos and death, but in actuality, they are rendered so tenderly that their gossamer, ethereal qualities acquire an openness that invites us to consider how carefully perceiving and appreciating fragile works of art and delicate human bodies remind us all of our responsibility to help and love each other even as we travel our own highly individual paths.[17]

Love, after all, remains the central theme of this novel, as with MacLaverty's earlier ones, but it is a love radically different from the mostly perverse personal and national loves that the previous ones explore. If Catherine can love her baby after wanting to kill her for a time, if she and her estranged mother can reconcile and love each other again, then perhaps even the most intransigent bigots of Northern Ireland can learn to love those they have hated.[18] The unexpected kind of unconditional love that Catherine finally offers her baby and that her mother offers Catherine soon before she returns to Glasgow suggests this love, like grace in all its connotations, is freely given with no expectation of reciprocity. In describing what he terms "the insanity of grace," the ability of Jesus Christ and, to a much lesser degree, Desmond Tutu, to forgive those who tortured them, former Bishop of Edinburgh Richard Holloway has noted that "this absolutely gratuitous conduct . . . comes upon us, when it comes at all, without condition. It is done for its own sake, out of the pure joy and love of doing it."[19] The hard work of political rapprochement and reconciliation in Northern Ireland clearly cannot be accomplished solely through such acts, but their graceful appearance in the novel suggests the delightful and leavening impact they can have in such societies.

This sense of grace, moreover, is not limited to seminal moments in the novel but is built into its comedic form, which in turn suggests the close relationship MacLaverty perceives between aesthetic form and ethics. *Grace Notes* is shot through with humor and travels an essentially comic trajectory in its return to order, a journey that suggests how the aesthetic conception of the novel evokes a renewed ethical compulsion. In this sense, it adheres to R. B. Gill's revelatory definition of both humor and comedy as gifts of grace. Gill suggests, "Humor and comedy are acts of grace, gifts of meaningfulness in a disordered world, given like religious grace without expectation of return."[20] Furthermore, Gill sees the comic plot as essential to promoting a recovery of justness and healthiness by "resolv[ing] the dissonances of a threatening world and restor[ing] its audience to the 'vital balance of justice and health.'"[21]

Part of this comic joy, I suggested early in this chapter, arises from a perception of beauty—particularly the beauty of Catherine's baby Anna and of Catherine's music, especially her symphony *Vernicle*—that ineluctably leads to a pursuit of justice, a crucial issue in such a novel that concerns itself with the suffering endemic in the Holocaust and Northern Irish conflict, among other narratives. How does perceiving the aesthetic beauty of Anna, Catherine's music, and, by extension, the symmetrical beauty of MacLaverty's novel lead toward justice? One way is through virtue of its form. Lukács has argued that whereas in other genres, "ethic is a purely formal pre-condition," in the novel, "the ethical intention . . . is visible in the creation of every detail and hence is, in its most concrete content, an effective structural element of the work itself."[22]

Significantly, the novel does not only preserve the author's "ethical intention," but also can lead to an enhanced appreciation of ethics on the part of the reader. In short, the many acts of perceiving beauty in the novel may lead to our heightened concern for the well-being of others and a desire to help them as fellow members of humanity. Denis Donoghue points out a compelling ethical reason for regarding beauty by noting that "looking at a beautiful thing for its beauty fosters in us certain intuitions that other forces in life have no time for—respect for intrinsic value, freedom, independence, selflessness."[23] Elaine Scarry goes further, arguing that the perception of an object or subject of beauty "is bound up with an urge to protect it, or act on its behalf, in a way that appears to be tied up with the perception of its lifelikeness."[24] Because of her apprehension of her baby's beauty, after some initial murderous urges experienced in the depths of her depression, Catherine feels strongly that she must protect her child.

More important, perhaps, for picturing a just social order in Northern Ireland through imaginative writing, is the subtle way in which perception of beauty exerts what Scarry terms "the pressure . . . toward the distributional."[25] She argues that the "quality of heightened attention" given "to the beautiful person or thing" is in turn, "voluntarily extended out to other persons or things. It is as though beautiful things have been placed here and there throughout the world to serve as small wake-up calls to perception, spurring lapsed alertness back to its most acute level. Through its beauty, the world continually recommits us to a rigorous standard of perceptual care."[26] In this way, carefully reading a work of beauty such as *Grace Notes* and attending to the persons of beauty such as Anna and the things of beauty such as Catherine's music in its pages lead us to a strengthened sense of other instances of the beautiful in our daily lives and a subsequent desire to protect them and, by extension, all things. Treading lightly and perceiving more closely the beauty of our world may well ensure that we treat other human beings as persons of beauty and serve them instead of ourselves.

Denying ourselves while delighting in the beauty of other human beings and even things can lead to what Scarry calls a "[r]adical decentering," a process that precedes the condition of "enjoying fair relations with others." "It is clear," she says, "that an *ethical fairness* which requires 'a symmetry of everyone's relation' will be greatly assisted by an *aesthetic fairness* that creates in all participants a state of delight in their own lateralness" (her emphases). In this condition of lateralness, which Catherine certainly occupies at significant moments in the novel, especially during her three major epiphanies, we occupy a site of beauty that moves from mere beholding to "the active state of creating—the site of stewardship in which one acts to protect or perpetuate a fragment of beauty already in the world or instead to supplement it by bringing into being a new object."[27] Although beauty may be fragile, Susan Sontag has argued that "the capacity to be overwhelmed by the beautiful is astonishingly sturdy and survives amidst the harshest distractions."[28] Our responsibility to preserve the beautiful, therefore, is elicited from our perception of its temporary condition, while our capacity to remain inspired by the beautiful may well outlast the object of perception itself. The beauty of Catherine McKenna's baby and music echoes the beauty of this deeply profound novel that intertwines a compelling ethical urge toward fairness for all with the aesthetic exhilaration of individual creation.

The Buoyant Beauty of a Belfast
Bildungsroman: The Anatomy School

T HIS PARTIALLY AUTOBIOGRAPHICAL NOVEL should confirm MacLaverty's place as the best fiction writer to emerge from Northern Ireland in the second half of the twentieth century, along with Brian Moore. Its popularity signals MacLaverty's growing appeal to a wide readership, having sold tens of thousands of copies in hardback in Britain and Ireland since its release in September 2001. His protagonist, Martin Brennan, comes of age in Belfast during the 1960s. Fruitful comparisons can be made between this younger child who grows up some before the current Troubles start and MacLaverty's earlier character Cal, whose coming of age is indelibly influenced by the conflict. Brennan is another figure of the artist, a budding photographer who takes exacting mental snapshots of the world around him in an attempt to capture moments of transcendence and potential.

With *The Anatomy School*, MacLaverty again writes through the perspective of a young Catholic male, this time with a wry and sometimes outrageous humor that surfaces at unexpected moments throughout the novel, a technique that should forever lay to rest the critical perception that MacLaverty is not a funny or joyful writer. In Part One, Martin Brennan is a young man of around 17 growing up in a poor neighborhood in 1960s Belfast. When Part Two opens, he is a lab technician around 20 years old at Queen's University, a detail that is at least partly autobiographical, because a slightly older MacLaverty worked the same job at Queen's in the 1960s and early 1970s when he was part of Philip Hobsbaum's creative writing group along with Seamus Heaney, Michael Longley, and Stewart Parker. He confessed some of these autobiographical details to the present author in an interview:

> There's a sort of comedic autobiography in there somewhere. It's the school
> I went to and all of those things. But it's that made-up truth again. There
> was a bunch of boys, friends, there were about five or six of us. I narrowed
> them down to three and they are kind of compartmentalized, portmanteau

characters. [laughter] All of those places and all of that upbringing are there. Martin's not too bright, therefore he needs help on his exams, like me. I ended up failing my A-level in English lit. and staying on a year, like Martin, and passing it the second time, by about two marks, whereas other friends of mine went on.[1]

But this is far from a mere self-portrait. Much like Joyce's famous bildungsroman *A Portrait of the Artist As a Young Man*, *The Anatomy School* successively details the growth of a fictional, sensitive mind as it encounters the world and seeks its place in that world. Irish bildungsromane are relatively rare because of the lingering influence of Joyce's work. As Michael R. Molino has pointed out, Joyce's *Portrait* has been so significant that "the few Irish novelists" such as Roddy Doyle in *Paddy Clark Ha Ha Ha* (1993) and MacLaverty in *The Antatomy School* "to take up the genre have felt compelled to acknowledge Joyce's novel."[2] Throughout the novel, we see through Martin's eyes as he observes the world around him. He aspires to be a photographer, a profession that calls for introspection and patience—qualities that he has in abundance and that MacLaverty displays in his own thoughtful prose.

As in many earlier works discussed in this study, *The Anatomy School* revolves around the dialectic of imprisonment, often symbolized by discussions of gravity, versus freedom, usually signified by discussions of buoyancy. Imprisonment is much less grim here, however, because Martin's home and school function as only mildly restrictive sites in the first part of the novel. For example, one day in physics class, the new boy, Blaise Foley, tells Martin and his best friend Kavanagh that "there's an element of imprisonment" to being a boarder rather than a day student. Their teacher, who is nicknamed "Cousteau," finally tells Foley to "stop talking out the side of your mouth like some sort of jailbird" (*AS* 58, 59). However, in the second half of the novel, parts of Belfast itself become imprisoning as the city literally begins to explode into street riots. Martin's major obstacle to attaining his freedom comes from within, because his lack of confidence and powerful interior life cause him to be impressionable and lack agency, especially in Part One. In Part Two, he gradually assumes a fuller, more dynamic and intentional selfhood as he moves away from the orbit of Blaise and Kavanagh. Freedom comes to him, too, through his continuing exploration of photography and through his first sexual experience, with the Australian girl in Part Two.

The Anatomy School shares with *Grace Notes* great humor, a similarly comedic trajectory, and an expansiveness that formally signal Martin's growing freedom and development. Although typical examples of the genre, such as Joyce's *Portrait*, involve the portrayal of the protagonist's life from birth or at least from early childhood through late adolescence or early maturity, *The Anatomy School* nevertheless qualifies as a bildungsroman because it displays major characteristics of the genre such as the adolescent hero's movement toward freedom and his search for a guiding principle. Weldon Thornton has noted that the freedom typical of the genre is a "complex psychological and spiritual matter," because it involves the hero's desire to escape "being dictated to by the ideas and ideals of others—of his family, his church, his social class, or his state."[3] MacLaverty's Martin Brennan eventually feels trapped by his family, the Catholic church, and his relative poverty, and seeks escape through adventures with his friends while he is still in school during Part One and through other means after he is working in the anatomy school at Queen's University in Part Two.

Both before and after he leaves school, however, he continues to search for meaning in his life, a search that is grounded in the father-son relationship MacLaverty has often portrayed in his fiction. He has always taken pains to explore variations on this relationship, as in, for example, Owen Kane's relationship with his "adopted" father Michael Lamb in *Lamb* and Cal McCluskey's more positive relationship with Shamie in *Cal.* As is typical of many of MacLaverty's adolescent male characters, Martin's father is dead. Like many protagonists of the bildungsroman, Martin undergoes a journey, not so much to find an actual father figure, but to discover a symbolic one, "a principle by which he can live."[4]

Martin's search for such a principle courts aspects of beauty similar to those pursued by Catherine McKenna in *Grace Notes* and realized in her creation of beautiful music and her lovely child. However, what becomes his guiding principle of beauty is grounded in a pursuit of the quotidian, the apprehension of which leads similarly to the ineffable. These two novels constitute an extended exploration of the beautiful, ranging from the extraordinary to the everyday and from the perception of the professional to the amateur, although of course, Catherine often finds beauty in the commonplace and Martin commonly discovers it in high art or the Catholic mass. Their respective creative trajectories, however, are toward creating art of high order and art of a so-called lower order, photography.

MacLaverty has long been interested in issues of the parochial, in the Irish writer Patrick Kavanagh's rehabilitated sense of the term that considers the local to be valuable and even universal if it is precisely rendered. In an interview, he cites Chekhov, Kavanagh, and the Glaswegian writer James Kelman as exemplars of parochial writing that transcends itself, concluding, "It's the heightening of the parochial which is so interesting, and if you portray it with exactitude then the parochial is universal."[5] Through his carefully practiced observation throughout *The Anatomy School,* Martin Brennan develops a trained eye for detail that gives his schoolboy and later experiences an exactitude that lifts them out of the context of 1960s Belfast and into a believably universal human experience.

For a time, Martin believes his guiding principle of beauty can be found in his faith, especially if he becomes a priest himself. Whereas Joyce's Stephen Dedalus tries on a series of clearly delineated life approaches, beginning with the social, then moving to the sensuous, the religious, and finally settling on the aesthetic,[6] Mac-Laverty's Martin Brennan begins with a religious approach, which then is elided and replaced by a social approach to life blended with aspects of the aesthetic and the sensuous, all in Part One. In Part Two, Martin, still interested in social and aesthetic approaches to the world, fully explores the sensuous approach.

As the novel opens, Martin is awakened by his mother to prepare for a spiritual retreat he is attending for several days, in part an homage to the long retreat scene in chapter 3 of Joyce's *Portrait*. While Joyce only gives us a limited amount of information about Stephen Dedalus's mother in *Portrait*, MacLaverty details Martin's relationship with his mother in a series of conversations they have throughout the novel. In this opening scene, we learn how dependent Martin still is on his mother—so much so that she still offers to cut the crusts off the sandwich she is making for him. As he journeys to the retreat and settles in there, we discover just how important this particular retreat is for him. While Stephen, after his early debauchery in *Portrait*, briefly considers, then rejects the priesthood after a retreat leads him to repent of his sins and return to the church, Martin has not left the church and is using the retreat as both a means of discovering whether or not the Lord wants him to enter the priesthood and as a chance to pray earnestly that he will pass his exams for university that he has failed the previous year.

Early on in the retreat, as he thinks of his faith, we realize that, despite his attempt to discern whether he is spiritually called to the priesthood, he is also seeking fiscal security in considering that vocation and mentally blends his projected sacrifice to Christ, couched in terms of beauty, with expected material comfort. He reflects, "It would be a beautiful thing to be a priest—give yourself to Christ for the rest of your life. Have a good comfortable house with big rooms and all the facilities. And a housekeeper. Maybe write poems. Say mass every day. He'd feel good coming back to the parochial house for his breakfast. 'Hello Missus So-and-so.' Maybe a big fry with bacon and eggs and potato bread. But there were terrible responsibilities as well. Anointing the dead after car crashes" (18). Martin is dismayed that his ruminations on the beauty of being a priest—giving oneself to Christ, writing poems, saying mass—are dashed by the intrusions of material terror, such as anointing the dead after road accidents. Like Joyce's Stephen Dedalus, he believes that becoming a priest would at least occasionally puncture the ideal he has built up in his mind, not realizing that any vocation would involve hard work and responsibility.

His only consistent interest that seems not to be hard work is his photography. Martin shows great artistic promise as he evinces a growing interest in this craft, which is one way in which he is able to access and capture fleeting moments of beauty, although he certainly would not consider this hobby a guiding principle based on beauty at this point in his life. His passion for photography is seen first at the retreat when he hilariously captures the "almost horizontal line" of vomit "along the side of the bus" that one of the students leaves there on the twisted road to the retreat house (7). Already, Martin is drawn to take pictures of striking images. More important, his affinity for the camera is juxtaposed explicitly against what should be his contemplation of taking up the priesthood the first afternoon of the retreat. Rather than reading spiritual books or examining himself about this vocation, he takes pictures of the various boys against the backdrop of the sea. "It was good for pictures, everyone being on their own—with guys standing here and there all over the gardens. Like statues. Martin went back inside for his camera. There was still some snow where it had blown into corners. The whirr and clunk of the shutter mechanism was satisfying as he took picture after picture" (27–28). Rather than reflecting, Martin takes pictures of others contemplating—caught in moments of stillness that render them as statues. He absorbs himself in the scene to such a degree that time seems to stop. Father Albert, however, enters the scene and tells him that what he is doing breaks the vow of silence and is an activity that "distracts—the noise of the shutter" (28). Martin actually is evincing a reverence toward his subjects that probably surpasses that of the other boys who are supposedly meditating, but the priest urges him toward silence and inactivity and, more crucially and indirectly, to think of himself. Taking pictures, he had momentarily forgotten himself because he was absorbed in his subjects, a posture of forgetful service that generally exemplifies the life of a priest.

At the end of this first chapter, Martin goes to the chapel to say penance and meditate, then walks outside to search in the sky for an answer about being a priest. This vocation was one of only a few available to young Catholic males in Northern Ireland in the 1950s and 1960s. Others would have included agricultural work for males in rural areas and, as the decade ended and the next began, violent republicanism. Because he has grown up in a household that hosts the local priest on a regular basis and has attended a parochial school all his life, it is natural for Martin to consider becoming a priest. But as he smokes a cigarette this night, he asks God whether or not he should take orders and his answer is rendered in a typically wry fashion. He is told, "En Oh. NO. . . . He wondered was the no an answer to the question he had asked himself—could this be a sign?—or the overall question of whether or not to become a priest. No. There it was again. From outer space—a message. It must apply to the big problem and not to the problem within a problem. . . . In the beginning was the Word and the Word was with God and the Word was NO" (40). This personal paraphrase of the first verse in chapter 1 of the Gospel according to John convinces him that the God who spoke the world into being is telling him to not become a priest. The sky itself that he stares at during this revelation confirms it with its beauty that inspires a piercing joy in him. As he watches, "Suddenly a meteor blazed across the sky—quick as a nib scrape.[7] And a joy shot through him. Everything was the right colour and in the right place and his feelings were in defiance of gravity" (40). This stellar vision of ordered beauty convinces him that all is right in the universe, and he is figuratively buoyed, in an indirect reference to St. Joseph of Cupertino, the patron saint of exams who could also levitate, to whom his mother has asked him to pray for help in passing his exams this year (17). Now, Martin temporarily "levitates" in both the relief afforded him and the excitement of realizing his guiding principle is still before him. The relieved teenager is now free to seek another vocation, but first he must negotiate the intricate web of relationships among the boys at his Catholic school and pass his exams.[8]

In the rest of this part of the novel, Martin attempts to become better friends with Kavanagh, who is a year younger than him. When a mysterious and worldly student named Blaise arrives at the school, the dynamic of the two boys' relationship changes, and Martin struggles to maintain his position with Kavanagh in the face of Blaise's attacks on his intellect. At times, he retreats into his penchant for photography as both an enjoyable way of perceiving beauty and an escape from others' control over him, the latter of which is part of his general trajectory toward freedom, according to the conventions of the bildungsroman.

Although Blaise and Kavanagh are only fleetingly interested in beauty, Martin is fascinated by it, especially by such simple, glancing moments of trivial observation that can be captured by film, as in the Cartier-Bresson photograph at which he gazes in the library. He is struck by the way in which the camera eye captures the pending impact of a man's heel, which is about to hit a puddle. He realizes that "The photograph is of a split second. A man attempting to leap a large puddle. . . . His heel is cocked like a gun and about to strike its own reflection in the water. The man is moving so fast that he is out of focus, fudged, but somehow his reflection seems sharper" (79). Just as Catherine McKenna is drawn to write a musical symphony that largely mirrors itself and to gaze into a mirror at the reflection of her and her daughter, Martin is mesmerized by reflective surfaces, especially when they give greater insight into the identity of others. Despite the futility and the speed of the man's attempt to leap over the water, the power of his heel coming toward its own reflection delineates him as singular, more fully realized.

Martin's penchant for looking indirectly at things, exemplified by this picture of quotidian beauty, is highlighted by his gaze at a lovely girl almost immediately after he views this particular Cartier-Bresson image. His perception of her is photographic or even cinematographic, as he approaches her slowly, panning his eyes as it were over her body. "She was half crouched, holding back her hair from her face in case it interfered with what she was looking at. Martin slowed the pace of his descent right down: he wanted to have her in his sights for as long as possible. He could adore her" (79–80).

Quickly, however, he decides to "have a look in the glass case" to observe her indirectly, as he had the man's heel in the surface of the water in the photograph. He sees her profile "reflected on the glass at a mirror angle," a sort of double indirection, viewing her profile through the mirror of the glass, a point of view that enables him to see her more fully:

> The girl moved around to the opposite side, concentrating on the display, totally unaware of him. She was tanned and her hair was streaked with blonde. She had soft, deep brown eyes. There were spotlights focused inside the case and he saw her profile reflected on the glass at a mirror angle. She was lovely from both sides. Like an Italian film star whose name he couldn't remember. He could see through one of her images in the case, making her seem like a ghost. The image was paler than her reality. An apparition. (80)

He cannot handle her direct gaze, however, when she looks up. "Then she raised her eyes and looked up at Martin. Looking at her. He nearly died. The girl's eyes were so deep and dark. . . . He swooned—saw himself cartwheel and tumble down the marble of the staircase" (80). His voyeurism exposed, Martin nearly faints with such direct visual contact, an imagined event that suggests his problem in dealing directly with people and his penchant for staying on the surface of relationships. As she leaves, he implicitly compares her footsteps on the marble to the poised step of the man above the surface of the water in the Cartier-Bresson photograph, perceiving her as climbing "the staircase with just the soles of her shoes coming in contact with the marble. Her heels made no contact" (81).

Despite his tendency to romanticize such fleeting moments, Martin's photographic gaze here and elsewhere in the novel, although superficial in certain ways, is altogether more artistic and dynamic than Cal's in that novel, in part because Martin always chooses to view images of great beauty or loveliness, while Cal often seems drawn to images of horror such as the customers lying on the floor when the door to the off-license swings open during Crilly's robbery. There is a careful and meditative manner to Martin's imagined and actual picture taking that makes Cal's figurative cameralike glimpses seem uncomposed and spontaneous, recordings of an already-past event. Martin's eye is concerned to evoke the potential in the moment and seeks to create artistically thoughtful compositions of something about to happen. We might say, then, that while Cal's "pictures" are always analeptic, suggesting the relatively restricted arc of most of his movements, Martin's pictures are always proleptic, implying his more progressive maturation. Although the form of *Cal* does look forward, as I argued in the chapter on that novel, to a time of confession, healing, and incorporation into community, his backward glances, usually rendered photographically, create a tension between forward-looking form and backward-looking content that is absent from *The Anatomy School*. Both the trajectory of the later novel toward freedom and Martin's ability to capture still moments of pending progression work together to create a harmony of movement at the macro level of structure and the micro level of content.

Juxtaposing achingly lyrical passages like this one in the library that focuses on Martin's sensitive and intuitive mind with imagined, then real conversations like the ones with his friend Kavanagh written in a self-deprecating tone that immediately follow allows MacLaverty to show us Martin's rich interior life even as that life quickly recedes because of his reentry into a public world that militates against contemplation. Although Martin is considered by Blaise and Kavanagh to be less intelligent than they are, he clearly has the sort of profound inner life with which his creator identifies.

Although Martin's burgeoning interest in photography based on an aesthetic of the beautiful as a guiding principle is explored winsomely and with great nuance by MacLaverty, a great deal of the action in the first half of the novel seems to take the focus away from this central aspect of Martin's development. For example, the endless conversations between Martin's mother, Nurse Gilliland, and Mary Lawless in Martin's house *are* hilarious, often canvassing a series of theological niceties that at times makes the local Catholic priest, a frequent visitor, throw up his hands in despair. However, they relegate Martin to the sidelines, rendering him an object of observation. Yet his patience, his passivity, and his careful study of the participants in the conversations will enable him to become a better photographer. Just as his ear becomes used to calibrating the nuances of their particular Belfast patter, so his eye becomes more attentive to the visual particularity of his surroundings and the talkers. When he studies during these evenings, he learns to be ever more selective, filtering out their background noise and focusing on his work, developing the skill of concentration that will similarly lead him to take more striking pictures.

Martin's affinity for photography leads him into two dangerous situations in this first half of the novel, however: one in which he photographs an advance copy of the forthcoming examination and the other in which he gazes at pornographic pictures that Blaise brings to school. His realization that both activities are not only wrong, but also sinful, confirms him in his belief that photography should capture poised beauty and not promote harmful behavior, whether it be cheating or lusting after pornographic images. Both Martin's pictures of the exam and Blaise's pornography are connected to demonstrate the appeal of this forbidden knowledge to the boys. While Martin takes pictures of the questions in the exam papers, Kavanagh idly mentions that the only thing better would be "a big girl lying on her back," and Blaise promises to get such pictures for them (189). Martin tentatively decides that even though he has seen the English exam, he will not look at the photographs of the exams in other subjects, while the other boys have looked through all the exams and taken notes.

The priest Condor soon arranges for the members of the school Gaelic football team to beat Blaise up for distributing the pictures. The scene of the attack, particularly the way in which Blaise's head hits the toilet bowl, recalls a flashback scene in *Cal* when the protagonist recalls Crilly beating up an older boy who also had shown around naked photographs of women. "Momentarily Martin saw it— saw Blaise's head as it bounced off the rim of the toilet bowl. . . . There was a sickening sound of bone on delf [sic]" (220). When Crilly hits the boy Smicker in the forehead, also in the bathroom, "The boy slewed sideways and banged his ear and the side of his head on the partition as he fell. Cal heard a dull bone noise as Smicker's back crunched on the delft horseshoe of the lavatory bowl" (*C* 19). Moreover, in each case, the priest uses a boy or boys who are especially nationalistic to punish a deviant boy, implying a collusion between Irish Catholicism and nationalism based on their joint interest in protecting sexual purity.

While Blaise is in the hospital, Martin and Kavanagh agree that Martin will destroy the pictures of the women, and Martin, more repulsed by them than ever, does so. As he burns the pictures late that night in the coal fire while his mother is in bed, Martin feels relieved, thinking, "he was burning them. At last. Getting rid of them" (233). As he continues burning them, he perceives them as the fragments of women they have been reduced to in these poses, in an implicit contrast to the girl at the library whom he saw fully. He sees "breasts and smiles and open cunts and bare backsides" (234). Having carried them around and lied about their whereabouts for several days has so unnerved Martin that he feels not only physically relieved, but also spiritually relieved by destroying them and also knowing that Kavanagh put the exams back. MacLaverty compares Martin's feeling of spiritual relief to "the feeling after confession" (234). He has been negatively taught that photography can be abused and that the gaze of the camera can coldly and clinically destroy what might have beauty in another setting.

After Part I closes with a mental projection by Martin of him taking his exams and barely passing, Part II opens with him studying slides in a night class, which is held "in the middle of the afternoon because of the Troubles" (239), and then riding his bicycle through a riot in the streets of Belfast as he prepares for a long night of conducting an experiment for Kavanagh in the science lab of the university, where Martin works for the school of anatomy. Despite a series of flashbacks in this section of the novel, it is compressed into the space of roughly twelve hours, giving it a compelling immediacy that the first, more languidly moving and expanded half does not always fully achieve. The change in pace between the sections is clearly meant to signify how the coalescence of political events and Martin's growing interest in the opposite sex create a charged and frenetic public and private atmosphere that nicely counterbalances that earlier, more leisurely time of adolescence.

As Martin takes part in his latest "photography" lesson, he gazes at part of "some poor bastard's brain" on a microscope slide and hears the wailing of another ambulance leaving the hospital to retrieve more wounded and dead from the ongoing street riots in Belfast. The conflation of brain matter and ambulance siren suggests the visual and aural gruesomeness of the Troubles, and Martin reflects that the "relatively new" American sirens "put the fear of God into people. A swooping sound—like a sensation in the gut when falling. Up and down like a sine wave" (239). This passage suggests the destructive tendency inherent in biology and in the Troubles to advance scientific and political causes, respectively, and becomes part of Part Two's dialectic between destruction and creation, a conflict that is finally resolved in its conclusion, when Martin resolves to become more serious about his photography and create carefully crafted pictures.

MacLaverty chooses to focus on Martin's perception of the violence occurring around him as he rides to Queen's, rather than attempting a broad overview of it that would not be attentive to local conditions. Because of this approach, we get a singularly searing view of the action that bewilders Martin as well as us:

> He looked over his shoulder and there in the road opposite was a phalanx of police and Land Rovers. Guys were running up to the brow of the bridge and chucking stuff across the road. . . . He spun round and retreated, bumping up on to the pavement where there was less crap lying on the ground. He stood on the pedals and flew down the hill. Something hit him on the back. A half-brick or something—he didn't know what. But he didn't feel it. He sensed it, but it wasn't painful. He turned the corner out of the line of fire and headed towards the City Hall as fast as he could, still on the pavement. (242)

This long passage also gives us a mini-geography of the city that MacLaverty obliquely employs to show the concentration of the violence in working-class areas over against the relative tranquility associated with the university area, which when Martin reaches it is described as "Trees, green lawns, birdsong" (242).

Before going in to the laboratory, Martin meets an Australian girl named Cindy whom he promises to see later that night at a jazz session in the building's basement. Their encounter there and afterward in the laboratory is handled especially well by MacLaverty as he sensitively shows Martin's apprehension and anxiety at being with a woman for the first time. In the funniest passage in this hilarious novel, Martin fears he has crippled or killed the girl when she writhes pleasurably on top of him while shots are fired outside the building. "She had her eyes closed and was shouting, threshing her hair from side to side. Jesus—she was having a fit of some sort. At a time like this, for fuck sake. . . . He wondered if he had done something to her, triggered some bad reaction. A heart attack? Her breathing was all over the place. . . . It scared the living daylights out of him. Or maybe she had been shot. A stray bullet had got her in the back" (314). Martin's violent lovemaking with Cindy eases his fears about sex, and he is soon able to relax afterwards, although the experience itself is ineffable, beyond words, an image of initial terror to him that becomes beautiful.

In the moving last scene, Martin briefly and negatively meditates on "these fucking Troubles [that] had gone on for years now," wondering "how long was it going to go on?" (347). Then he has two positive visions that bode well for his future. First, he meets the girl he first gazed at so reverently in the library long ago and gathers up the courage to invite her for a coffee the next morning. She agrees, and a delighted Martin rides into Shaftebury Square on his bicycle, carried aloft with his hope for the future. He feels buoyant, musing, "Pegasus was a horse with wings and as he cycled around the complexity of the Square it felt he was on such a creature, gliding. It was about gravity and defying gravity at the same time" (353).

Throughout the novel, MacLaverty employs discussions of gravity, buoyancy, and bodies falling or rising to convey Martin's state of mind when he has reached a major decision in his life. For example, after he decides not to become a priest, MacLaverty writes "The weight of the decision he had just made was beginning to lift" and "a meteor blazed across the sky" (40). In the sentence in this passage that signifies how Martin moves on to look for another guiding principle, we are told, "He had moved from one element to another" (40). Later, in chapter 6 of Part One, Martin, Blaise, and Kavanagh discuss falling rocks as they throw stones high into the air and watch them plop into the water. Blaise notes, "It's the sound of bursting from one element to another. . . . 'Breaking the sound barrier'" (143). After they wrestle with each other, they flop down on the grass and Martin has another buoyant epiphany of ordered beauty as he inhales his cigarette smoke and gazes again at the sky:

> For a moment his head felt light. Everything combined to give him a rush of intensity at the rightness of things. . . . His best friends were here, he was sure he would pass his exams this time. He identified the upward rush as happiness. . . . It was like the feeling he'd had in Ardglass when he decided not to be a priest. . . . Suddenly there was the sound of swans lifting and flying overhead. Moving from one stretch of water to another. The sound

> of moving from one element to another. The stone falling from air to water. The swans from here to there. Love was in it somewhere but he couldn't tell where or with whom. (145)

This passage signifies how Martin is confidently moving into becoming his own man, achieving the necessary agency and selfhood for moving out into the world and falling in love, even though he is content with his current situation. Just as he has earlier moved "from one element to another" in deciding not to become a priest, he is now on the cusp of manhood.

Now, in the novel's conclusion, a newly buoyant Martin, having entered manhood and put away childish things, ponders what vocation he should pursue, seizing on the striking sculptures adorning the wall of the Ulster Bank in Shaftesbury Square as signs of his future. Just as he considers himself to be astride Pegasus on his bicycle, the figures themselves soar. He notices that "The top body was horizontal, the lower one at 45 degrees to it appeared to be winged" (354). The joy and hopefulness of these uplifting figures counterbalance both the prone, but unseen bodies of the Troubles that presumably lie in the streets of Belfast that same day after the riots, and the dead bodies lying on the tables of the anatomy school that Martin has just left. As he rides by, looking up, he muses that contemplating and capturing such figures should become his profession. "He should really stop some day and take pictures—it was such a strong image. Two strong images. He had taken the laboratory job 'in the meantime' and the meantime had lasted too long. Maybe Cindy was right: he should look at something else. He should think about something in photography. In his bones he felt it as becoming more and more important to him" (354). As he ponders them, he thinks, "What is a photograph, after all, but an image which invites contemplation?" Then, quickly, he perceives them as "falling—like angels chucked out of heaven. Sent down—like Blaise. Falling apart and falling together." Martin realizes that he is falling apart from his friends even his career plans, his guiding principle founded on beauty, fall together. Finally, he decides that perceptions do matter—that life can be what we make it and decides that even as he is falling through space by living on earth, "the Frink statues were bodies rising—two of them, lofted, buoyed up on thermals of hope. About to come into bodily contact with one another," much like he may soon come into such contact with the girl from the library whom he has just met again (354).

Wondering if she will stand him up, he plays with that idea, but chooses a vision that redolently recalls Molly Bloom's affirmative decision at the end of Joyce's *Ulysses* to embrace Leopold. He imagines her "sitting across from him, her mouth red after a strawberry tart, playing with the spoon in the sugar bowl, occasionally looking up at him with those eyes and saying yes, I do want to make my life with you—even before you've asked me" (355). This is still an idealistic and naïve Martin Brennan, but his time in the anatomy school of life has irrevocably changed him. That this novel can stand even more sustained comparisons with Joyce's *A Portrait of the Artist As a Young Man* than those delineated here testifies to MacLaverty's exceptional fictional skills at detailing the growth of a mind, a body, a spirit, which together constitute an holistic human being assailed with a host of private and public pressures and triumphing over them. *The Anatomy School* fits Lukács's definition of the novel as "the story of the soul that goes to find itself, that seeks adventures in order to be proved and tested by them, and, by proving itself, to find its own essence."[9]

Martin's affirmation of his vocation of photography, based on an aesthetic of buoyant beauty, brings the trajectory of MacLaverty's four novels full circle. While Martin embraces and soars with this guiding principle that is the symbolic father figure he has intermittently pursued throughout this bildungsroman, his upward flight contrasts that of the fall of the Icarian Owen Kane who is let down, even betrayed, by his figuratively Daedalian father, Michael Lamb. Additionally, although there is gentle irony in MacLaverty's treatment of Martin, just as there is in Joyce's treatment of the fiercely independent Stephen Dedalus, unlike Stephen, Martin finally realizes that, despite needing to pull away from Blaise and Kavanagh to some degree, solipsism is not artistically or personally satisfying. He thus pursues a relationship with a woman he has previously thought unattainable. The greatest lesson Martin finally learns is not to pursue photography, but that he must pursue others, as he recognizes that the artist in isolation is doomed to a dying fall without the support of a community of friends and loved ones.

The Truth of Fiction:
Matters of Life and Death
and Other Stories

I N 2006, MACLAVERTY RELEASED *Matters of Life and Death and Other Stories*, a collection that is heralded on the front inside flap as "the finest collection yet from a contemporary master of the form." Curiously, although critical articles have continued to appear on MacLaverty, his own considerable accomplishments in the short story have not been recognized in recent assessments of the genre in Britain and Ireland.[1] But critics who have followed MacLaverty's career for many years are convinced of the permanence and subtlety of his art as exemplified in this new collection of short stories. For example, Tom Adair, in his May 13, 2006, review for *The Scotsman* newspaper, muses about the stories' similarity to those in *Secrets and Other Stories*, published almost thirty years before this collection. Browsing through that earlier book, he found, "The same quiet voice, both amused and musing, the diction tighter, a touch less relaxed. More punctuation then, more striving for effect, but the same uncanny, unerring gift for touching that part of us that's alive yet most often hidden: nerve and bone."[2] Anne Enright, reviewing the new collection for *The Guardian* on May 6, 2006, claims that MacLaverty's habit of lifting the ordinary into the extraordinary through virtue of his art places his work "in a line from Chekhov, via Frank O' Connor."[3] Peter Kemp, a sensitive critic who, like Adair, has followed MacLaverty's career with admiration for some time, argues that although he had "earn[ed] the right to cross-reference . . . Chekhov" in the story "The Clinic," the "short story writer he seems closest, to, though, is the James Joyce of *Dubliners*,"[4] which is high praise indeed.

It is not entirely true, as Simon Baker claims, that "the book's theme is solitude."[5] The deliberate placing of "On the Roundabout"—a shocking story about a man and his family who rescue a hitchhiker from murderous Ulster Defence Association (UDA) members in the early 1970s—as the first story in the collection suggests that community, biological and human, remains of paramount concern to

MacLaverty. All these characters find themselves in positions of solitude or loneli ness but also evince the need for human community after time alone. In this sense, these characters and those in MacLaverty's short fiction generally share with D. H. Lawrence's stories and tales a quality that Tom Paulin has argued makes them socially committed beings. Paulin notes that "those in Lawrence's stories are often redeemed from isolation by their commitment to a relationship. Instead of existing permanently on the fringes of society, they acquire through that commitment the living confidence we associate with characters in a novel."[6] Paulin's reference to characters "existing permanently on the fringes of society" recalls the dictum by Frank O'Connor explored in the introduction to this study as essential to understanding modern short fiction and MacLaverty's stories particularly. Although MacLaverty remains committed to exploring lives on the margins of Belfast and other locales in Northern Ireland, Scotland, and abroad, his constant focus on love over the course of his career suggests that solitariness, not solitude, can be an imprisoning trap out of which love can spring us. Solitude is, of course, necessary for introspection and meditation, but his characters need others badly, just as we all do.

"On the Roundabout" is based on a story told to MacLaverty by one of his friends about an incident that he was part of in 1972. MacLaverty has termed this friend capable of "incredible acts of bravery" and has confessed that, both times his friend has told him the story, "I was amazed by it." The story was written during a five-hour train journey to Liverpool, where MacLaverty would hold a post as a visiting professor of creative writing at John Moores University. Recalling this trip, MacLaverty remembers thinking, "Would it be interesting just once to get on the train and write a story? . . . So I did, and I got to the end just before I arrived in Liverpool." The terse quality of this story, one of MacLaverty's shortest in his oeuvre, undoubtedly was created by the compressed period of time he allotted himself to write it on his trip by train to Liverpool from Glasgow, but the train's driving rhythm must have also influenced the similarly pounding pace and frenetic activity of the story. Along with "Walking the Dog," it is his most direct story to date dealing with the Troubles, going far beyond the oblique political situation in "Father and Son" from *A Time to Dance* to deal with the intricacies of identity and explore how perception of human suffering can engender tenderly proffered care to those needing help. MacLaverty points out that the piece contains both the hope and horror endemic to the situation in the province at the time. "I hope the story encapsulates many of the things that Northern Ireland meant to me. . . . The horrors of it, the violence from both sides. The jolt this person and his family suffer to their Norman Rockwell kind of normality. And the legacy of that violence to the children."[7] The story's raising of a factual event to the level of fiction suggests MacLaverty's continuing conviction about the ability of narrative to convey essential human truths that transcend the harsh reality surrounding his characters.

Although the narrator plays down his rescue of the man who is attacked by the UDA members in the story, he is commendable for his bravery. He begins with a disclaimer, "I suppose it's about doing something without thinking. But it was nothing really. Anybody'd've done the same" (*MLD* 1). But would anybody have done the same? The narrator is returning from a family trip and has his wife and two kids in the car. Stopping to help the man who is attacked with a hammer in front of their eyes not only exposes them to danger at that moment, but also possible further reprisal in the future. The rescuer even perceives his wife at the hospital "looking ahead to me in the witness box facing the UDA across the court. We know your registration, we know your whole family" (4).

In an ironic similarity to the kidnapped man in "Walking the Dog," the man who is hit with the hammer, kicked, and punched by the UDA hooligans turns out to be Protestant, just like his attackers. Once he is bundled into the car by the narrator, with blood pouring profusely down his face, he tells them incredulously, "the funny thing is I'm Presbyterian" (3). As he and the narrator laugh uproariously at this identity confusion, the hitchhiker falls back and convulses violently. And just as "Walking the Dog" implies that no one will care if the kidnapped man reports this attack, the authorities at the hospital seem uninterested in prosecuting the offenders. Even though the narrator tries "to give my name and address . . . the doctors and nurses don't want to know." More surprisingly, he realizes "There's a Brit soldier there with his gun and he doesn't want to know." Frustrated, the narrator thinks, "I've just witnessed an attempted murder and nobody wants to know" (4). The implicit complicity of the medical staff and soldier in covering up the attack stands in sharp contrast to the narrator's risking of life and limb and family to save him. This passage suggests that such events were often omitted from official reports but live on in the hearts and minds of those personally involved, in effect functioning as an alternative history of the Northern Irish Troubles in which nameless individuals nonetheless instantiate deeply intimate relationships with unknown victims of violence.[8]

The parablelike quality of the story is reinforced in its closing lines, when the narrator recalls the letter written by the victim to the *Belfast Telegraph* in which "he was trying to thank the Good Samaritan who'd helped him on the roundabout that night. Wasn't that good of him? To tell the story" (4). Presumably, the family was Catholic and went out of their way to help the injured man, who turned out to be Presbyterian. Reaching beyond the religious barriers that still divide many communities in the North, the nameless man and his family turned an afternoon of hate into an afternoon of hope for the victim, who will never forget their help.

Just as important, he will keep telling this story and thus publicize their bravery and compassion to a province that would desperately need such stories in the midst of the worst moments of the conflict during the 1970s, when events like Bloody Friday (1) and the randomness of violence made everyone fearful to be around others who did not share their cultural and religious affiliations.[9] "On the Round-about" thus fictionalizes a factual event and lends it a continuing circulation in the minds of MacLaverty's readers, affirming once again the decency and strength of the human spirit.

Moreover, the last line of the piece—"To tell the story"—suggests a quality that MacLaverty's short and long fiction about atrocities committed during the Troubles shares with literature about the Jewish Holocaust: its recording of events for posterity as a graphic record of the importance of the individual despite the worst kind of dehumanizing, often mass murder.[10] MacLaverty's first depiction of the plight of Jews during the 1930s and 1940s occurs obliquely in *A Time to Dance* as he tenderly explores the character of the deracinated Miss Schwartz, Danny's Jewish piano teacher from "My Dear Palestrina" who had fled 1930s Poland as a little girl and now lives in rural Northern Ireland. In his later fiction, however, he develops an explicit connection between Northern Irish and Jewish suffering. For example, after musing on both the massacre of the Kiev Jews at Babi Yar by the Nazis and various killings from the Troubles, *Grace Note*'s Catherine McKenna is satisfied that "her act of creation, whether it was making another person or a symphonic work, defined her as human, defined her as an individual. And defined all individuals as important" (*GN* 128).

Yet there is also a communal, public dimension to writing about atrocity. Lea Fridman has argued in her study of narrative representations of the Holocaust that such writing collapses the traditional divide between art and life in its particular artistic objective. She suggests "The work of art that would represent historical horror is in a peculiarly complicated and vulnerable position. . . . Such a telling is no ordinary 'telling.' We ask that it tell us what cannot be told. We ask it to perform special communal and cultural tasks in society at large. We ask that it 'bear witness' when art is founded on the very opposite notion of a 'suspended disbelief' or separation between art and life."[11] Unlike Holocaust survival authors such as Elie Wiesel and Primo Levi, MacLaverty stands at a remove from the event described in "On the Roundabout," placing him in the tenuous position of writing fiction about an incident recounted to him by an eyewitness to it. However, the story's immediacy—achieved by its brevity, its breathless, first-person narrative once the family encounters the UDA attack on the victim they pick up, and its use of present tense except in the opening paragraph and closing passages—goes some way toward creating a sense that this is an eyewitness account. In the process,

MacLaverty largely achieves what one Jewish literary critic calls the imperative to render past atrocities immediate and real in our imagining of them: "the prior events, so distant, *must* be continually revived as a present."[12]

Furthermore, the narrator's desire to relate a sort of bedtime story to his children in the car as they drive back to Belfast in order to relax them before they fall asleep—"Tell them a story maybe"—contrasts the driving pace of the real story that occurs with its musing tone and use of past tense (1). MacLaverty seems to be implying that that narrative, which is never offered, would be fanciful, a children's story, but that the heart of "On the Roundabout" is factual, a story for adults. And yet, as we have seen, a certain comfort more lasting than any bedtime story results both from the telling of this story by the victim in his letter to the *Belfast Telegraph* (4) for the family who involved themselves in his life and by MacLaverty's retelling of the story to us. Both the horror of the event and, just as important, the bravery and humanity of the family who stop to help are searingly evoked and recalled every time the story is read. The value of the individual is affirmed but the need for community is as well. Fiction both enfolds us in its web of relationships and makes us realize our utter singularity.

The subject matter and circular motif in "On the Roundabout" link it to an account of a different trauma about a Scottish poet caught in a Midwestern snowstorm in "Winter Storm," the last story of the collection. Both narratives explore trauma in the context of solitariness and suggest that incorporation of the individual into community leads to a directed path out of dangerous repetitions—literally and metaphorically. Consider the traffic flow of the roundabout in the former story—or indeed, on any roundabout—and the similarly repetitious attempts by the narrator of the latter story to find his way out of the blizzard. Once the family in "On the Roundabout" enters the scene and picks up the victim, the narrator takes "the exit to the Royal" [Hospital] in Belfast (3) and thus helps the victim escape the repeated pounding he is likely to take from the UDA members if he stays on the roundabout. On a figurative level, the roundabout functions in much the same way as the image of stasis signaled by the titular yo-yoing move of "Walking the Dog." The UDA and supporters of violence generally in the province are caught up in an endless cycle of sectarianism that leads nowhere and prevents escape into the province's future of dynamic, give-and-take dialogue. Hope lies in reaching out toward others, a selfless maneuver that is also offered on a much smaller scale in "Winter Storm," where a Native American cleaning woman rescues the visiting Scottish poet from his circular steps and "helped him to his feet" (232). Although the poet thinks he has been walking in a straight line, he has deluded himself and is in real danger of frostbite, even death. The final line of the story makes clear that individual striving with no clear direction is folly, but that help from outside can often lead to clarity and survival. The poet is described as sheltering "in her wake as she walked the blizzard in a straight line to the buildings on the far side" (232).

If "On the Roundabout" demolishes sectarian shibboleths held by Protestant loyalists in the province by inscribing a contemporary parable of help and hope, the next story, "The Trojan Sofa," focuses on the prejudices of Catholic nationalists and republicans during the Troubles and their paranoia toward the British Army and security forces. It shares with the first story a feeling of enclosure and stasis that is epitomized by the furniture in which the young protagonist hides to rob unsuspecting customers within their own homes. The titular theme conveys the betrayal that such Catholics felt was often lurking around the corner from their own or from outsiders, while its hilarity confirms MacLaverty's penchant for comedy, especially in the midst of difficult, even deadly situations.

Niall Donnelly, the boy narrator, has a father much like the IRA leader Skeffington in *Cal*, who is steadfast in his belief that any actions taken against the British are always legitimate economic blows struck in the overall struggle for nationalist liberation. He tells Niall repeatedly, "The wrong done to this country was so great that we can do *anything* in retaliation"; that "a broken phone is a British liability"; and "so's a burnt bus. They're things that have to be replaced—by the English exchequer" (6). MacLaverty's portrayal of the father's and uncle's nationalist sentiments verges on caricature, and one wonders if such hyperbolic sentiments would really have been held at the time. For example, when the boy's father first asks him to hide inside a sofa to be delivered to a rich Protestant's house and cut himself out the next day so he can let the father and uncle in to rob the place, he hilariously tells the lad the decision is up to him, stating "but I must say it is for Ireland," while his Uncle Eamon exclaims "Ireland the Brave" (7).

Although Niall sees his services to his father and uncle as more of a lark than anything, there are dangerous signs he is being infected by their propaganda. As he lies inside the sofa during the night in question, having been delivered to the supposed British major's house earlier, he listens to the radio and disdains any expression of grief for an officer at Long Kesh Prison who is killed, but laments the shooting of a youth who is presumably an IRA volunteer and is thankful that the IRA's protocol of warnings before bombings has saved more lives. He reflects, "a prison officer who worked at the Maze tried to start his car and it blew up and he got killed. Boo-hoo. Lend me a hanky. The other was a drive-by shooting on the Antrim Road. A boy of seventeen had been shot and died on the way to hospital. If it's the Antrim Road he'll be one of ours. There was three explosions but nobody was hurt because there were warnings" (11). The IRA has long considered British Army soldiers, Royal Ulster Constabulary (now the Police Service of Northern Ireland) officers, and prison guards to be legitimate targets in its campaign to form a united Ireland through force, while making martyrs out of IRA volunteers who die for the cause. Niall's feelings about these different events perfectly mimic the IRA's propaganda and suggest he has not yet learned to think for himself or consider the humanity of "the other side."

The sectarian energies of Irish nationalism have long been condemned by MacLaverty in novels such as *Cal* and his rejection of them may be grounded in a belief that perverse understandings of masculinity drive this hatred. In fact, Catherine's very femininity in *Grace Notes* and the way in which she transforms the harsh music of lambeg drums into a joyful noise suggest MacLaverty's belief that women offer solutions to violence through their much-lauded capacity as listeners.[13] He told Anne Simpson in an interview after *Grace Notes* came out, "Women with their particular sensitivities, achieve great things in Northern Ireland whenever they manage to gain a modicum of power," mentioning as an example their "work at the grassroots which is very impressive in both communities. The other day I heard a programme about women in the Shankill [Road in Belfast, a loyalist enclave], learning Irish. That would have been impossible a few years ago, so among ordinary folk there are shifts in opinion."[14] MacLaverty's belief in women's power to influence the cultural shifts taking place in even loyalist strongholds like the Shankill implies that the republican leanings of the narrator of "The Trojan Sofa," along with that of his father and uncle, and the violent loyalism of the UDA thugs in "On the Roundabout" constitute understandable, but dead-end forms of masculinized protest that belong largely to the province's sectarian past.

Moreover, MacLaverty juxtaposes two types of darkness in *Grace Notes*—Catherine's depression and the interior of her womb and mind—to convey the dichotomy between two attitudes associated with women that are important for understanding how darkness functions symbolically in "The Trojan Sofa." Catherine's biological and artistic creative powers represent positive femininity, while her black depression connotes a defeatist posture focused on inward, circular, repetitious thinking, a position that many male Irish nationalists have adopted in their pursuit of martial glory for the sake of an imagined, feminized Ireland. Because Niall Donnelly has no mother and evinces a penchant for hiding in the inside of sofas, he may be searching for a mother, or at least unconsciously for a womblike darkness in which to symbolically return to his mother. Irish nationalism has often used images of women and the mother such as Mother Ireland to rally masculine, martial support for the cause. The darkness of the furniture in which Niall hides cannot compete with the images of Ireland as a distressed woman needing rescue by men still found on republican murals in the province, but it nonetheless conveys the boy's need to embrace the nationalist cause by electing to remain in an uncomfortable posture in utter darkness—a literal position that suggests his embrace

133

of the republican cause despite having limited knowledge about the vagaries of the conflict. When he is in the sofa, he mentions that "I couldn't see a watch it's so dark," and indeed, his "life" inside the sofa and other furniture symbolically blinds him to a more balanced view of the conflict in the province (9).

Despite his father's having taken up with a new woman with the resonantly nationalist name of Rosaleen after his mother's death, Niall still misses his biological mother terribly. After lamenting her passing the night he spends in the major's sofa, he wistfully notes, "I don't have very many friends. Most of them are grown up—like Uncle Eamon and the ones who come back to the house after the pub [closes]" (15). Lonely boys like Niall, cut off from redeeming images of women and in extended states of mourning, are easy pickings for men who would appropriate them for political causes. Along with hearing republican propaganda from the lips of his father and uncle, he surely hears more of the same from Uncle Eamon's friends. Fighting for a cause, even if it involves burgling houses, goes some way toward filling the empty void in Niall's heart.

Darkness works in another powerful way in the story as well: to symbolize the paranoia and miscommunication between nationalists and unionists in the province. When the alleged British major realizes that Niall is in the sofa and calls the police, the boy quickly cuts his way out and is interrogated by the man, who first asks him, "Who put you up to this?" and then, "Who are you working for?" (18, 19). After Niall escapes by running from the house shortly afterward, he is confronted later by the police but gets off because of his young age. He finds out that the major was not even a soldier but a noted English architect, a fact his father believes is merely cover for the man's position in the British intelligence services. He recalls, "Still my Dad said the architecture was a cover story—everybody in Intelligence work had one. They like to keep us in the dark, he said" (24). Dunstan Luttrell, the architect, is not in intelligence, however, and has even been recently commended for "designing an oratory for some nuns," a commission that pleased the press, who "made a big thing about it. English architect, Irish nuns. Protestant-Catholic co-operation" (23–24, 24). Similarly, Niall is not a member of the IRA, although he works for a father and uncle who believe that their thievery is justified because of British oppression. Because daily exchanges at the time between British unionists and Irish nationalists were so fraught with suspicion, the story implies that fictions about the other flourished, with an attendant loss of comprehending motives. If Niall continues to immerse himself in the literal darkness of his father's Trojan sofas, he will end up not only betraying the trusting customers to whom they are delivered, but also himself, because he will likely become dark and clouded in his thinking about all unionists and Protestants, his eyes never adjusting to the light that accompanies cultural understanding.[15]

Violence, of course, is never merely confined to the political arena, and the longest story in the collection, "Up the Coast," explores how violence lingers and changes the life of the sensitive woman who is raped in her retreat and refuge from the world. Years after she has thinks she has healed, she exhibits some paintings from her time spent in the coastal area of Scotland where she was raped, partly as a defiant gesture against her forced submission. However, the story concludes with a chillingly nonchalant rejection of her identity as a woman and an artist that threatens to send her into a spiral of depression.

The story is metatextual, mainly featuring the artist reading excerpts from the diary she kept on her trip up the coast, the pages of which are part of her multimedia retrospective display. She has always been interested in the lot of the dispossessed villagers of Inverranich, Scotland, and as she gazes at four of the paintings from her time in that lonely spot, she muses on the "homesickness—the wrench from the land and everything dear to them" (142). Drawn to the landscape of these dispossessed, she becomes stripped herself by the young man who rapes her of "everything dear to" her. As she stares at her rendering of the submissive villagers and the "strong" stones of the rocky terrain around them in the present (142), she recalls "the anger at their making—the cross-hatching, the savaging of the paper surface." She had returned to her camp the summer after the rape and retrieved "the sketches and notebooks," which were the basis for the paintings. The paintings, she believes, "were part of the healing process" (143).

The iterated narrative of the Inverranich stones, whose "story must be told" (142), in an echo of the phrase "To tell the story" from "On the Roundabout," also signifies the continued importance of telling the story of the woman's rape. As she reads progressive pages from her diary written days before the rape, she is catapulted back in time, and the entire story becomes a flashback juxtaposing the naïvete of her wish to be at one with nature, represented by the diary excerpts, with the cynical mind and cruel cunning of the rapist, who desires to subjugate nature and women. Just as she romanticizes the rugged, isolated beauty of the coastal area where she is dropped by a fishing crew and her own art, the rapist views his environment and himself naturalistically, as part of a struggle for dominance and survival. While the female artist, who significantly remains unnamed, symptomatic of her lost identity, takes great pleasure in the quality of light and the variegated colors of the sky on the coast, the young male rapist is chillingly rendered reading the sky as propitious for his purposed conquest. He is portrayed thinking, "The light was clear and harsh. It would be a good day. The sea was the right colour" (145). Later, shortly before he attacks her, he revels in controlling the sun by flashing it in her eyes with his knife. He gleefully realizes, "He had the power to aim the sun, to aim

CHAPTER 9

it into her tent—to flick it over the walls, at the girl's face, down between her legs—anywhere he liked" (170).

She quickly learns her lesson and comes to view nature pragmatically and harshly. Ironically, the rapist, committed to survivalist principles and raised by the sea, cannot even swim, and after he rapes her, she lures him to an overlook above the sea and pushes him in, drowning him. By the end of the incident, she is the survivor, he the defeated. But what price does she pay for this freedom? Although she rises above this incident to produce superb landscape art, her retrospective exhibit is remarkable for its lack of human beings represented on her canvases, except for her "grandchild series" (142). She has clearly learned to trust enough to have a family, but her attitude toward others outside this tight, familial circle is wary at best and sometimes smolders with barely suppressed anger. When the older Canadian man and his wife view her paintings in the present, she lingers to hear their praise. When the man "leaned towards her as she tried to sidle past him and said, 'Such images. Such vital images he's managed to capture,'" however, she becomes very angry and rightly so. Staring at him, she asks "He?" (195). The man can barely believe that a woman painted the works, and when she replies that she is actually the artist, he tells her how wonderful that is and both he and his wife congratulate her. The last sentence is chilling in its evocation of her altered state. We are told, "She began to make her escape, self-conscious that her block heels were making too much noise on the wooden floor" (196).

Having escaped the rapist once, she is forced to flee from her own exhibit, outraged by a kindly man who nevertheless reflects a continuing assumption on the part of many people that creativity is a male province. The story stops, but we cannot help but wonder if this incident will constitute a severe setback for the woman, who will almost certainly retreat within herself again for a while. "Up the Coast" demonstrates MacLaverty's continuing sensitivity to women's issues and his general conviction that the hurt inflicted on innocent victims of violence continues on for years, perhaps even for a lifetime. This realistic view of abuse and the way in which it continues to produce harmful psychological effects on the abused is consistent with the effect on children of the circular, entrapping attitudes expressed in the actions of the UDA thugs in "On the Roundabout"[16] and of the boy's father and uncle in "The Trojan Sofa."

The story's trajectory toward solitariness, not life-affirming solitude or community, places it in a dialectic with other stories in the volume that stress the importance of others in our lives, such as "On the Roundabout," both parts of "Learning to Dance," "The Clinic," and "Winter Storm." Although MacLaverty fully realizes our human potential to become solipsistic, lonely beings, he even more strongly believes that we need each other to fully be our individual selves.

"On The Roundabout" and "The Clinic" also demonstrate the truth of Anne Enright's contention that the volume shows MacLaverty "putting a greater emphasis on truth and truth-telling, leaning in places toward non-fiction."[17] If "On the Roundabout" often privileges fact over fiction in its attempt to give a sense of how atrocities sometimes impinged on daily life during the Troubles, "The Clinic" instead values the consoling power of fiction over threatening facts and official rhetoric. The nameless protagonist of "The Clinic," the loveliest story in the volume, and one of the best in MacLaverty's oeuvre, knows the importance of relationships, finding it vicariously in a Chekhov story and in his need for his wife in a quick phone call to her after his appointment at a diabetes clinic is concluded. The emotional impact of the story accrues from our belief that the man is single and able to find emotional solace solely in literature; when he calls his wife with the good news that he is not diabetic, however, we are swept out of the loneliness of the waiting room, which, despite its many patients, is grim and bleak, and back into the warm, domestic life the man shares with his wife. Thus, the fiction of the Chekhov story proves more true to the man's life than does the harsh reality of the waiting room.

MacLaverty admitted in an interview that "The Clinic" was inspired by his recent trip to the doctor and suggested that the reality of the waiting room cannot compete with the fictional truth of the Chekhov story, noting, "in reality you're sitting among people who are ill and unsexy. . . . and every time you look up you're still waiting to piss in a jar or have your blood taken. But when you look down again, you're back inside the story."[18]

The story is another metatextual study, subtly showing how various types of writing compete for the man's attention before he finally, lovingly, settles on reading the Chekhov short story, "The Beauties," which hints at MacLaverty's own continued interest in portraying the ordinary and extraordinary beauty of our lives. As the man waits, he sees a series of magazines, which beckon him alluringly. "All the men's magazines were about golf or cars. He picked up Vogue and flicked through it. Beautiful half-naked sophisticated women clattering with jewelery. But he couldn't concentrate to read any of the text." The version of escapism represented by the magazines' text and pictures cannot compete with the officialese of the letter that has summoned him to the clinic this day. It tells him, "*your family doctor has referred you to the Diabetic Clinic to see if you are diabetic. To find this out we will need to perform a glucose tolerance test.*" These words, and others he has read in reference books since receiving the letter, frighten him into fearing he could lose his "eyesight" and perhaps even his "extremities." Taken together, the words of the letter, the medical books, and the "yellow outpatient card" constitute a form of discourse too chilling to be ignored (50).

And yet, once the man submits to the long round of drinking, urinating, and having his blood tested, he is able to escape this official discourse with its grim prophecies and be drawn into the fictional world Chekhov has created in his ten-page story. "The Clinic" itself only runs a bit under twelve pages, and MacLaverty is presumably trying to put readers through a similar experience to the one he actually must have had in the clinic reading Chekhov's similarly short story. The spareness of MacLaverty's writing invites comparison with that of Chekhov. In another writer's hands, such a maneuver might seem audacious. But just as the man realizes Chekhov "draws you in. He writes as if the thing is happening in front of your eyes" (53), so does MacLaverty, managing to capture the beauty of a young couple in love, surrounded by images of nineteenth-century rural Russia. In the process, he successfully juxtaposes, through chiasmus, the fleeting happiness of this fictional scene and its more lasting sadness with the fleeting fears of the possibly diabetic man and his lasting happiness with his wife. After a boy and his grandfather travel through the "summer heat and dust of the countryside," they stop at a farm and the boy stands transfixed by the beauty of the girl who brings them tea. "Then tea is brought in by a barefoot girl of sixteen wearing a white kerchief and when she turns from the sideboard to hand the boy his cup she has the most wonderful face he has ever seen. He feels a wind blow across his soul" (53). The image is pictorial, the first part of the sentence recalling Vermeer's domestic paintings of solitary women, and obliquely, Catherine McKenna's new suite of piano pieces dedicated to Vermeer in *Grace Notes*. Yet this girl, in reaching out to and looking up to the lad, instantiates a moment of communication with him, changing his life and hers. Swept off his feet by her beauty, he experiences an aesthetically rendered conversion to her beauty and a corresponding spiritual conviction that he must be with her.

Although the boy is smitten, "when confronted with the girl in the white kerchief feels himself utterly inferior," and as she turns away into the reality of her own life, she recedes from him and he is filled with an ineffable sadness. He knows that he is "sunburned, dusty and only a child. But that does not stop him adoring her and having adored her his reaction is one of—sadness. Where does such perfection fit into the world?" Just as she "disappears into a grimy outhouse which is full of the smell of mutton and angry argument," the man quickly is pulled out of the story and into the "talk of medical stuff" in the diabetes clinic (56).

This pattern is reversed when, after urinating again, the man returns to the Chekhov story and experiences "the room gradually disappear[ing]" (57). The second incident recounted in the story involves a student, the boy from earlier who has now grown up. He stops at a train station and walks around, suddenly captivated by the beauty of the stationmaster's daughter. As he watches her, he realizes that so are all the other men on the platform, and her unattainable position reminds him of the serving girl long ago and the mixture of pleasure and pain he felt at that time, which then blends with the pleasure of the man reading the story and the repeated pain and discomfort of the procedures he is going through in the clinic and his anticipated pain of having diabetes. "The youth remembers the Armenian's daughter, the girl with the white kerchief, and the sadness it brought him. Again he experiences the whoosh of feeling and tries to analyze it but cannot. . . . What chance for someone like him? The stationmaster's daughter wouldn't look at him twice" (58). The narrator loves the blurring of the boundaries between life and art, reveling in them and even desiring the stationmaster's daughter himself. We are told that Chekhov's presentation "was so immediate, the choice of words so delicately accurate, that they blotted out the reality of the present. He ached now for the stationmaster's daughter the way the student aches. It's in his blood" (58).

Although he questions Chekhov's presentation of the silent, worshipped women in the story after giving another urine sample and wonders, "Was this not about women as decoration?" he nonetheless knows its fictional truth about beauty's ineffability and clings to it. Again emerging from the story, he drinks some water and fearfully reads the text about diabetes on posters on the wall, whose ominous words compete with the delicate power of Chekhov's story. "He could barely bring himself to read them. They made him quake for his future. . . . The poster warnings were for the worst cases. *Diabetic retinopathy*—can lead to permanent loss of vision. *Blindness.* Never to be able to read again. *Atherosclerosis* leading to *dry gangrene.* Wear well-fitting shoes, visit your chiropodist frequently. Care for your feet" (59). Although he knows his own condition is not likely to be this bad, the man fears the worst, allowing this discourse to have temporary power over the exquisite beauties of Chekhov's story.

As "The Clinic" concludes, the man gives his final blood sample, finishes "The Beauties," which ends with the sadness of the student on the departing train and the "figure of the guard coming through the train beginning to light the candles" (60), another mixed image of despair and hope that prefigures the man's state at the end of the story. He is told that does not have diabetes but does have "impaired glucose tolerance," which he must work to prevent through diet and exercise. His relief is palpable. Walking outside, he stares "up at the blue sky criss-crossed with jet trails. People traveling. Going places, meeting folk" (61). We share his relief but lament what we perceive as his loneliness, then are surprised by his phone call to his wife, who has purposely not been mentioned throughout the story to enhance our affection for this tenderly rendered man we fear is all alone. He still feels about her like the young boy in Chekhov's story did about the serving girl, repeating the fictional language of the Russian master's story to convey the reality of his own present in which he actually got the girl. "He had seen her across a dance floor forty years ago and felt the wind blow across his soul" (61). The man allays his wife's anxiety and concern, telling her simply, "I'm OK" (61). And he is. And we are. And we shall be, MacLaverty seems to suggest, as long as we trust the power of fiction to give us pictures of our lives that are truer and more real than the fear and despair to which we occasionally succumb.

Afterword

T HE BODY OF BERNARD MACLAVERTY'S FICTION—five collections of short stories and four novels—suggests an enviable staying power among fiction writers from Ireland and Northern Ireland. Only William Trevor, the recently deceased John McGahern, Brian Moore, Jennifer Johnston, and John Banville have written over a longer period of time. MacLaverty's popularity can be traced to the appealing qualities of his style and his timeless convictions about human nature. In 1988, he told Deirdre Purcell in an interview that he preferred a perspicuous style, noting that writing stories for broadcast on the BBC and being forced to pare them down to fit into a short time slot early in his career made him realize that "invariably, the leaner story would be the better one."[1] He went on to claim, "Words should be 'like plain ordinary glass, so that you can look through them to see what's behind them. If they're too ornate they become like stained glass windows so you focus on the window itself and not on what's outside.'"[2] The richness of MacLaverty's created worlds resides instead in his richly drawn images and in the delightful dialects of many of his characters. His spare prose style enhances his vivid imagery and dialogue by largely eschewing description and free indirect discourse in favor of the direct and the spoken.

Tom Adair, one of MacLaverty's best critics, has noted in his review of *Grace Notes* that MacLaverty's prose "is shriven, plaintive, stealthy, and paradoxical, coupling lavishness at moments of magpie glitter . . . with restraint. It's the ultimate Northern Irish prose style, all Catholic curlicues and Calvinistic spareness."[3] In this fascinating stylistic blend of decoration and simplicity, his fiction implicitly suggests a common ground of humanity for all the citizens of Northern Ireland who, despite fairly superficial differences, share a love for apt characterization and spirited conversation. Protestant culture in Northern Ireland has long been linked to what David Brett has termed "the plain style," an inheritance dating back to the

Reformation, which is particularly reflected in a penchant for decentralized authority and the suspicion of imagery, the latter of which is manifested in its architecture and graveyards. And yet even this conception of Protestant identity in the province holds true largely only in religious practice. As Brett argues, people in Northern Ireland "display rather few cultural differences and a great preponderance of similarities. Those differences, moreover, seem to mirror one another, each being mutually necessary to one another."[4] The retreat of the imperially supported nation-state, as the British government continues to extract itself from Northern Ireland, is particularly consonant with Protestant, especially Presbyterian, notions of decentralized government, as Brett notes, and may afford grassroot participation from all communities in the province. Moreover, reclaiming positive aspects of the Protestant suspicion of images may enable us to escape our image-saturated culture and attend to deeper realities.[5]

As part of the devolving literary culture of Northern Ireland, MacLaverty's fiction establishes a radical, human egalitarianism, not unlike that imagined by some of the early church reformers, although, of course, their view of salvation would unfortunately exclude Catholics and former Catholics such as MacLaverty. In his own inimitably plain style, laced with ornateness, he suggests the continuing pleasure and pain of being human and the promise of being bound in community to each other. He, like the Protestant reformers, is properly suspicious of images, because they can be so easily manipulated by republicans and loyalists, as they are in *Cal.* And yet, his healthy skepticism toward images makes his own carefully chosen ones all the more telling and resonant. Who can forget the crumpling, genuflecting Robert Morton in *Cal*, or the buoyant, soaring images on the bank building at the end of *The Anatomy School?* The former image employs a traditional Catholic devotional practice to engender our sympathy for the murdered Protestant man, while the second reflects Martin Brennan's choice to soar over his riotous surroundings and become a photographer of moments of potential.

As we have seen, many of MacLaverty's early works favor the visual over the oral, especially in their large-scale development—a process that culminates in the ekphrastic novel *Cal* with its striking artistic and iconographic images, some of which are static, while others are dynamic. Starting with *The Great Profundo* and culminating in the laudable soundscape of *Grace Notes*, however, he increasingly employs noises, sounds, and musical motifs to not only convey the emotions of his characters, but also to scaffold the very structure of his work. In the current stage of his career, beginning with *The Anatomy School* and continuing through *Matters of Life and Death*, he seems to be moving back toward privileging striking visual imagery to represent key moments in characters' lives.

But reproducing the sonic qualities of human language remains an abiding concern. Besides focusing on carefully chosen images to render heightened states of mind, another part of MacLaverty's genius manifests itself in his lifting the vernacular rhythms and telling phrases of everyday Northern Irish speech into the realm of written art, rendering the ordinary extraordinary, as one of his exemplars, Joyce, did. His clear zest in elevating this speech to the status of art permeates his fiction. Recognizing his joy in dialogue and in words generally should go some way toward changing the critical perception that he is dour and grim; so, too, should understanding his levity and great humor.

Despite representing atrocity and horror in his work—from the murder of Owen Kane at the conclusion of *Lamb* to the emotionally eviscerating rape in "Up the Coast"—MacLaverty consistently employs a finely calibrated sense of humor that delights in the unexpected visual image. This humor becomes more pronounced in the later work until it reaches a crescendo in *The Anatomy School*. The uproarious humor of the large dog of the composer Melnichuck that attempts to mount Catherine McKenna as she plays for the famous man in *Grace Notes* exemplifies MacLaverty's penchant for visually creating laughter through juxtaposing the crude with the refined.

On the other hand, he is equally capable of evoking laughter through cleverly rendered conversation, as an episode from *The Anatomy School* demonstrates. When Nurse Gilliland queries the local Catholic priest Father Farquharson at one of the evening gatherings at Martin's house about how he has managed to maintain his lifelong abstinence from alcohol, given that he imbibes alcohol during the mass, he retorts, "I'm amazed at you asking such a question," and goes on to explain to her, "By the time I'm consuming it, its essence has changed. . . . It looks like wine, smells like wine—but it has been changed. To the Precious Blood. In essence" (*AS* 97). Unruffled, Nurse Gilliland proceeds to ask him about what would happen to ordinary, store-bought bread if it were brought into the mass and "exposed" to the words of consecration. "When the priest says the words of the consecration why doesn't . . . what's to stop her bread turning into the . . . Lord, the Precious Body?" (98) The exasperated priest takes refuge in the phrase "sacerdotal intentionality," (98) but on seeing the blank looks on the faces of his parishioners, takes refuge in more quotidian language, saying finally, "The words are spoken to—what he holds between his fingers—the host. The miracle doesn't leak out, as it were, to bread within the vicinity" (99). The hilarity of this episode shows MacLaverty's delight in the way that common sense often runs up against mercilessly logical authority and suggests his deep sympathy with those who would question tradition.

Given his resistance to authority figures such as many of the priests that populate his fiction, and his rejection of the authority of victimhood, represented in his critique of loyalism and republicanism, how, then, does MacLaverty's art achieve its own considerable authority? The answer, in brief, seems to be his ability to render the truth of the human condition realistically across a range of nationalities, ages, and stages of life and to show us both the follies and cruelty and the empathy and love we are capable of expressing. The conflict between imprisonment and love remains his favorite dialectic. Although he certainly believes that we will continue to imprison ourselves and others, especially through our slavish adherence to warped ideologies, he more strongly feels that we desire freedom to release ourselves and others from our contemporary malaise of selfishness, thereby developing relationships and even finding love. In our reaching out to others, we are, after all, most fully ourselves and most fully human. In Bernard MacLaverty's fiction, we see ourselves as others see us, and, perhaps, ourselves as we might yet be. Despite the tendency in our current critical environment to view art as largely incapable of providing a moral design for our lives, revealing such insights constitutes a very considerable achievement.

NOTES

INTRODUCTION

1 Ben Forkner, introduction, *Modern Irish Short Stories* (New York: Penguin, 1995), 41.

2 Trevor, who is the best living Irish short story writer, includes MacLaverty, along with the lesser-known Desmond Hogan, as the only two Irish short story writers born after the start of World War II in his far-ranging collection of short fiction from Ireland dating back to the oral tales. In his introduction to *The Oxford Book of Irish Short Stories* (Oxford: Oxford University Press, 1989), xvi, Trevor suggests MacLaverty and Hogan as examples of the generation succeeding writers born in the 1920s and 1930s, arguing that this new generation is "now confidently moving from promise to achievement."

3 See Fionnuala O'Connor, *In Search of a State: Catholics in Northern Ireland* (Belfast: Blackstaff Press, 1993). As an example of a Northern Irish Catholic who feels neither British nor Irish but something in between and stateless, see the brief interview with then fifty-nine-year-old Hugh, a businessman and supporter of the moderate Catholic party, the Social Democratic Labour Party (SDLP). Hugh told O'Connor that Irishness "is in continual flux. It was hugely anti-Britishness, and it certainly isn't that any longer. . . . you start thinking again about Ireland, and Irishness—and you realize you're neither fish nor flesh. You're not part of the Britishness and you're not part of the Irishness that goes as far as the Provos" (352, 353). In "False Faces," in *False Faces: Poetry, Politics, and Place* (Belfast, Lagan Press, 1994), 58, the poet and critic Gerald Dawe points out that there has been a "general switchoff in the Republic to the north itself. The place seems stuck in a groove few in the Republic have much private time for—the old historical business of fighting the Brits has not, as Sinn Fein knows, cut any parliamentary ice in the 26 counties."

4 Denis Donoghue, "The Literature of Trouble," in *We Irish: Essays on Irish Literature and Society* (New York: Knopf, 1986), 193.

5 Alex Houen, *Terrorism and Modern Literature, from Joseph Conrad to Ciaran Carson* (Oxford: Oxford University Press, 2002), 25. Houen's emphasis.

6 Qtd. in Dominic Head, *The Modernist Short Story: A Study in Theory and Practice* (Cambridge: Cambridge University Press, 1992), 190.

7 In *North* (London: Faber, 1975), 53, Heaney laments "The famous // Northern reticence, the tight gag of place / And times" in his poem "Whatever You Say Say Nothing."

8 "Whatever You Say Say Nothing," Transmission date July 24, 1994. BBC Northern Ireland Radio Archives. Museum number 4010. Cultra, Northern Ireland.

9 Elmer Kennedy-Andrews, *Fiction and the Northern Ireland Troubles since 1969: (de-)constructing the North* (Dublin: Four Courts Press, 2003), 7.

10 Michael L. Storey, *Representing the Troubles in Irish Short Fiction* (Washington, DC: Catholic University of America Press, 2004), 14. Storey cites only a handful of stories to substantiate this claim, including ones by Val Mulkerns and David Park, along with the only story dealing with the Troubles by the inimitable William Trevor, "Attracta," which is a departure from Trevor's usual fictional focus on rural southern Ireland. Later, Storey exaggerates greatly when he claims, "In the 1970s and 1980s Irish writers made sectarian violence and terrorism the primary focus of their stories" (151). In "First Impressions: 1968–1978," 65, Maurice Harmon, a veteran observer of the literary scene north

and south of the border, has argued more believably that "when the violence in Northern Ireland appears in the contemporary story, it does so as context and background, and as something to get away from." In *The Irish Short Story,* ed. Patrick Rafroidi and Terence Brown (Atlantic Highlands, NJ: Humanities Press, 1979).

11 One author who has written short stories dealing directly with the Troubles in a realistic vein is Eugene McCabe, discussed in Storey's study, who published a suite of such stories—"Cancer," "Heritage," and "Victims"—in 1976, which was also televised. After the real-life local man on whom "Heritage" was based was assassinated in 1980, McCabe stopped writing for some years. This incident demonstrates the dangers inherent in creative writing based too closely on reality at that time in the province.

12 See Eamonn Hughes, "Fiction," in *Stepping Stones: The Arts in Ulster, 1971–2001*, ed. Mark Carruthers and Stephen Douds (Belfast: Blackstaff, 2001), 79.

13 Eve Patten, "'Flying to Belfast': Audience and Authenticity in Recent Northern Irish Fiction," in "Nations and Relations: Writing across the British Isles," ed. Tony Brown and Russell Stephens, special issue, *New Welsh Review* (2000): 30–31.

14 John Wilson Foster, *Forces and Themes in Ulster Fiction* (Dublin: Gill and Macmillan, 1974), 47.

15 Edward Said, *Reflections on Exile and Other Essays* (Cambridge, MA: Harvard University Press, 2000), 186.

16 Gerry Smyth, *The Novel and the Nation: Studies in the New Irish Fiction* (London: Pluto Press, 1997), 117.

17 Qtd. in ibid., 116.

18 Hughes, "Fiction," 87, 88. Hughes argues specifically about MacLaverty's fiction, however, that while stories such as "Walking the Dog" and novels such as *Grace Notes* feature characters that rise above the rhetoric and violence of the conflict, *Cal* "fails in subordinating the lives of its characters to the Troubles," 94, an argument that I challenge in the present study's chapter on that book.

19 "An Interview with Richard Rankin Russell," *Irish Literary Supplement* 26, no. 1 (Fall 2006): 22.

20 Ibid., 22. See the incorporation of this autobiographical memory in *Cal*, 78, when Cal and Shamie move in with Shamie's cousin Dermot Ryan after their house is firebombed and destroyed by loyalists. Cal, lying on the floor near the fire, recalls, "He had been ill once in their first house in Clanchatten Street and they had moved his bed down beside the range. The fire door was usually kept open at night to keep the room warm and he would lie listening to his mother's voice talking to a neighbour or his father, feeling the heat from the fire on his back."

21 Philip Hobsbaum, "The Belfast Group: A Recollection," *Eire-Ireland* 32, no. 2–3 (Summer–Fall 1997): 180.

22 Glenn C. Arbery, *Why Literature Matters: Permanence and the Politics of Reputation* (Wilmington, DE: ISI Books, 2001), 19.

23 Mikhail Bakhtin, "Discourse and the Novel," in *The Dialogic Imagination: Four Essays by M. M. Bakhtin*, ed. Michael Holquist, trans. Caryl Emerson and Michael Holquist (Austin, University of Texas Press, 1981), 259.

24 Ibid., 259.

25 Theodor Adorno, *Aesthetic Theory*, ed. Gretel Adorno and Rolf Tiedemann, trans. Robert Hullot-Kentor (Minneapolis, University of Minnesota Press, 1997), 5.

26 Ibid., 5.

27 "Interview with Russell," 22.

28 Ibid., 22. The loneliness of McLaverty's characters wandering the margins of Belfast has also powerfully influenced the younger writer. MacLaverty told Gregory McNamee in "Capturing the Whirlwind: An Interview with Northern Irish Writer Bernard Mac-Laverty," *The Bloomsbury Review* 5, no. 9 (June 1985): 20, that "my regard for the short story began with reading Michael McLaverty."

29 "Bernard MacLaverty," interview by Rosa González, *Ireland in Writing: Interviews with Writers and Academics* eds. Jacqueline Hurtley, Rosa González, Inés Praga, and Esther Aliaga (Amsterdam: Rodopi, 1998), 24.

30 Ibid., 25.

31 Frank O'Connor, *The Lonely Voice: A Study of the Short Story* (London: Macmillan, 1963), 19.

32 Ibid., 20.

33 In this regard, Clare Hanson's remarks in her introduction to Clare Hanson, ed., *Re-reading the Short Story* (New York: St. Martin's, 1999), 6, suggest how short fiction functions as an alternative history to the official one. "The formal properties of the short story—disjunction, inconclusiveness, obliquity—connect with its ideological marginality and with the fact that the form may be used to express something suppressed/repressed in mainstream literature."

34 Ian Reid, *The Short Story* (London: Methuen, 1977), 64. Stories of this sort, of course, depart from Edgar Allan Poe's formulations of the short story in his reviews from the 1830s and 1840s. For example, in his 1842 review of Nathaniel Hawthorne's *Twice-Told Tales*, reprinted in Charles E. May, ed., *The New Short Story Theories* (Athens: Ohio University Press, 1994), 60, Poe argues for the "unity of effect or impression" as a central quality of the short story, further noting that this unity is only possible because of the story's brevity relative to that of the novel. Poe points out "this unity cannot be thoroughly preserved in productions whose perusal cannot be completed at one sitting." The pervasiveness of this nineteenth-century short story model established by Poe and his successors also obtained in Ireland into the 1970s, as Harmon, "First Impressions," 65, has shown. Harmon observes, "The classic form of the short story, as practiced by Mary Lavin, Frank O'Connor, Liam O'Flaherty, and Sean O'Faolain, is still the accepted mode. This involves a chronological narrative, with minimal characterization, careful attention to setting, one or two incidents, a taut control of tone and development, and the general sense of all the ingredients moving towards a moment of insight."

35 Trevor, introduction, *Irish Short Stories*, ix.

36 Patrick Grant, *Breaking Enmities: Religion, Literature, and Culture in Northern Ireland, 1967–1997* (New York: St. Martin's, 1999), 147.

37 Said, *Reflections on Exile*, 185.

38 Georg Lukács, *The Theory of the Novel* (Cambridge, MA: MIT Press, 1971), 61.

39 John Cronin, "Prose," in *Causeway: The Arts in Ulster*, ed. Michael Longley (Belfast: Arts Council of Northern Ireland, 1971), 76.

40 Liam Harte and Michael Parker, eds. in their introduction to *Contemporary Irish Fiction: Themes, Tropes, Theories* (New York: St. Martins, 2000), 4, citing Seamus Deane, argue that "contemporary Northern Irish fiction, like the cultures it serves and the histories it traces, is itself a miscegenated discourse, the complex product of a society 'neither Irish nor British while also being both.'"

41 Foster, *Forces and Themes*, 121.

42 Lukács, *Theory of the Novel*, 60.

43 Denis Donoghue, "Teaching Literature: The Force of Form," *New Literary History* 30, no. 1 (1999): 13.

44 See Alan Spiegel, *Fiction and the Camera Eye: Visual Consciousness in Film and the Modern Novel* (Charlottesville: University of Virginia Press, 1976), 71–82. Spiegel argues convincingly that Joyce "was cinematographic in his literary procedure before the cinema; . . . he was, in fact, at a very early age, developing and perfecting the cinematographic variety of concretized form . . . previous to, and quite apart from, the invention of the motion picture camera" (77).

45 "Bernard MacLaverty," interview with Sharon Monteith and Jenny Newman, in *Contemporary British and Irish Fiction: An Introduction through Interviews*, eds. Sharon Monteith, Jenny Newman, and Pat Wheeler (London: Arnold, 2004), 116.

CHAPTER 1

1 Weldon Thornton, *D. H. Lawrence: A Study of the Short Fiction* (Boston: Twayne's, 1993), 87.

2 Brander Matthews, "The Philosophy of the Short Story," in *New Short Story Theories*, 77.

3 Reid, *Short Story*, 59.

4 Robert Hogan, "Old Boys, Young Bucks, and New Women: The Contemporary Irish Short Story," in *The Irish Short Story: A Critical History*, ed. James F. Kilroy (Boston: Twayne, 1984), 193–94.

5 In her otherwise sensitive and thoughtful review of *Secrets*, "Secrets and Other Stories," *The New Republic* 191 (November 26, 1984): 39, Anne Tyler misreads the conclusion of this story when she claims that its effectiveness lies in "the implied ending that lies just beyond the actual ending—that moment not too far in the future when, faced with another such incident, the son will have to admit the truth to himself."

6 Martin Brennan, the protagonist of MacLaverty's later novel *The Anatomy School*, is also told by his mother to pray to St. Joseph of Cupertino, and on researching this saint, is delighted to find that "he levitated . . . rose up in the air at unexpected times, causing considerable inconvenience to the other members of his order" (17).

7 Tom Paulin, "A Necessary Provincialism: Brian Moore, Maurice Leitch, Florence Mary McDowell," in *Two Decades of Irish Writing: A Critical Survey*, ed. Douglas Dunn (Chester Springs, PA: Dufour, 1975), 243.

8 Gregory McNamee, "Capturing the Whirlwind: An Interview with Northern Irish Writer Bernard MacLaverty," *The Bloomsbury Review* 5, no. 9 (June 1985): 14.

9 Arnold Saxton, "An Introduction to the Stories of Bernard MacLaverty," *Journal of the Short Story in English*, no. 8 (Spring 1987): 118, points out that "the relevance of the aside is clear—the protagonist is 'maimed for life' as a result of 'chasing it'."

10 Said, *Reflections on Exile*, 177.

11 Edna Longley, "'A Barbarous Nook': The Writer and Belfast," in *The Living Stream: Literature and Revisionism in Ireland* (Newcastle, UK: Bloodaxe, 1994), 87.

12 Ibid., 88.

13 Indeed, his escape may have been necessary to preserve his psychological health and well-being. Although he has said his reasons for leaving Belfast when he did also involved purposeful exile as a creative tool and being offered a teaching post in Edinburgh, his third reason was that "in the early 1970s, Belfast was a tense and uncomfortable place to live" ("Capturing the Whirlwind," 15).

14 Anne Tyler remains the only critic to have noted the importance of the letters, although

she does not suggest their value in maintaining an enabling fantasy life. "She notes, how-ever wrong the nephew was to have invaded her privacy, he did her a strange kind of service. After she dies he alone carried her secret, and he alone realizes its value. His mother, on the other hand, tosses the dead woman's letters into the fire without a thought" (Tyler, "Secrets and Other Stories," 39).

15 Thomas Kelly, "*Secrets and Other Stories*, by Bernard MacLaverty," *Eire-Ireland* 16, no. 1 (1981): 156.

16 Ibid., 157.

17 Reid, *Short Story*, 62.

18 Hogan, "Old Boys, Young Bucks, and New Women," 194.

19 Ibid., 194.

20 Tyler, "Secrets and Other Stories," 39.

21 Ibid., 39.

22 Ibid., 40.

CHAPTER 2

1 George Watson, "The Writer on Writing," in *Lamb*, ed. Hamish Robertson, Longman Literature Series, (Essex, UK: Longman, 1991), vi.

2 Ibid., vii.

3 MacLaverty has noted in interview with Deirdre Purcell, "The Glass Word Game," *The Sunday Tribune,* September 25 1988, that he began with the ending of the novel and worked backward from there.

4 Declan Kiberd, *Inventing Ireland: The Literature of the Modern Nation* (Cambridge, MA: Harvard University Press, 1995), 382.

5 Foster, *Forces and Themes in Ulster Fiction*, 257.

6 Ibid., 258.

7 Watson points out in "Writer on Writing," vii, that there are important differences be-tween the actual St. Malachy's Grammar School in Belfast that MacLaverty attended and the fictional school in the novel, but that there are also important continuities. Watson writes, "MacLaverty enjoyed his time at St. Malachy's and . . . it is and was a very different place from Brother Benedict's Catholic Borstal, ironically called *Home* in his novel. Nevertheless, any Irish Catholic will recognize the authenticity of the author's portrait of the clerical domination of education; of its rituals of obedience; of its stress on discipline (*discipline is love disguised*, as Benedict tells Sebastian; very well disguised, we may add); its general authoritarian repressiveness."

8 See Stephen Watt, "The Politics of Bernard MacLaverty's *Cal*," *Eire-Ireland* 28, no. 3 (1993): 138–40, for a reading of *Lamb* (and the later novel *Cal*) as challenges to "the entire liberal-humanist notion of a freely choosing subject. . . . both Michael and Cal may seem doomed from the outset, their fates determined by forces over which they can exert no control" (139). He qualifies this deterministic view, however, by suggesting that such a reading cannot "account for Michael's quite conscious, even selfish, scheming to abduct Owen" (139).

9 C. S. Lewis, *The Four Loves* (San Diego, CA: Harcourt Brace, 1988), 95.

10 Ibid., 33.

11 Weldon Thornton, *The Antimodernism of Joyce's "Portrait of the Artist as a Young Man"* (Syracuse, NY: Syracuse University Press, 1994), 142 and 137–45.

12 Ibid., 144, 145.

13 Penelope Reed Doob, *The Idea of the Labyrinth from Classical Antiquity through the Middle Ages* (Ithaca, NY: Cornell University Press, 2001), 1.

14 Watt, "Politics of Bernard MacLaverty's *Cal*," 139–40.

15 Lewis, *Four Loves*, 41.

16 Ibid., 50.

17 Ibid., 51.

18 "In the Beginning Was the Written Word: Paul Campbell Interviews Bernard MacLaverty," *The Linenhall Review* (Winter 1984/85): 5.

19 One symbol of this freedom is, as MacLaverty has noted, "the fish in the London Aquarium" that Michael and Lamb see together (Ibid., 5).

20 Neil Corcoran, in *After Yeats and Joyce: Reading Modern Irish Literature* (New York: Oxford University Press, 1997), 156, argues that "Michael and Owen transgress . . . into a relationship which has strong overtones of the *doppelganger*, since Michael's surname, 'Lamb,' is, we are told, the translation of the Irish 'Owen.' In this sacrifice of the Lambs, therefore, we may read a realism aspiring to the level of the allegorical."

21 MacLaverty told Rosa Gonzalez in conversation that "*Lamb* was an attempt to write about it [the Troubles] obliquely, yet there is . . . a bleak image . . . where a man who destroys the thing he loves [and] sees that something misdirected his love, saying 'I love this child,' or in the case of some people who say, 'I love this country and I'm going to destroy it'" ("Bernard MacLaverty," interview by Rosa Gonzalez, *Ireland in Writing*, 24). Fully apprehending this analogy between the character Michael Lamb and the IRA suggests that, while MacLaverty may well see him as "slightly stupid and very naïve," as George Watson argues in "The Writer on Writing," he is certainly not "a wholly convincing picture of a good man" (x). The stupid and the naïve—both fictional characters and national liberation movements—can pursue a misguided ideal and in the process, activate a latent part of their depravity, resulting in evil actions.

22 Gary Brienzo, "The Voice of Despair in Ireland's Bernard MacLaverty," *North Dakota Quarterly* 57, no. 1 (Winter 1989): 68.

CHAPTER 3

1 Hogan, "Old Boys, Young Bucks, and New Women," 194.

2 Ibid., 194.

3 John Conroy, *Belfast Diary: War as a Way of Life* (Boston: Beacon Press, 1987), 8.

4 As the essayist and novelist Robert (McLiam) Wilson, himself raised Catholic in West Belfast, has put it in his study of Belfast's poor, *The Dispossessed* (London: Picador, 1992), 165, "It is Belfast's poorest who suffer the worst effects of the city's violence, economically and physically. The death toll among the Belfast bourgeoisie in no way matches that sustained by the city's working class. And then there's the inordinate prosperity that Belfast's highest earners still enjoy. The privileges of Belfast's suburbia seem to protect them from most of the cost and most of the dying."

5 Hogan, "Old Boys, Young Bucks, and New Women," 194.

6 Elaine Scarry, *Dreaming by the Book* (New York: Farrar, Straus, Giroux, 1999), 146–47, argues that "a map of the relative size of body parts as they exist not in the body but in neural activity shows by far the largest body part is the hand (rivaled in size only by the lips and feet)" and thus, "since we know that mental picturing uses the same neuronal paths in the brain that sensory perception uses, it may be that alluding to the hand brings large resources of the brain to bear on the project of making an image move."

7   Austin Wright, "Recalcitrance in the Short Story," in *Short Story Theory at a Crossroads*,
    ed. Susan Lohafer and Jo Ellyn Clarey (Baton Rouge: Louisiana State University Press,
    1989), 116.

8   Ibid., 120.

9   Ibid., 120.

10 A close variation of this phrase is used in *Cal*, when the title character puts down the
    public phone after informing the police that the local library has an IRA bomb in it.
    We are told, "he put the phone down as if it was a black garden slug and left the phone
    box" (*C* 151). In this latter case, Cal does the right thing by informing on the IRA, but
    is disgusted with himself for doing so, unlike the boy's father in "Father and Son," who
    rightly rejects the pistol and is comfortable with this rejection.

11 In *Door into the Dark*, (London: Faber, 1969), 7, the anvil of Heaney's blacksmith is
    described as "an altar / Where he expends himself in shape and music."

12 See Watt, "The Politics of Bernard MacLaverty's *Cal*," for a different, more negative read-
    ing of Danny's development as an artist under the tutelage of the blacksmith and Miss
    Schwartz. Watt argues that the story "depicts an educational setting that offers refresh-
    ing possibilities for the story's central character until it is destroyed by the social setting's
    repressive mores" (142). He further holds, "In the case of Marysia Schwartz and her pro-
    tégé, local ideological commitment to the principles of marriage and family squelch artis-
    tic potential, effectively ending Danny's dreams of a career as a concert pianist" (142–43).

13 C. J. Ganter, "Bleakness and Comedy: Stoic Humor in Bernard MacLaverty's Short Sto-
    ries," *International Fiction Review* 26, no.1–2 (1999): 6, holds that the story, with its pun
    on "A.J. Ayers's positivist treatise *Language, Truth, and Logic* (1936)" and its juxtapo-
    sition of "an eccentric caste [sic] of philosophers (commonly taken to be representa-
    tives of an intellectual elite) and linguistically restricted handicapped people (commonly
    taken to be representatives of human abnormality), enables MacLaverty to interrogate
    "the primacy of language postulated by twentieth-century positivism and [to] remind . . .
    us of the disastrous shortcomings in the anthropological quest for criteria of human
    'normality.'"

CHAPTER 4

1   As Joseph Ruane and Jennifer Todd note in *Dynamics of Conflict in Northern Ireland:
    Power, Conflict, and Emancipation*, "In 1971, Catholic men were 2.6 times as likely to
    be unemployed than their Protestant equivalents and remained at that level through
    the mid-1980s" (Cambridge: Cambridge University Press, 1996), 167. For the period
    1983–85, John McGarry and Brendan O'Leary, *Explaining Northern Ireland: Broken
    Images* (Oxford: Blackwell, 1995), 285, note that partly because of discrimination
    against them by Protestants, the overall Catholic unemployment rate was 35.1%, while
    it was 14.9% for Protestants.

2   Laura Pelaschiar, *Writing the North: The Contemporary Novel in Northern Ireland* (Tri-
    este, Italy: Edizioni Parnaso, 1998), 63, points out that Shamie McCluskey "is one of
    the few positive father figures to be encountered in Northern Irish fiction. . . . The total
    lack of rhetoric in MacLaverty's depiction of him and his simple resistance make him into
    one of the few really heroic and tragic figures in the fictional world of the Troubles."

3   MacLaverty has revealed in "Bernard MacLaverty," interview with Monteith and New-
    man, 112, that he also has some knowledge of photography. He recalled, "My father
    had a darkroom set up in the house, and I had a summer job in a photo works cutting
    up negatives."

4   As Bill Rolston has noted in the introduction to his first collection of political murals in Northern Ireland, *Drawing Support: Murals in the North of Ireland* (Belfast: Beyond the Pale Publications, 1992), iii, because of the history of nationalist repression in the province and its subsequent marginalization, "Nationalists traditionally did not paint murals." Rolston argues, "The emergence of murals on the nationalist side dates from the hunger strike[s] carried out by republican prisoners in 1981 in pursuit of their demand for political prisoner status" (iii). See plates 53, 57, 58, and 64, on 28, 30, 30, and 33, respectively, for Christian and specifically Catholic images of hunger strikers. Plate 64 is particularly striking, showing a hunger striker crucified on a Union Jack flag.

5   Rolston, introduction, *Drawing Support*, vii.

6   Although I arrived at this conclusion on my own, I was pleased to find it confirmed in general by Richard Haslam, "'Designed to Cause Suffering': *Cal* and the Politics of Imprisonment," *Nua: Studies in Contemporary Irish Writing* 3, no. 1–2 (2002): 48: "*Cal* . . . seeks to come to terms with (and finds terms for) the sacrificial discourse of imprisoned republicans between autumn 1976 (when the blanket protest commenced) and 1981 (when the second hunger strike ended). Though the novel is written in the preterite and apparently set in the period from autumn to Christmas Eve, 1976, its intimated tense is the future perfect, setting out aspects of what will have been from 1977 to 1981 (two years before *Cal* was published)."

7   John Wilson Foster, "Irish Fiction 1965–1990," in *The Field Day Anthology of Irish Writing*, ed. Seamus Deane (Derry, Northern Ireland: Field Day Publications, 1991), 3: 940.

8   Seamus Deane, *A Short History of Irish Literature* (Notre Dame, IN: University of Notre Dame Press, 1986), 244.

9   Martha Bayles, review of *Cal, The New Republic,* September 19, 1983, argues that the novel successfully departs from what by then had become a convention in fiction about Northern Ireland of depicting either flat characters who are "symbols of pure evil" or "rounded characters" as mere "victims" in its portrayal of Cal's complicity in the violence. Bayles argues that such fiction dealing with the Troubles up until *Cal* set up a false dichotomy between the "violent and nonviolent" in the province, but points out that in fact, "Northern Ireland is full of decent people who do support the violence, or at least display the sort of mental compartmentalization by which deeply ingrained hatred for the other side may coexist with kindness toward its individual members, not to mention lofty ideals" (30). Although she does not mention Cyril Dunlop in her discussion, this last point aptly describes both Dunlop's hatred for most Catholics and his kindness toward Cal.

10 See Joe Cleary, "'Fork-Tongued on the Border Bit': Partition and the Politics of Form in Contemporary Narratives of the Northern Irish Conflict," *South Atlantic Quarterly* 95, no. 1 (1996): 249, for a persuasive reading of this lone appearance of the border between the Republic of Ireland and Northern Ireland in the novel: "Crossing the border into 'the real Ireland,' then, offers no reprieve from the 'original sin' of the policeman's murder, which has cost Cal any hope of achieving genuine happiness. The function of this single incident is therefore an essentially negative one: its purpose is to seal off the border in narrative terms, to underscore the fact that the Republic can offer Cal no sanctuary; having sinned against the Northern Irish State, it is there that his sin must be expiated."

11 Lukács, *Theory of the Novel,* 72–73.

12 Ibid., 61–62.

13 *Pelaschiar, Writing the North,* 19. See Pelaschiar, ibid., 19–22, for a helpful overview of the Northern Irish thriller. See Aaron Kelly, *The Thriller and Northern Ireland since 1969:*

Utterly Resigned Terror (Aldershot, UK: Ashgate, 2005), for the definitive study of this subgenre. Kelly classes *Cal* as a thriller that "attempt[s] to debunk the mythic motivations of modern Nationalism," but argues that "the heroism which it tries to attribute to the people of the North becomes reducible . . . to a stoic ineffectuality" (65). Cleary, "'Fork-Tongued on the Border Bit,'" 250–51, shows that *Cal* actually mimics a specific type of this thriller—the romance-across-the-barricades—in Cal's initial attraction to Marcella, whom he thinks is Protestant. On Cal's discovery that Marcella is Catholic like himself, she loses none of the exotic aura with which he had invested her, and their subsequent romance explodes the neat conventions of this subgenre. Cleary argues, "The relationship between Cal and Marcella is transgressive, then, not because it crosses a traditional communal divide, but because it is *conducted over the grave of exactly that kind of union*, one which it effectively cancels out by recovering *Catholic Marcella* from *Protestant Robert* and restoring her to the embrace of *Catholic Cal*" (Cleary's emphases).

14 Pelaschiar, *Writing the North*, 20, quotes Eamonn Hughes, *Culture and Politics in Northern Ireland* (Milton Keynes, UK: Open University Press, 1991), 6, for a stirring assessment of how the static form of such thrillers enforces the cultural inertia of the societies they depict. Hughes suggests, "At its most mechanical the thriller moves to a closure which projects its locale as a closed but always unresolved system: the Cold War can never end, the forces of corruption can never be defeated, and the problems of Northern Ireland will inevitably endure."

15 M. M. Bakhtin, "Epic and Novel: Toward a Methodology for the Study of the Novel," in *Dialogic Imagination*, 7. See David Lloyd, *Anomalous States: Irish Writing and the Post-Colonial Moment* (Durham, NC: Duke University Press, 1993), 153, however, for an argument that "Bakhtin's account of the novel" is "tied to a merely mimetic notion of representation" and thus unable to address "the importance of the novel as an active force in processes of social transformation." *Cal* both reflects the changing reality of Northern Ireland and acts as a transformative work in imagining the future of its protagonist and his society, as we will see.

16 Lukács, *Theory of the Novel*, 127.

17 Terrence Doody, *Confession and Community in the Novel* (Baton Rouge: Louisiana State University Press, 1980), 4.

18 Kennedy-Andrews, *Fiction and the Northern Ireland Troubles since 1969*, intriguingly argues that Cal "inhabits the kind of contemporary society that Michel Foucault describes in his book, *Discipline and Punish* (1975), a disciplinary, highly regulated society which relies for its success on its capacity to produce people who subject themselves to its terms." For Kennedy-Andrews, the surveillance endemic in Cal's society resembles Foucault's concept of the panopticon, a "central watch tower surrounded by a series of individual cells which were separate from each other but always visible from the central tower. The central tower could be seen from the cells, but not the watcher in the tower. Through this technique of surveillance, assessment, supervision and correction, the individual feels that he is being continually watched—regardless of whether or not he really is—and so eventually comes to regulate his own behavior in accordance with the demands of the dominant society" (89).

19 Stephen Watt, "The Politics of Bernard MacLaverty's *Cal*," 146. I take issue with Watt's final analysis of such moments, however, because he refuses to see how the novel and Cal's proleptic future featuring his beating, confession, and reentry into an imagined community and society implies a trajectory of freedom. Instead, he believes such moments as Cal's lonely walking in the countryside away from the restrictions of the town and his lovemaking with Marcella are isolated but still worthwhile occurrences of liberty in

the novel, arguing that "any triumph of love or the human spirit, no matter how ephemeral, must count for something" (146).

20 W. J. T. Mitchell, *Picture Theory: Essays on Verbal and Visual Representation* (Chicago: University of Chicago Press, 1994), 152.

21 The murderous disturbance of Morton from his domestic bliss, particularly the detail of his slipper, recalls the final atrocity in the Northern Irish poet Michael Longley's poem "Wounds," in *An Exploded View: Poems 1968–1972* (London: Victor Gollancz, 1973), 40–41, about a bus conductor who is shot in his own home. "He collapsed beside his carpet-slippers / Without a murmur, shot through the head / By a shivering boy who wandered in / Before they could turn the television down / Or tidy away the supper dishes."

22 Benjamin Griffith, "Ireland's Ironies, Grim and Droll: The Fiction of Bernard Mac-Laverty," *The Sewanee Review* 106, no. 2 (Spring 1998): 335, has noted that "The word *knee* in the novel, whether referring to the kneeling at Mass or the smashing of an enemy's patella, leads Cal to recall the 'genuflection' of the dying husband as he falls on his doorstep, screaming for his wife." Cal kneels during his attendance at Mass in the church at Magherafelt (*C* 36), surely reminding him of Robert Morton's posture in death; he must be similarly reminded of Morton's collapsing body when hearing Crilly tell on page 147 of the knee-capping he gave to a sixteen-year-old boy who stole a car and severely injured Skeffington's old father. Crilly exclaims "Both knees he wanted, and your man on the ground squealing like a stuck pig with Skeffington sitting on his head."

23 Peter Brooks, *Troubling Confessions: Speaking Guilt in Law and Literature* (Chicago: University of Chicago Press, 2000), 2.

24 Cleary, "'Fork-Tongued on the Border Bit,'" 252.

25 Spiegel, *Fiction and the Camera Eye*, 32.

26 Qtd. in Karen Jacobs, *The Eye's Mind: Literary Modernism and Visual Culture* (Ithaca, NY: Cornell University Press, 2001), 14, 20.

27 Ibid., 21.

28 Rudolf Arnheim, *Art and Visual Perception: A Psychology of the Creative Eye,* rev. ed. (Berkeley: University of California Press, 1974), 43.

29 Elaine Scarry, *Dreaming by the Book*, 244.

30 The painting dates from the *Insenheim Altar*, c. 1512–16 and is oil on wood. It resides at the Musee d'Unterlinden in Colmar, France.

31 Richard Haslam, "'The Pose Arranged and Lingered Over': Visualizing the 'Troubles,'" in Harte and Parker, *Contemporary Irish Fiction*, 200, 203.

32 Jeanette Shumaker, "Rivalry, Confession, and Healing in Bernard MacLaverty's *Cal*," *Notes on Modern Irish Literature* 9 (1997): 12, argues that because Cal does not know Gaelic, he is forced to resort to cursing himself in both "Black English," "as though he were a slave protesting the factional loyalties that own him," and in French, "mixing in a little English, apparently feeling the centuries-old link between the French and the Irish Catholics." But Shumaker misunderstands these moments as articulations of rage and marginalization when they are often playful immersions in other cultures undertaken to escape a particular crisis in which Cal has just been involved, such as when he realizes for the first time who Marcella is (*C* 13–14) and when he is beaten up by the loyalist youths on his street (47). See Lauren Onkey, "Celtic Soul Brothers," *Eire-Ireland* 28, no. 3 (1993): 157, for an interesting outline of the type of imagined community that Cal might join based on his love of blues songs such as the "negro work song" he sings when splitting the wood blocks at the Morton farm (*C* 43) and his view of himself

as black at significant moments in the novel such as when his lips are bruised and swollen from the fight with the loyalists (*C* 47). Onkey suggests, "It seems that an alliance with a group outside Ireland, like African Americans, is one of the few ways Cal can find a place for himself in Northern Ireland. Both the immediacy of Cal's political situation and MacLaverty's more muted use of the Irish and African-American alliances make that alliance more credible and potentially productive."

33 Cleary, "'Fork-Tongued on the Border Bit,'" 255. Kennedy-Andrews, *Fiction and the Northern Ireland Troubles since 1969*, 91, shares Cleary's belief that the novel is not sufficiently political, terming it a "blend of fairytale" and Catholic theology (which presumably Kennedy-Andrews feels is also mythical) that relies "on a predictable plot and stereotyped emotional configurations." Needless to say, Kennedy-Andrews rejects outright the confessional trajectory of the novel and its implication that Cal's series of confessions will lead him back into a newly imagined community.

34 Bakhtin, "Epic and Novel," 7.

35 Adorno, *Aesthetic Theory*, 1.

36 Ibid., 2.

37 Ibid., 2.

38 Doody, *Confession and Community in the Novel*, 4.

39 Karl F. Morrison, "Constructing Empathy," *Journal of Religion* 84, no. 2 (April 2004): 267.

40 Patrick Grant, *Literature, Rhetoric and Violence in Northern Ireland, 1968–1998: Hardened to Death* (New York: Palgrave, 2001), 3.

CHAPTER 5

1 A small, but significant number of Protestants in Northern Ireland belong to less sectarian denominations of Presbyterianism than Paisley's Free Presbyterian Church, while others belong to the Church of Ireland, the Methodist Church, the Baptist Church, or other denominations. Still others eschew loyalism in favor of socialism or even nationalism. For an anecdotal overview of the complexities within Northern Irish Protestantism, see the interviews with 40 different people from Protestant backgrounds in Marilyn Hyndman, *Further Afield: Journeys from a Protestant Past* (Belfast: Beyond the Pale, 1996). For more rigorous statistical analysis of this complexity, see Ruane and Todd, *Dynamics of Conflict in Northern Ireland*, 54–65. For example, Ruane and Todd note on 54 that in "1991, Presbyterians formed 42 per cent of the Protestant population, Church of Ireland 35 per cent, Methodists 7.5 per cent . . . with smaller sects proliferating and gaining more adherents. Each of the main denominations is itself internally divided between fundamentalists, liberals, and an intermediate group of 'liberal-conservatives.'" A 1991 survey shows some ideological diversity: "two-thirds of Protestants now identify themselves as British, a quarter as either Ulster or Northern Irish, and a small minority (3 per cent) as Irish" (59–60).

2 David Parker, *Ethics, Theory, and the Novel* (Cambridge University Press, 1994), 6, has cogently argued that "literature ought to be regarded as theory's resistant Other, having anticipated many of its major moves and implying compelling answers to these." In this general sense, the fictional son's attitude in "No Surrender" anticipates later theoretical calls for increased, constructive cultural activity on the part of Northern Irish Protestants, such as that envisioned by Brian Graham, "The Imagining of Place: Representation and Identity in Contemporary Ireland," in *In Search of Ireland: A Cultural Geography*, ed. Brian Graham (New York: Routledge, 1997), 210. "They cannot continue to say no

but must instead formulate the positive cultural iconography necessary to imagine and thereby legitimate their place for all its people. Inevitably, such a construct must take them closer to Ireland but only to a revised and pluralist representation of that society, defined by regional and cultural heterogeneity, notions of hybridity, and the equality of rights of citizenship embodied in civic nationalism."

CHAPTER 6

1 Mark Wormald, "Not Far Away from Home," *The Times Literary Supplement,* June 6, 1994, n.p. See, too, the misleading anonymous review in *The Virginia Quarterly Review,* vol. 71, no. 4 (Autumn 1995): 129, which wrongly states, "In the magnificent title story a man is kidnapped by IRA hit men while out walking his dog at night."

2 Michael L. Storey, " *Walking the Dog and Other Stories,*" *Studies in Short Fiction,* vol. 34, no. 4 (Fall 1994): 527.

3 Ibid. To be fair, in his expanded reading of the story for *Representing the Troubles in Irish Short Fiction,* 224, Storey argues that the ellipses John Shields inserts after being asked directly if he is Protestant or Catholic, "I'm . . . I don't believe any of that crap," "indicate a careful hesitation in an effort to say the right thing but perhaps also imply a repudiation of which tradition he has belonged to," although Storey strangely maintains that it is impossible to verify to which tradition Shields has formerly belonged.

4 Seamus Heaney, *Death of a Naturalist* (London: Faber, 1966), 44.

5 Seamus Heaney, *Field Work* (New York: Noonday Press, 1979), 15.

6 Ibid., 15.

7 Daniel Tobin, *Passage to the Center: Imagination and the Sacred in the Poetry of Seamus Heaney* (Lexington: University of Kentucky Press, 1999), 151.

8 Stuart Gilbert, *James Joyce's* Ulysses: *A Study* (New York: Vintage, 1955), 53.

9 Samuel Beckett, *Waiting for Godot* (New York: Grove Press, 1982). Pozzo's full sentence is as follows: "They give birth astride of a grave, the light gleams an instant, then it's night once more" (103).

10 Charles E. May, "The Nature of Knowledge in Short Fiction," *The New Short Story Theories,* 137.

11 Percy Lubbock, *The Craft of Fiction* (London: Jonathan Cape, 1921), 1–2.

12 Tom Adair, "Orange Turns towards Green: *Walking the Dog,*" *The Independent Weekend,* Books Section, July 23, 1994, 27.

13 Patricia Waugh, *Metafiction: The Theory and Practice of Self-Conscious Fiction* (London: Methuen, 1984), 2.

14 Ibid., 7.

15 Trevor, introduction to *Oxford Book of Irish Short Stories,* xv.

16 Waugh, *Metafiction,* 18.

17 Ibid., 100.

CHAPTER 7

1 Marilynn Richtarik, "A Review of Bernard MacLaverty's *Grace Notes,*" *Nua: Studies in Contemporary Irish Writing,* vol. 1, no. 2 (Spring 1998): 89. MacLaverty himself, in interview with Monteith and Newman, 109, cautions against an overly optimistic reading of the novel. He observes, "The fact that there are two parts to the book's structure means you can end on a high note before you realize that the actual end has been in the middle

of the book when she relapsed into another depression. But it wasn't as bad as what she first suffered, so some small progress has been made—in the human condition, the way out of the blackness."

2 "An Interview with Richard Rankin Russell," 22.

3 R. B. Gill, "Why Comedy Laughs: The Shape of Laughter and Comedy," *Literary Imagination,* vol. 8, no. 2 (Spring 2006): 250.

4 Elaine Scarry, *On Beauty and Being Just* (Princeton University Press, 1999), 62.

5 Bernard MacLaverty, "Lost in Music," interview with Helen Meany, *The Irish Times,* July 3, 1997.

6 Gaston Bachelard, *The Poetics of Space* (Boston: Beacon, 1994), 132.

7 Joe Cleary, *Literature, Partition, and the Nation State: Culture and Conflict in Ireland, Israel, and Palestine* (Cambridge: Cambridge University Press, 2002), 141. I say "somewhat" because Cleary is clearly suspicious of novels of individual hope. To wit, he says on 141, "This is not uncritically to endorse these more recent narratives; in some the stress on individual redemption endures."

8 E. M. Forster, *Aspects of the Novel* (1927; repr., San Diego, CA: Harcourt Brace, 1955, 167.

9 Ibid., 169.

10 Nancy Anne Cluck, ed., introduction to *Literature and Music: Essays on Form* (Provo, UT: Brigham Young University Press, 1981), 2–3. Recall Lukács's contention in *Theory of the Novel* that the novel, of all forms, "appears as something in process of becoming" (72–73).

11 Cluck, ed., introduction to *Literature and Music,* 3.

12 Susan Sontag, *Regarding the Pain of Others* (New York: Picador, 2003), 115.

13 Although I arrived at this conclusion on my own, I was pleased to find that Patrick Grant, *Literature, Rhetoric and Violence in Northern Ireland: 1968–1998: Hardened to Death* (New York: Palgrave, 2001), 146, similarly argues about *Grace Notes*, "In so far as music in the novel both symbolizes and effects the kind of reconciliation that answers a deep human desire, it stands opposed especially to mechanical repetition, which symbolizes and effects the alienations confirmed by violence."

14 See Linden Peach, *The Contemporary Novel: Critical Readings* (Basingstoke, UK: Palgrave, 2004), 206–7, for a compelling argument that this triumph is specifically feminized. Peach suggests that "The wispy, barely audible nature of the opening, encapsulates the disempowerment of female being and desire in a male-dominated society. The silence that follows the first intervention of the Lambeg drums is like that 'induced by a slap in the face or the roarings of a drunk' (*GN* 271). It is a musical metaphor for the way in which what was a haunting presence—masculinist violence—at the outset becomes even more aggressive and dominating. But it is also the silence that follows their intervention that is significant for in it, we are made conscious of what is lying dormant waiting to erupt and interrupt. The violent and aggressive first movement is haunted by the potential joy that emerges, explosively, in the second movement. When the Lambeg drums re-enter in this context, they have been changed, feminized, by the fortissimo."

15 Grant, *Literature, Rhetoric and Violence in Northern Ireland,* 149, convincingly argues that "the novel suggests a pattern of interlacements, a 'co-inherence,' as Charles Williams says, whereby art becomes the type and pattern of redeemed relationships. What happens to the lambeg drums in the musical composition is what might happen also in a polity marked by a reconciliation of old and violent differences." Finally, Gerry Smyth, "'The Same Sound but with a Different Meaning': Music, Repetition, and Identity in

Bernard MacLaverty's *Grace Notes,*" *Eire-Ireland: A Journal of Irish Studies,* vol. 37, no. 3–4 (Fall–Winter 2002): 22–23, argues specifically about the political possibilities engendered by the many repetitions in the novel that "every repetition represents, despite itself, a transformation, and . . . this contributes to a liberation from the notion that effective identity resides only in the ritualized repetition of originary essences."

16 Stephen Watt, "Beckett, Late Modernism, and Bernard MacLaverty's Grace Notes," *New Hibernia Review,* vol. 6, no. 2 (Summer 2002): 60, reads Catherine's affirmation of art and the individual in the context of Theodor Adorno's claim that, after Auschwitz, art's efficacy and the integrity of the individual are destroyed. Watt holds that for Catherine, "music turns Adorno's abject subject—who consists of 'nothing but the wretched realities of their world, which has shriveled to bare necessity'—into an individual, one who has the determinative power of agency, delimited though it may be, to transform 'wretched realities' into [positive] non-spaces," thus reversing Adorno's argument.

17 The only reviewer of the novel who seems to have noticed its emphasis on both Catherine's frailty and that of Northern Ireland is Hugo Hamilton, "Living through a Mother Ireland Nightmare," *Sunday Independent,* August 16, 1997. Hamilton correctly points out the importance of Catherine's "frail psychology" and "the inherent frailty of Northern Ireland," although he exaggerates by saying that the province's frailty "takes central place in the narrative." Clearly, Catherine's frailty is foregrounded by the description of, for example, the bombed hometown to which she returns for her father's funeral.

18 In an interview with Monteith and Newman, 109, MacLaverty affirms the role of love in *Grace Notes,* quietly insisting that, "My whole idea of redemption has changed over time. . . . What was it that Raymond Carver said? Something like—to love and be loved, that is as much as we can hope for."

19 Richard Holloway, *On Forgiveness: How Can We Forgive the Unforgivable?* (Edinburgh: Canongate, 2002), 88.

20 Gill, "Why Comedy Laughs," 249.

21 Ibid., 243. See Watt, "Beckett, Late Modernism, and Bernard MacLaverty's *Grace Notes,*" 62–64, for an interesting, although not completely convincing, discussion of the way in which the novel affirms MacLaverty's insistence on the integrity of the individual by the similarity of its grotesque and bodily humor to that of Beckett.

22 Lukács, *Theory of the Novel,* 72.

23 Denis Donoghue, *Speaking of Beauty* (New Haven, CT: Yale University Press, 2003), 24.

24 Elaine Scarry, *On Beauty and Being Just,* 80.

25 Ibid., 80.

26 Ibid., 81.

27 Ibid., 114.

28 Susan Sontag, "An Argument about Beauty," in *At the Same Time: Essays and Speeches,* ed. Paolo Dilonardo and Anne Jump (New York: Farrar, Straus and Giroux, 2007), 12–13.

CHAPTER 8

1 "An Interview with Richard Rankin Russell," 22.

2 Michael R. Molino, "Bernard MacLaverty," in *Dictionary of Literary Biography* (First Series), vol. 267, *British Novelists of the Twenty-first Century,* ed. Michael R. Molino (Detroit, MI: Gale Research Group, 2003), 179.

3 Thornton, *Antimodernism of Joyce's "Portrait,"* 78.

4 Ibid., 70.

5 "In A Coat with a Measure of Guilt," interview with Anne Simpson, *The Herald,* September 29, 1997.

6 See Thornton, *Antimodernism of Joyce's* "Portrait," 90, for a structural pattern of these approaches.

7 This simile is usually used by MacLaverty to convey great, unexpected pleasure, as it does later in the novel, when the Australian girl takes Martin's underpants off as a prelude to making love, and he touches her, then ejaculates prematurely: "quick as a pen scrape, he came" (308).

8 The major subplot of taking exams and praying to St. Joseph of Cupertino—though not Blaise's plan to steal an advance copy of them—recalls elements first adumbrated in "The Miraculous Candidate" from *Secrets.* The group of Martin, Kavanagh, and Blaise recalls the three friends in "Hugo," also from *Secrets,* although in that story, the narrator does not fail as Martin did the first time. The allegedly brilliant Blaise's later disappearance and dissolution in Part Two also is anticipated by the downfall of the supposedly intelligent Hugo.

9 Lukács, *Theory of the Novel,* 89.

CHAPTER 9

1 MacLaverty is excluded, for example, from Cheryl Alexander Malcolm and David Malcolm ed., *Dictionary of Literary Biography: British and Irish Short-Fiction Writers, 1945–2000* (Detroit, MI: Thomson-Gale, 2006): 319. Another Irish short-story writer sometimes linked with MacLaverty, Desmond Hogan, as he is in William Trevor's introduction to *The Oxford Book of Irish Short Stories,* is included, however.

2 Tom Adair, "Inside Stories," review of *Matters of Life and Death, The Scotsman,* May 13, 2006.

3 Anne Enright, "A Herringbone Walk," review of *Matters of Life and Death, The Guardian,* May 6, 2006.

4 Peter Kemp, "A Thrilling Sense of Urgency," review of *Matters of Life and Death, The Sunday Times,* May 14, 2006.

5 Simon Baker, "Studies in Solitude," review of *Matters of Life and Death, New Statesman,* June 26, 2006.

6 Tom Paulin, "Formal Pleasure: The Short Story," in *Writing to the Moment: Selected Critical Essays, 1980–1996* (London: Faber, 1996), 213.

7 "Interview with Stephen Phelan," *The Sunday Herald,* May 25, 2006.

8 This function of the story accords with Clare Hanson's argument in her introduction to *Re-reading the Short Story,* 6, that the genre "gives us the other side of 'the official story or narrative.'"

9 "Bloody Friday" is the moniker given to the events of July 21, 1972, in which twenty-six Irish Republican Army bombs exploded in Belfast, killing eleven people and injuring 130. The bombs were so destructive that body parts were collected in plastic bags.

10 The phrase, "to tell the story" has acquired a special resonance in literature about the Holocaust. A famous example occurs in Holocaust survivor Elie Wiesel's prologue to *The Gates of the Forest* (New York: Holt, Rinehart, and Winston, 1966), when Rabbi Israel of Rizhyn speaks to God about the misfortune threatening the Jews as part of an Hasidic parable. "All I can do is to tell the story, and this must be sufficient." The phrase appears in at least one title about the atrocities as well. Polish Holocaust survivor Yala Korwin's collection

of poetry is entitled *To Tell the Story: Poems of the Holocaust* (New York: Holocaust Library, 1987).

11 Lea Wernick Fridman, *Words and Witness: Narrative and Aesthetic Strategies in the Representation of the Holocaust* (Albany: State University of New York Press, 2000), 100, 101.

12 Daniel R. Schwarz, *Imagining the Holocaust* (New York: St. Martin's Press, 1999), 14. Schwarz's emphasis.

13 Catherine even thinks, immediately before reciting her mental litany of the atrocities from the Troubles, that "it was a map which would not exist if women made the decisions" (*GN* 127). But Peach, *Contemporary Irish Novel*, 202, rightly points out that Catherine's assertion here is selective, "ignoring the part that female freedom fighters and paramilitaries have played in the Troubles and in the Anglo-Irish Wars, let alone the part played by a female British prime minister [Margaret Thatcher]."

14 "In a Coat with a Measure of Guilt," Interview with Anne Simpson, *The Herald,* September 29, 1997, 14.

15 Tellingly, MacLaverty calls Niall "the exploited boy" in "An Interview with Richard Rankin Russell," 22.

16 Although the narrator claims, "The kids weren't affected," he immediately admits, "Sean doesn't remember a thing about it—he was too young—but wee Kate does. She was really scared and timid for a long time" (4).

17 Enright, "Herringbone Walk."

18 "Interview with Stephen Phelan."

AFTERWORD

1 "The Glass Word Game," interview with Deirdre Purcell, *The Sunday Tribune,* September 25, 1988.

2 Ibid.

3 Tom Adair, "Pints of Bitterness," review of *Grace Notes, The Observer,* July 6, 1997.

4 David Brett, *The Plain Style: The Reformation, Culture, and the Crisis in Protestant Identity* (Belfast, black square books, 1999), 108.

5 Ibid., 121–24.

Primary Works

Matters of Life and Death and Other Stories. Belfast: Blackstaff, 2006; London: Jonathan Cape, 2006; New York: Norton, 2006.

The Anatomy School. Belfast: Blackstaff, 2001; London: Jonathan Cape, 2001; New York: Norton, 2002.

Grace Notes. Belfast: Blackstaff, 1997; London: Jonathan Cape, 1997; New York: Norton, 1998.

Walking the Dog and Other Stories. Belfast: Blackstaff, 1994; London: Jonathan Cape, 1994; New York: Norton, 1995.

The Bernard MacLaverty Collection, ed. Hamish Robertson. Harlow, UK: Longman, 1991.

The Best of Bernard MacLaverty: Short Stories, New Windmills Series. Oxford: Heinemann, 1990.

The Great Profundo and Other Stories. Belfast: Blackstaff, 1987; London: Jonathan Cape, 1987; New York: Grove Press, 1988.

Cal. Belfast: Blackstaff, 1983; London: Cape, 1983; New York: Braziller, 1983.

A Time to Dance and Other Stories. Belfast: Blackstaff, 1982; London: Jonathan Cape, 1982; New York: Braziller, 1982.

Lamb. Belfast: Blackstaff, 1980; London: Jonathan Cape, 1980; New York: Braziller, 1980.

Secrets and Other Stories. Belfast: Blackstaff, 1977; New York: Viking, 1984; London: Allison and Busby, 1984.

"A Legacy and Some Gunks."
www.bernardmaclaverty.com/works/short_stories/a_legacy.htm.

Adaptation for Televison

The Real Charlotte. Granada/Gandon (UK), 1989.

Children's Books

Columba. Edinburgh: Scottish Children's Press, 1997.

Andrew McAndrew. Cambridge, MA: Candlewick Press, 1993; London: Walker Books (UK), 1988.

A Man in Search of a Pet. Illustrations by Bernard MacLaverty. Belfast: Blackstaff, 1978.

Radio Plays

Grace Notes. Radio Scotland, 1999; BBC Radio 3, 2003.

Lamb. BBC, 1992.

Some Surrender. BBC, 1988.

The Break, adapted by MacLaverty from his short story of that title in *The Great Profundo.* BBC, 1988.

No Joke, adapted by MacLaverty from his short story of that title in *A Time to Dance.* BBC, 1983.

Secrets, adapted by MacLaverty from his short story of that title in *Secrets.* BBC, 1981.

My Dear Palestrina, adapted by MacLaverty from his short story of that title in *Secrets.* BBC, 1980.

Screenplays

The Cone-Gatherers, adapted by MacLaverty from Robin Jenkins's novel of that title. In pre-production with Saltire Pictures (UK). Director Michael Caton-Jones. Projected shooting date of 2008.

Bye-Child, adapted by MacLaverty from Seamus Heaney's poem of that title. Director MacLaverty. Poetry in Motion (UK), 2003.

The Dawning, adapted from Jennifer Johnston's novel *The Old Jest*; cowritten with MacLaverty. Director Robert Knights. Lawson Productions (UK), 1988.

Lamb, adapted by MacLaverty from his novel of that title. Director Colin Gregg. Flickers Productions and Limehouse Pictures in association with Channel Four Films (UK), 1986.

Cal, adapted by MacLaverty from his novel of that title. Director Pat O'Connor. Enigma (UK), 1984.

Television Plays

Hostages. HBO (USA), 1993; Granada (UK), 1992.

Elephant. BBC Northern Ireland, 1989.

Sometime in August. BBC, 1988.

The Daily Woman. BBC, 1986.

Phonefun Limited. BBC, 1982.

My Dear Palestrina. BBC, 1980.

Interviews

"An Interview with Richard Rankin Russell." *Irish Literary Supplement* 26, no. 1 (Fall 2006): 21–22.

"Interview with Stephen Phelan." *The Sunday Herald,* May 25, 2006.

"Bernard MacLaverty." Interview with Sharon Monteith and Jenny Newman. In *Contemporary British and Irish Fiction: An Introduction through Interviews,* eds. Sharon Monteith, Jenny Newman, and Pat Wheeler. London: Arnold, 2004, 103–18.

"Bernard MacLaverty." Interview by Rosa González. In *Ireland in Writing: Interviews with Writers and Academics,* eds. Jacqueline Hurtley, Rosa González, Inés Praga, and Esther Aliaga. Amsterdam: Rodopi, 1998, 21–38.

"In a Coat with a Measure of Guilt." Interview with Anne Simpson. *The Herald,* September 29, 1997, 14.

"Lost in Music." Interview with Helen Meany. *The Irish Times,* July 3, 1997.

"Whatever You Say Say Nothing." Museum number 4010. Transmission date 7–24–94. BBC Northern Ireland Radio Archives. Cultra, Northern Ireland.

"The Glass Word Game." Interview with Deirdre Purcell. *The Sunday Tribune,* September 25, 1988.

"Capturing the Whirlwind: An Interview with Northern Irish Writer Bernard MacLaverty." By Gregory McNamee. *The Bloomsbury Review* 5, no. 9 (June 1985): 14–15, 20.

"In the Beginning Was the Written Word: Paul Campbell Interviews Bernard MacLaverty," *The Linenhall Review* (Winter 1984–85): 4–6.

Other Works

Adair, Tom. "Inside Stories." Review of *Matters of Life and Death. The Scotsman,* May 13, 2006.

———. "Orange Turns towards Green: *Walking the Dog.*" *The Independent Weekend,* Books Section, July 23, 1994.

———. "Pints of Bitterness." Review of *Grace Notes. The Observer,* July 6, 1997.

Adorno, Theodor. *Aesthetic Theory.* Edited by Gretel Adorno and Rolf Tiedemann. Translated by Robert Hullot-Kentor. Minneapolis: University of Minnesota Press, 1997.

Anonymous. Review of *Walking the Dog and Other Stories. Virginia Quarterly Review* 71, no. 4 (Autumn 1995): 129–30.

Arbery, Glenn C. *Why Literature Matters: Permanence and the Politics of Reputation.* Wilmington, DE: ISI Books, 2001.

Arnheim, Rudolf. *Art and Visual Perception: A Psychology of the Creative Eye.* Rev. Ed. Berkeley: University of California Press, 1974.

Bachelard, Gaston. *The Poetics of Space.* Boston: Beacon, 1994.

Baker, Simon. "Studies in Solitude." Review of *Matters of Life and Death. New Statesman,* June 26, 2006.

Bakhtin, Mikhail. *The Dialogic Imagination: Four Essays by M. M. Bakhtin.* Edited by Michael Holquist. Translated by Caryl Emerson and Michael Holquist. Austin: University of Texas Press, 1981.

Bayles, Martha. Review of *Cal. The New Republic,* September 19, 1983: 30–32.

Beckett, Samuel. *Waiting for Godot.* New York: Grove Press, 1982.

Brett, David. *The Plain Style: The Reformation, Culture, and the Crisis in Protestant Identity.* Belfast: black square books, 1999.

Brienzo, Gary. "The Voice of Despair in Ireland's Bernard MacLaverty." *North Dakota Quarterly* 57, no. 1 (Winter 1989): 67–77.

Brooks, Peter. *Troubling Confessions: Speaking Guilt in Law and Literature.* Chicago: University of Chicago Press, 2000.

Cleary, Joe. "'Fork-Tongued on the Border Bit': Partition and the Politics of Form in Contemporary Narratives of the Northern Irish Conflict." *South Atlantic Quarterly* 95, no. 1 (Winter 1996): 227–76.

———. *Literature, Partition, and the Nation State: Culture and Conflict in Ireland, Israel, and Palestine.* Cambridge: Cambridge University Press, 2002.

Cluck, Nancy Anne, Introduction to *Literature and Music: Essays on Form,* ed. Cluck Provo, UT: Brigham Young University Press, 1981.

Conroy, John. *Belfast Diary: War as a Way of Life.* Boston: Beacon Press, 1987.

Corcoran, Neil. *After Yeats and Joyce: Reading Modern Irish Literature.* Oxford: Oxford University Press, 1997.

Cronin, John. "Prose." In Michael Longley, ed. In *Causeway: The Arts in Ulster.* Belfast: Arts Council of Northern Ireland, 1971, 71–82.

Dawe, Gerald. "False Faces." In *False Faces: Poetry, Politics, and Place.* Belfast, Lagan Press, 1994, 58–61.

Deane, Seamus. *A Short History of Irish Literature.* Notre Dame, IN: University of Notre Dame Press, 1986.

Donoghue, Denis. "The Literature of Trouble." In *We Irish: Essays on Irish Literature and Society.* New York: Knopf, 1986, 182–94.

———. *Speaking of Beauty.* New Haven, CT: Yale University Press, 2003.

———. "Teaching Literature: The Force of Form." *New Literary History* 30, no. 1 (1999): 5–24.

Doob, Penelope Reed. *The Idea of the Labyrinth from Classical Antiquity through the Middle Ages.* Ithaca, NY: Cornell University Press, 2001.

Doody, Terrence. *Confession and Community in the Novel.* Baton Rouge: Louisiana State University Press, 1980.

Enright, Anne. "A Herringbone Walk." Review of *Matters of Life and Death.* The *Guardian,* May 6, 2006.

Forkner, Ben. Introduction to *Modern Irish Short Stories.* New York: Penguin, 1995, 21–42.

Forster, E. M. *Aspects of the Novel.* 1927. Reprint, San Diego, CA: Harcourt Brace, 1955.

Foster, John Wilson. "Irish Fiction 1965–1990." In Seamus Deane, ed. *The Field Day Anthology of Irish Writing,* Vol. 3. Derry, Northern Ireland: Field Day Publications, 1991, 937–43.

————. *Forces and Themes in Ulster Fiction.* Dublin: Gill and Macmillan, 1974.

Fridman, Lea Wernick. *Words and Witness: Narrative and Aesthetic Strategies in the Representation of the Holocaust.* Albany: State University of New York Press, 2000.

Ganter, C. J. "Bleakness and Comedy: Stoic Humor in Bernard MacLaverty's Short Stories." *International Fiction Review* 26, no. 1–2 (1999): 1–7.

Gilbert, Stuart. *James Joyce's* Ulysses: *A Study.* New York: Vintage, 1955.

Gill, R. B. "Why Comedy Laughs: The Shape of Laughter and Comedy." *Literary Imagination* 8, no. 2 (Spring 2006): 233–50.

Graham, Brian. "The Imagining of Place: Representation and Identity in Contemporary Ireland." In Brian Graham, ed. *In Search of Ireland: A Cultural Geography.* New York: Routledge, 1997, 192–212.

Grant, Patrick. *Breaking Enmities: Religion, Literature, and Culture in Northern Ireland, 1967–1997.* New York: St. Martin's, 1999.

————. *Literature, Rhetoric and Violence in Northern Ireland, 1968–1998: Hardened to Death.* New York: Palgrave, 2001.

Griffith, Benjamin. "Ireland's Ironies, Grim and Droll: The Fiction of Bernard MacLaverty." *Irish Literature Today.* Special issue, *The Sewanee Review* 106, no. 2 (Spring 1998): 334–38.

Hamilton, Hugo. "Living through a Mother Ireland Nightmare." *Sunday Independent,* August 16, 1997.

Hanson, Clare, ed. *Re-reading the Short Story.* New York: St. Martin's, 1999.

Harmon, Maurice. "First Impressions: 1968–1978." In Patrick Rafroidi and Terence Brown, eds. *The Irish Short Story.* Atlantic Highlands, NJ: Humanities Press, 1979, 63–77.

Harte, Liam and Michael Parker, eds. *Contemporary Irish Fiction: Themes, Tropes, Theories.* New York: St. Martin's, 2000.

————. Introduction. In *Contemporary Irish Fiction,* 1–12.

————. "Reconfiguring Identities: Recent Northern Irish Fiction." In *Contemporary Irish Fiction,* 232–54.

Haslam, Richard. "'Designed to Cause Suffering': *Cal* and the Politics of Imprisonment," *Nua: Studies in Contemporary Irish Writing* 3, no. 1–2 (2002): 41–56.

————. "'The Pose Arranged and Lingered Over': Visualizing the 'Troubles.'" In Harte and Parker, *Contemporary Irish Fiction,* 192–212.

Head, Dominic. *The Modernist Short Story: A Study in Theory and Practice.* Cambridge: Cambridge University Press, 1992.

Heaney, Seamus. *Death of a Naturalist.* London: Faber, 1966.

————. *Door into the Dark,* London: Faber, 1969.

————. *Field Work.* New York: Noonday Press, 1979.

———. *North.* London: Faber, 1975.

Hobsbaum, Philip. "The Belfast Group: A Recollection." *Eire-Ireland* 32, no. 2–3 (Summer–Fall, 1997): 173–82.

Hogan, Robert. "Old Boys, Young Bucks, and New Women: The Contemporary Irish Short Story." In James F. Kilroy, ed. *The Irish Short Story: A Critical History.* Boston: Twayne, 1984, 169–215.

Holloway, Richard. *On Forgiveness: How Can We Forgive the Unforgivable?* Edinburgh: Canongate, 2002.

Houen, Alex. *Terrorism and Modern Literature, from Joseph Conrad to Ciaran Carson.* Oxford: Oxford University Press, 2002.

Hughes, Eamonn. *Culture and Politics in Northern Ireland.* Milton Keynes, UK: Open University Press, 1991.

———. "Fiction." In Mark Carruthers and Stephen Douds, eds. *Stepping Stones: The Arts in Ulster, 1971–2001.* Belfast: Blackstaff, 2001, 79–102.

Hyndman, Marilyn. *Further Afield: Journeys from a Protestant Past.* Belfast: Beyond the Pale, 1996.

Jacobs, Karen. *The Eye's Mind: Literary Modernism and Visual Culture.* Ithaca, NY: Cornell University Press, 2001.

Joyce, James. *A Portrait of the Artist as a Young Man*, Viking Critical Edition, ed. Chester Anderson. New York: Penguin, 1977.

Kelly, Aaron. *The Thriller and Northern Ireland since 1969: Utterly Resigned Terror.* Aldershot, UK: Ashgate, 2005.

Kelly, Thomas. "*Secrets and Other Stories* by Bernard MacLaverty." *Eire-Ireland: A Journal of Irish Studies* 16, no. 1 (Spring 1981): 155–58.

Kemp, Peter. "A Thrilling Sense of Urgency." Review of *Matters of Life and Death. The Sunday Times,* May 14, 2006.

Kennedy-Andrews, Elmer. *Fiction and the Northern Ireland Troubles since 1969: (de-)constructing the North.* Dublin: Four Courts Press, 2003.

Kiberd, Declan. *Inventing Ireland: The Literature of the Modern Nation.* Cambridge, MA: Harvard University Press, 1995.

Korwin, Yala. *To Tell the Story: Poems of the Holocaust.* New York: Holocaust Library, 1987.

Lewis, C.S. *The Four Loves.* San Diego, CA: Harcourt Brace, 1988.

Lloyd, David. *Anomalous States: Irish Writing and the Post-Colonial Moment.* Durham, NC: Duke University Press, 1993.

Lohafer, Susan and Jo Ellyn Clarey, eds. *Short Story Theory at a Crossroads.* Baton Rouge: Louisiana State University Press, 1989.

Longley, Edna. "'A Barbarous Nook': The Writer and Belfast." In *The Living Stream: Literature and Revisionism in Ireland.* Newcastle, UK: Bloodaxe, 1994, 86–108.

Longley, Michael. *An Exploded View: Poems 1968–1972*. London: Victor Gollancz, 1973.

Lubbock, Percy. *The Craft of Fiction*. London: Jonathan Cape, 1921.

Lukacs, Georg. *The Theory of the Novel*. Cambridge, MA: MIT Press, 1971.

Malcolm, Cheryl Alexander and David Malcolm, eds. *Dictionary of Literary Biography: British and Irish Short-Fiction Writers, 1945–2000*, Vol. 319. Detroit, MI: Thomson-Gale, 2006.

Matthews, Brander. "The Philosophy of the Short Story." In May, *New Short Story Theories* 73–80.

May, Charles, ed., "The Nature of Knowledge in Short Fiction." *New Short Story Theories* 131–43.

———. *The New Short Story Theories*. Athens: Ohio University Press, 1994.

———. *The Short Story: The Reality of Artifice*. New York: Twayne's, 1995.

McGarry, John and Brendan O'Leary. *Explaining Northern Ireland: Broken Images*. Oxford: Blackwell, 1995.

Mitchell, W. J. T. *Picture Theory: Essays on Verbal and Visual Representation*. Chicago: University of Chicago Press, 1994.

Molino, Michael R. "Bernard MacLaverty." In *Dictionary of Literary Biography* (First Series). Vol. 267, *British Novelists of the Twenty-first Century*. Detroit, MI: Gale Research Group, 2003, 172–80.

Morrison, Karl F. "Constructing Empathy." *Journal of Religion* 84, no. 2 (April 2004): 264–69.

O'Connor, Fionnuala. *In Search of a State: Catholics in Northern Ireland*. Belfast: Blackstaff Press, 1993.

O'Connor, Frank. *The Lonely Voice: A Study of the Short Story*. London: Macmillan, 1963.

Onkey, Lauren. "Celtic Soul Brothers." *Eire-Ireland: A Journal of Irish Studies* 28, no. 3 (Fall 1993): 147–58.

Parker, David. *Ethics, Theory, and the Novel*. Cambridge: Cambridge University Press, 1994.

Patten, Eve. "'Flying to Belfast': Audience and Authenticity in Recent Northern Irish Fiction." In Tony Brown and Russell Stephens, eds. *Nations and Relations: Writing across the British Isles*. Special issue, *New Welsh Review*. Cardiff, Wales, 2000, 30–41.

Paulin, Tom. "Formal Pleasure: The Short Story." In *Writing to the Moment: Selected Critical Essays, 1980–1996*. London: Faber, 1996, 208–14.

———. "A Necessary Provincialism: Brian Moore, Maurice Leitch, Florence Mary McDowell." In Douglas Dunn, ed. *Two Decades of Irish Writing: A Critical Survey*. Chester Springs, PA: Dufour, 1975, 242–56.

Peach, Linden. *The Contemporary Novel: Critical Readings*. Basingstoke, UK: Palgrave, 2004.

Pelaschiar, Laura. *Writing the North: The Contemporary Novel in Northern Ireland*. Trieste, Italy: Edizioni Parnaso, 1998.

Poe, Edgar Allen. "Poe on Short Fiction." In May, *New Short Story Theories,* 59–72.

Reid, Ian. *The Short Story.* London: Methuen, 1977.

Richtarik, Marilynn. Review of *Grace Notes. Nua: Studies in Contemporary Irish Writing* 1, no. 2 (Spring 1998): 89–92.

Rolston, Bill. *Drawing Support: Murals in the North of Ireland.* Belfast: Beyond the Pale Publications, 1992.

Ruane, Joseph and Jennifer Todd. *The Dynamics of Conflict in Northern Ireland: Power, Conflict, and Emancipation.* Cambridge: Cambridge University Press, 1996.

Russell, Richard Rankin. "A Review of Bernard MacLaverty's *The Anatomy School." Nua: Studies in Contemporary Irish Writing* 5, no. 1 (Fall 2006): 151–55.

Said, Edward. *Reflections on Exile and Other Essays.* Cambridge, MA: Harvard University Press, 2000.

Saxton, Arnold. "An Introduction to the Stories of Bernard MacLaverty." *Journal of the Short Story in English,* no. 8 (1987): 113–23.

Scarry, Elaine. *Dreaming by the Book.* New York: Farrar, Straus, Giroux, 1999.

———. *On Beauty and Being Just.* Princeton, NJ: Princeton University Press, 1999.

Schwarz, Daniel R. *Imagining the Holocaust.* New York: St. Martin's Press, 1999.

Shumaker, Jeanette. "Rivalry, Confession, and Healing in Bernard MacLaverty's *Cal." Notes on Modern Irish Literature* 9 (1997): 9–15.

Smyth, Gerry. *The Novel and the Nation: Studies in the New Irish Fiction.* London: Pluto Press, 1997.

———. "'The Same Sound but with a Different Meaning': Music, Repetition, and Identity in Bernard MacLaverty's *Grace Notes." Eire-Ireland: A Journal of Irish Studies* 37, no. 3–4 (Fall-Winter 2002): 5–24.

Sontag, Susan. "An Argument about Beauty." In Paolo Dilonardo and Anne Jump, eds. *At the Same Time: Essays and Speeches.* (New York: Farrar, Straus and Giroux, 2007, 3–13.

———. *Regarding the Pain of Others.* New York: Picador, 2003.

Spiegel, Alan. *Fiction and the Camera Eye: Visual Consciousness in Film and the Modern Novel.* Charlottesville: University of Virginia Press, 1976.

Storey, Michael L. *Representing the Troubles in Irish Short Fiction.* Washington, DC: Catholic University Press, 2004.

———. *"Walking the Dog and Other Stories." Studies in Short Fiction* 34, no. 4 (Fall 1994): 527.

Thornton, Weldon. *The Antimodernism of Joyce's 'Portrait of the Artist as a Young Man."* Syracuse, NY: Syracuse University Press, 1994.

———. *D. H. Lawrence: A Study of the Short Fiction.* Boston: Twayne's, 1993.

Tobin, Daniel. *Passage to the Center: Imagination and the Sacred in the Poetry of Seamus Heaney.* Lexington: University of Kentucky Press, 1999.

Trevor, William. Introduction to *The Oxford Book of Irish Short Stories*. Oxford: Oxford University Press, 1989. ix-xvi.

Tyler, Anne. "Secrets and Other Stories." *The New Republic,* November 26, 1984, 39–40.

Watson, George. "The Writer on Writing." In Hamish Robertson, ed. *Lamb.* Longman Literature Series. Essex, UK: Longman, 1991, v–xii.

Waugh, Patricia. *Metafiction: The Theory and Practice of Self-Conscious Fiction.* London: Methuen, 1984.

Watt, Stephen. "Beckett, Late Modernism, and Bernard MacLaverty's *Grace Notes.*" *New Hibernia Review: A Quarterly Record of Irish Studies* 6, no. 2 (Summer 2002): 53–64.

———. "The Politics of Bernard MacLaverty's *Cal.*" *Eire-Ireland: A Journal of Irish Studies* 28, no. 3 (Fall 1993): 130–46.

Wiesel, Elie. Prologue to *The Gates of the Forest.* New York: Holt, Rinehart, and Winston, 1966.

Wilson, Robert and Donovan Wylie. *The Dispossessed.* London: Picador, 1992.

Wormald, Mark. "Not Far Away from Home." *The Times Literary Supplement,* June 6, 1994.

Wright, Austin M. "Recalcitrance in the Short Story." In Lohafer and Clarey, *Short Story Theory,* 115–29.